CLEFT CAPITALISM

Stanford Studies *in* Middle Eastern *and* Islamic Societies *and* Cultures

CLEFT CAPITALISM

The Social Origins of Failed Market Making in Egypt

Amr Adly

STANFORD UNIVERSITY PRESS
Stanford, California

STANFORD UNIVERSITY PRESS
Stanford, California

Printed in the United States of America on acid-free, archival-quality paper

Library of Congress Cataloging-in-Publication Data
Names: Adly, Amr, author.
Title: Cleft capitalism : the social origins of failed market making in Egypt / Amr Adly.
Other titles: Stanford studies in Middle Eastern and Islamic societies and cultures.
Description: Stanford, California : Stanford University Press, 2020. | Series: Stanford studies in Middle Eastern and Islamic societies and cultures | Includes bibliographical references and index.
Identifiers: LCCN 2019051225 (print) | LCCN 2019051226 (ebook) | ISBN 9781503608917 (cloth) | ISBN 9781503612204 (paperback) | ISBN 9781503612211 (ebook)
Subjects: LCSH: Economic development—Egypt. | Capitalism—Egypt. | Egypt—Economic conditions—1981– | Egypt—Economic policy.
Classification: LCC HC830 .A5548 2020 (print) | LCC HC830 (ebook) | DDC 330.962—dc23
LC record available at https://lccn.loc.gov/2019051225
LC ebook record available at https://lccn.loc.gov/2019051226

Cover photo: Downtown Cityscape view in Cairo, Egypt, February 25, 2010. Baloncici | iStock
Cover design: Rob Ehle

Typeset by Kevin Barrett Kane in 10.5/14.4 Brill

To Noha and Ibrahim

Contents

Figures

Tables

Acknowledgments

THIS BOOK WAS INSPIRED BY MY EARLIER WORK ON "REFORMING the Entrepreneurship Ecosystem in Post-Revolutionary Egypt and Tunisia," a report published by the Centre on Democracy, Development and the Rule of Law at Stanford University in April 2014. The report was supported by the Centre of International Private Enterprise (CIPE). I thank Lina Khatib, Larry Diamond, Kim Betcher, and Gregory Simpson for their continuous support and guidance throughout the process of doing the fieldwork in 2013, writing the report, and backing the idea of writing this book.

In Egypt, I benefited from the help of Randa Zoghby, Saif Khawanki, and Lobna Afifi at the CIPE Cairo bureau. I am also thankful to Mohamed Gad, Ahmed Gad, Ahmad Shams, Yeyha Shawkat, and Karim Ibrahim.

I especially thank Joel Beinin and Kate Wahl for shepherding this work through the long process of writing, editing, and publication. Many others have carefully read, considered, and thoughtfully criticized the work in its various incarnations, including the late Ellis Goldberg, Nathan Brown, Robert Springborg, Mohamed Menza, Samer Atallah, Ibrahim Awad, Mohamed Gabr, and especially Dina Elkhawaga. Thanks also to Thomas Hinkel and Shaza Eliwa for their help through the editing process.

Finally, I will always be indebted to many friends who supported me before, during, and after the research for this book.

Acronyms

AFLPO	Armed Forces Land Projects Organization
CAPMAS	Central Agency for Public Mobilization and Statistics
CBE	Central Bank of Egypt
CICs	Capital investment companies (Egypt)
EU	European Union
FDI	Foreign direct investment
GAID	General Authority for Industrial Development
GARPAD	General Authority on Rehabilitation Projects and Agricultural Development
GCC	Gulf Cooperation Council
GDP	Gross domestic product
GEM	Global Entrepreneurship Monitor
GNI	Gross national income
GOPP	General Organization for Physical Planning
IDSC	Information and Decision-Making Support Center
IFI	International financial institutions
IMC	Industrial Modernization Center
IMF	International Monetary Fund

MENA	Middle East and North Africa
MFCs	Microfinance companies
MNCs	Multinational corporations
NBE	National Bank of Egypt
NCPSL	National Center for Planning State Land
NDP	National Democratic Party (Egypt)
NGO-MFIs	Nongovernmental organizations–microfinance institutions
NIB	National Investment Bank
NPLs	Nonperforming loans
NUCA	New Urban Communities Authority
NSPO	National Service Project Organization
OECD	Organization for Economic Cooperation and Development
SAP	Structural Adjustment Program
SFD	Social Fund for Development
SMEs	Small and medium enterprises
SOEs	State-owned enterprises
SSEs	Small-scale establishments
TDA	Tourism Development Agency
TVEs	Township and village enterprises (China)
UNDP	United Nations Development Program
UNIDO	United Nations Industrial Development Organization
USAID	US Agency for International Development
VoC	Varieties of capitalism

CLEFT CAPITALISM

Chapter One

SUCCESSFUL TRANSITION TO FAILED CAPITALISM

THIS IS A BOOK ABOUT THE SOCIAL AND POLITICAL CONDITIONS for economic development. Why does market-based development work in some societies and fail in others? Although it focuses on Egypt, it is not intended solely for those specialized in Egypt or the Middle East and North Africa (MENA). Egypt is a country in the Global South that has undergone significant economic liberalization under the auspices of the International Monetary Fund (IMF), the World Bank, the US Agency for International Development (USAID), and the European Commission. However, four decades of economic reform have failed to meet popular expectations for inclusive growth, better standards of living, and high-quality employment.

The mainstream political economy literature, informed by neoclassical institutionalism, has assigned blame to crony capitalism, rent seeking, and corruption. These critics have held that the regime of Egypt's longstanding dictator, Ḥosni Mubārak (1981–2011), stifled the liberalization and privatization processes in favor of its cronies, raising the barriers to entry for other businesses, and thus sacrificing competition and efficiency. However, this argument does not fully explain the failure of Egypt's attempted market making. Indeed, many other countries in the Global South have delivered development to significant segments of their populations despite the prevalence of cronyism and corruption. Even in the absence of formal market institutions such as the universal rule of law and secured property rights, these economies have developed other institutional rules that have brought about a vibrant, dynamic, and broad private sector that has led to wider engagement of the population in the production and exchange of economic value. The question is why Egypt has not followed suit, and specifically why its four-decade effort to develop a private sector–based economy has failed.

In pursuit of an answer, this book adopts an interdisciplinary approach that combines economic sociology with political economy. It establishes a detailed account of the institutional features of capitalism in Egypt—formal, informal, and semiformal, as well as public and private. This is done through developing, theoretically and empirically, the concept of cleft capitalism as an institutional explanation for Egypt's failed market making and then offers a political-economic explanation of the factors that led to the rise of cleft capitalism. Although the focus is on Egypt's transformation into a market economy since the mid-1970s, its central concept of cleft capitalism may prove to be beneficial in explaining other cases of arrested development in the Global South, with a special focus on MENA.

Egypt's transformation has been part and parcel of a general change in the Global South since the 1970s, and the country's recent political economic history bears considerable resemblance to other parts of the world, including South Asia, Latin America, and non-oil economies in North Africa like Tunisia and Morocco.

A PRIVATE SECTOR– DOMINATED ECONOMY

After two decades of adopting state-led development policies under Gamāl ʿAbdel-Nāṣer (1954–1970), President Anwar al-Sadāt (1970–1981) launched an economic liberalization initiative in 1974 that inaugurated Egypt's market-making process and transformation toward a private sector–dominated economy. In the following decades, an undeniable shift toward greater economic liberalization, deregulation, and privatization took place. These changes were part of the global transformation that was occurring under the ideological hegemony of neoliberalism, especially the Washington consensus after the end of the Cold War. Although these changes were part of the global neoliberal turn, domestic forces and influences also shaped Egypt's institutional path.

Using the Heritage Foundation's economic freedom index, a conservative source that refers to the ability to enter and operate a private business with the least amount of state regulation, Egypt showed continuous progression from the middle of 1995, jumping from 55 percent to 60.2 and 64.5 percent in 2008 and 2010, respectively.[1] Freedom of trade showed a more dramatic increase, from 25 percent in 1995 to 57.2 percent in 2002 and 74 percent in 2010, which tracked with the world average. This was largely a result of Egypt's compliance with the IMF and World Bank conditions in return for funding, as well as its growing relationship with its principal trade partner since the 1980s: the European Union (EU). The two economies signed an association agreement in 2001 that went into effect in 2004 and included the gradual phasing out of tariff and nontariff barriers with the aim of mutual trade liberalization and, eventually, the establishment of a free trade area by 2020.

This trade liberalization and deregulation opened new areas for the development of private enterprises. At the same time, the state provided direct and indirect subsidies to private enterprises, especially in the sectors of manufacturing, tourism, financial services, telecommunications, agricultural exports, and real estate and construction. These took the form of tax rebates, investment incentives, below-market rate land allocation, and generous energy subsidies.

Private sector expansion proceeded concurrently with the contraction of state-owned enterprises (SOEs), particularly in their share in output and employment, due to chronic financial problems and lack of investment along with privatization and divestiture (Adly, 2012a). Overall, the share of private sector enterprises of all sizes underwent continuous expansion in terms of total output, investment, and employment, assuming the largest share in most productive sectors by the early 2000s. This trend was accelerated further as of 2004 when Mubārak appointed a neoliberally inclined cabinet that was committed to intensifying the liberalization of trade and capital movement, as well as further privatizing SOEs and supporting foreign direct investment (FDI).

Throughout this period, private sector enterprises expanded their shares in key sectors. According to the World Bank (2009, 26), the private sector held around 75 percent of Egypt's nonhydrocarbon GDP. In the manufacturing sector, privately owned enterprises pushed their share from 58 percent in 1991 to 79 percent in 1995/1996, and eventually to 85 percent by 2001(Central Bank of Egypt, 2017, cited in Adly, 2017, 6). This large share remained constant through 2010.

The story is not much different in the construction sector, where the share of the private sector grew from 71 percent in 1991 to 88.4 and 89.1 percent in 2006 and 2010, respectively. The private sector also dominated retail and wholesale trade, as well as tourism, with shares growing from 85 percent in the 1990s to 99 percent in 2010 (Central Bank of Egypt, 2017, cited in Adly, 2017, 6).

On the investment front, the private sector's share also exceeded that of the public sector in terms of gross capital formation as a percentage of GDP—increases in the fixed assets of an economy, including land improvement; the purchase of machinery, plants, and equipment; the construction of transportation infrastructure and facilities; and increases in inventories of goods used for production. Gross capital formation from the private sector rose from 7 percent between 1990 and 2000, to 10.3 percent from 2001 to 2010, whereas in the public sector, it declined from an average of 14.7 percent in the 1990s to 8.7 percent in the next decade (World Bank, 2017a).

The same trend applies to employment. By 2007, the overall share of the private sector, including wage laborers, the self-employed, and employers, stood at 65.3 percent versus 34 percent in the public sector (CAPMAS, 2007, cited in al-Merghani, 2010,144–146). Furthermore, the vast majority of state employees (5.4 million) worked for the bureaucracy rather than for SOEs (a mere 3.6 percent of the total labor force), rendering productive sectors in the hands of privately owned enterprises.

Capitalist Transformation

These transformations in Egypt were indeed part of the global neoliberal turn. Neoliberal influences found their way to the Egyptian economy through three principal linkages (Stallings, Haggard, and Kaufman, 19921):

1. *Hierarchical*, through conditionality by international creditors and sponsors such as the IMF, the World Bank, and USAID and Arab Gulf development funds
2. *Market*, primarily by the integration of the Egyptian economy into global trade and capital flows via foreign direct investments and commercial credit

3. *Ideational,* especially in the 2000s when a coherent collection of neoliberally oriented teams of technocrats and businessmen came to dominate economic policymaking for the first time (Hanieh, 2013, 52; Roccu, 2013, 65)

These neoliberal transformations were neither uniform nor local implementations of some universal agenda. In contrast, the domestic political economy weighed heavily as to the scale, pace, and scope of such changes, as well as to the definition of the final outcome of such market-making processes. The Egyptian state was by no means a mere transmission belt (Cox, 1992), with domestic factors shaping the reforms as much as any external linkages or influences (Roccu, 2013, 111). Therefore, it would be more accurate to say that the Egyptian economy since the 1990s has become a national variety of globalized neoliberalism (Panitch and Gindin, 2012, 4).

The rise of neoliberalism, with its call for deregulation, privatization, and liberalization as the means to ending stagflation, coincided almost perfectly with the reintegration of the second and third worlds into the capitalist world order. The end of the Cold War reaffirmed the trend that began in the 1970s and underscored the ideological primacy of neoliberalism to a degree that even gave rise to illusions about the end of history (Fukuyama, 1989). This book, however, holds that capitalist transformation is a much broader process than neoliberalization.

At the country level, domestic institutions, and the sociopolitical coalitions that uphold them, matter (Weiss, 2003). Even in an increasingly integrated world and American-led globalization-cum-neoliberalization, there was room for a variety of national and regional capitalisms (Panitch and Gindin, 2012, 202–203). For example, China's capitalist transformation initiated by Deng Xiao Ping's reforms of the late 1970s proceeded on Chinese terms with almost no presence of IMF or World Bank conditionality. In contrast, Chinese trade liberalization was guided by a mercantilist approach aimed at generating a large trade surplus and the accumulation of massive foreign reserves. This included a large role for the state in relation to the market, as well as networks permeating the public and private sectors. On the central and subnational regional levels, the government continued to run public sector enterprises alongside semipublic and semiprivate firms. In the end, China was undoubtedly integrated into the global division of labor; however, this unfolded largely along particular Chinese lines and resulted in the production of a variety (or many varieties) of national, and possibly even regional, capitalism(s) (McNally, 2006; Peck and Theodore, 2007, 57; Peck and Zhang, 2013).

Even with countries that had less international leverage than a large, powerful country like China, domestic institutions and coalitions were crucial in shaping the terms of transformation. This makes it very difficult to tackle neoliberalism as a uniform power active on the global scale. Rather, it was more of an ingredient that is channeled through market, hierarchical, and ideational linkages in order to shape domestic capitalist transformations. The result was the rise of a great variety of institutions and outcomes across and within nations in the Global South. In Egypt, they have mediated and shaped the influences of neoliberal globalization, defining to different extents the pace, scope, and scale of the transformation. Domestic forces have also defined the institutional basis for the capitalist transformation on the national level.

A Record of Poor Market Development

Nevertheless, Egypt's resultant market-based development performance has been rather humble, a fact that is seldom contested. In fact, myriad indicators reveal that little improvement has occurred in terms of the standard of living for a large majority of Egyptians. Economic growth has hardly kept pace with population growth. Whereas the average per capita GDP growth rate was 2.6 percent between 1990 and 2012, average population growth for the same period was 1.7 percent. In the 1990s, GDP per capita growth averaged 3.7 percent versus a population growth rate of 2.2 percent (World Bank, 2017b).

In addition, growth generation and distribution have been concentrated in a handful of capital- and energy-intensive sectors that are dominated by big business— private domestic, multinational, and within the public sector.[2] For instance, most high-growth enterprises prior to the 2011 revolution were in capital-intensive sectors such as cement, iron and steel, aluminum, glass, fertilizers, financial services, and telecommunications, in addition to extractive industries (natural gas and oil). These high-growth sectors were based on Egypt's traditional competitive edge in providing cheap energy through generously subsidized fuels, which ultimately proved unsustainable: Egypt became a net oil importer in 2006 and net energy importer (including natural gas) by 2012.

With these humble growth rates and the confinement of growth generation to a handful of capital-intensive sectors, the capacity of the Egyptian economy to generate productive and well-paying jobs was quite limited. In response, the majority of job seekers found employment in microenterprises or became self-employed in the menial and marginal service sectors. In other words, the majority of the Egyptian labor force was caught between unemployment and underemployment, further exacerbating the problems of income generation and distribution. The jobs created were either insufficient in number or unsatisfactory in quality due to their low productivity, low wages, and job insecurity (UNDP, 2011; Barsoum, Ramadan, and Mostafa, 2014; Sahnoun et al., 2014). According to the World Bank vulnerable employment indicator, the average percentage of vulnerable employment in Egypt between 1997 and 2007, as a percentage of total employment, was as high as 24.09 percent (World Bank, 2017c).

THE QUESTION CONCERNING MARKET INTEGRATION

There is very little agreement among scholars when it comes to answering the question of why market-based development has not delivered in Egypt. Thinkers on the right, in particular the centers of neoliberal discourse production and policymaking (e.g., international financial institutions, aid agencies, and right-wing think tanks and universities), have sought explanations in the specific ways that reforms were (or were not) implemented. According to them, Egypt's dismal performance was the result of a neoliberalization process that either did not go far enough or was implemented poorly. Indeed, throughout the 1980s and 1990s, neoliberal scholars and commentators did view Egypt's track record as sluggish and reticent (Richards, 1991; Waterbury, 1992). This was no longer the case by the 2000s, when Egypt quickly became a model reformer in the eyes of the IMF (2007, 5). This reform period, however, did not come to a happy ending.

As the 2011 revolution exposed the sociopolitical vulnerabilities of the previously praised economic model, the mainstream literature shifted the blame onto crony capitalism and rampant rent seeking and corruption. According to this argument, successive episodes of liberalization, privatization, and deregulation did not give way to the emergence of a competitive market (King, 2009; Adly, 2012a, 2012b; Chekir and Diwan, 2014). Instead, it created a nonmarket-based capitalism dominated by private monopolies and cartels that used (or, rather, abused) their political influence to generate unnatural profits at the expense of consumers, smaller businesses, the state budget, and the economy as a whole. This literature drew a strong correlation between this cronyism and predation, on the one hand, and the authoritarian dynamics of the ruling regime, on the other. The lack of democratic accountability provided the ripe political context for an unholy alliance between wealth and power, as well as increased the appetite of the former dictator and his family and allies to translate their monopoly over political power into economic gains.

Undoubtedly, cronyism—in the form of the uneven distribution of property rights—has been a prevalent feature of the failed capitalist order that emerged in Egypt and other MENA countries after the mid-1970s. However, the prevalence of crony capitalism and the absence of functioning formal market institutions do not explain the ultimate inability of Egypt's economic system to deliver growth and development for the majority of the population. Many successful cases of capitalist transformation have occurred in the Global South, especially in Asia, in environments of unevenly distributed property rights and the absence of functioning formal market institutions. Yet they have been able to generate impressive growth and investment rates that have ultimately led to economic development and political stability—all despite (or perhaps thanks to) special state-business ties.

Of course, the resultant capitalist order in Egypt was exclusionary and failed to create jobs that were adequate in quantity and quality for the increasingly educated young population. But this can hardly be attributed simply to cronyism or the uneven distribution of property rights, which cannot account for unemployment and other forms of social marginalization and exclusion on its own. Close state-business relations did feed the resentment against the regime as being corrupt; however, it would be far too simplistic to ignore the powerful factors, such as the institutions reigning over education and vocational training, health care, industrial relations, and taxation, that undermined the ability of the Egyptian economy to produce and distribute high economic value. Egypt has been underperforming on these fronts, especially compared to East and Southeast Asia, and China (Achcar, 2013, 15).

In terms of the Left, the problem of Egypt's development was not perceived so much as a failure to live up to the expectations of free market development or as mere deviation from "true market capitalism"; rather, the very precepts of the neoliberal development model, deeply carved into neoclassical economic tenets, were seen as flawed and nondevelopmental. As David Harvey argued (2007), neoliberalism was a global project that varied in its tools and policies but had one principal objective: the upward redistribution of income and wealth on a world scale. This project was held to be truly global and to have firmly extended its influence to the Middle East (Mitchell, 1999; Hanieh, 2013). According to these leftist critics, neoliberalism has effectively led to the dismantlement of welfare structures and Keynesian macroeconomic policies that were designed to limit inequality and socioeconomic marginality (Jessop, 1990). Thus, marginalization and impoverishment were the logical outcomes of such a capitalist transformation rather than some pathological deviation.

These authors further note that despite all claims of shrinking the state in order to allow more market freedom, what actually unfolded was the redefinition of the role of the state rather than its size. The state ended up moving away from delivering welfare services to the poor and middle classes, while taking a more active role toward sustaining the market through tax cuts, subsidies to large businesses, and the massive bailouts in the aftermath of the market meltdown of 2008.

According to this analysis, neoliberal measures led to increasing inequality and poverty in Egypt, especially in the countryside, as social protections were slashed (Bush, 1999). Meanwhile, income and wealth flowed up to a limited clique of businesspeople and corrupt officials in the name of market making and private sector development. It was a clear case of market making by dispossession (Elyachar, 2005), and it unfolded precisely as it was supposed to.

These leftist accounts nevertheless underplay the fact that the Egyptian economy had failed on the production front as much as on the distribution and redistribution ones. (See Hansen, 1991, 23, 161–163 for a historical account of the low-productivity problem in contemporary Egypt.) In this light, Gilbert Achcar's work (2013) on capitalist transformation in MENA stands out: he focuses on the failure to generate sustainable and long-term growth rather than the simple scourges of corruption and rent seeking or the maldistribution of income and wealth due to neoliberal influences. He thus underscores the problem of production, noting that the dependence on external rent, principally derived from oil and other raw materials, combined with weak public investment due to international financial institutions' conditionality and (neo-)patrimonial political regimes, ultimately led to MENA's "fettered development" (35, 51–53).

The Centrality of Firm Capitalization

This book employs a similar approach. Like Achcar, it does not dismiss capitalism altogether as inherently nondevelopmental in the periphery, nor does it perceive neoliberalism as a monolithic global force that emanates from beyond the region and that no local or national actor can resist. Indeed, Achcar stresses the potential role of the Arab state to use public investment to play a more decisive role in transformation, much like what was witnessed in the more successful cases in East, Southeast, and South Asia where capitalist transformation was able to deliver growth and development. Finally, Achcar does not overemphasize cronyism, rent seeking, and corruption as the principal factors behind the failed transformation. Instead he invokes more structural factors like low investment and saving rates, providing institutional and political explanations for these restraints.

Although this book builds on Achcar's institutional approach, I also seek to transcend its rather traditional scope that focuses on states and regimes, external rents, big businesses, international financial institutions, and workers. Using the tools of economic sociology, I carefully examine the different components of the Egyptian private sector, which has come to possess the biggest percentage of output and employment since the country's infitāḥ, or economic opening in 1974, and how its interaction with the state could provide a more comprehensive explanation to failed market making.

The failure of the Egyptian economy to generate growth rates that could catch up with population increases and ultimately lead to higher per capita incomes stems from its larger failure to integrate social forces and relations into the market. This was not the result of a lack of liberalization measures; rather, it was that only a small number of Egyptians were involved in the generation of economic value, which subsequently undermined the ability of the economy to distribute the returns of growth. This took place amid the general inability of a majority of active Egyptians to take part in the production, and hence distribution, of economic value as workers, entrepreneurs, or the self-employed—what I call "market integration," or the process through which social actors (groups as well as individuals) become market actors. This takes place not only through the old classical route of the proletarianization of peasants and the urban poor but also through the rise of a robust base of small to medium private sector enterprises (SMEs) capable of creating value and exchanging it on the market. Both of these complementary routes to capitalist transformation were taken in the most successful cases in East and Southeast Asia throughout the past four decades.

There is nothing utopian about market integration, but there is little diabolical about it either. It is not the end of social conflict (not to mention the end of history). Rather, it simply means that more people, more social relations, and more interactions pass through market-based production, exchange, and consumption of economic value. There will always be elements of unevenness between workers and capitalists, as well as among workers and consumers themselves. Questions of justice and equality will persist, or may even escalate, as political issues rather than merely economic matters. This has been the case with earlier capitalist transformations in Europe and North America, and it remains the case with many Asian countries that are currently undergoing these transformations. The main difference here is that more and more people will participate in the creation of value as well as get returns from it, whether just and equitable or not.

Contrary to (neo)dependency theories, socioeconomic development under market-based capitalism is possible and does exist. (See Amsden et al., 2003, commenting on Arrighi, Silver, and Brewer, 2003a, and their response, 2003b. See also Sánchez, 2003; Evans, 2012, 6–8; and on the Middle East, Khafaji, 2013, 36–39.) In fact, globalization in terms of the intensifying movement of goods, services, information, technology and capital, and, to a lesser extent, people has benefited a number of countries in the Global South tremendously and allowed them to upgrade to producing higher-value-added products (Panitch and Gindin, 2012, 195–196, 211). China and the other countries of East Asia stand out as the most dramatic cases of market-based development through the integration of their national economies into the global division of labor. These economies managed to upgrade their industrial bases and achieve a high level of competitiveness, while also making considerable improvements in standards of living for sizable percentages of their populations.

Egypt's Unintegrated Market

Like many other countries in the Global South incapable of negotiating the terms of integration into the world economy, Egypt has faced many external constraints. However, it also enjoyed opportunities thanks to its geopolitical importance, especially following its strategic realignment with the Western bloc in the mid-1970s. Egypt enjoyed remarkable access to capital inflows that were seldom available to other low- or lower-middle-income countries. According to World Bank data (2017f), Egypt received a staggering $61 billion in official development assistance between 1990 and 2012, a figure that does not include the $1.3 billion in annual military aid that has flowed into the country since 1979, representing a rough cumulative total of $40 billion (Sharp, 2009). To these figures, we must also add the massive debt forgiveness Egypt enjoyed in 1990 and 1991 as part of the deal with the Paris club that secured Egypt's participation in the international coalition for the liberation of Kuwait. This debt agreement included the cancellation of 50 percent of Egypt's external debt (around $45 billion) and the rescheduling of the remaining half (Ikram, 2007, 150).

These public foreign capital inflows were supplemented by private inflows in the form of workers' remittances, which are private incomes that Egyptian expatriates send home. Egypt received a massive $166.56 billion in remittances between 1989 and 2012: $5 billion annually, a sum far greater than that received by countries of similar or greater population sizes, such as Turkey or Brazil (World Bank, 2017d, author's calculations).

Why these massive and sustained inflows of capital did not translate into higher rates of saving and investment is a question that begs an institutional answer. In other words, the weak investment rates and prevalence of a consumption-driven development model since the 1970s are themselves results of institutional arrangements—social, economic, and political—rather than mere structural constraints. This example shows that developmental breakthroughs require a combination of functioning domestic institutions and favorable external conditions.[3]

China represents the most obvious case, achieving a robust annual growth over four decades that led to the largest movement of people out of poverty in history in both relative and absolute terms. Of course, there is no romanticizing the model in China, which remains one of the most inequitable countries in the

Global South, despite the absolute reduction in poverty, and is under the control of a repressive one-party state (Fan, Zhang, and Zhang, 2002; Ravallion and Chen, 2007). Nevertheless, it stands as a clear example that market-based development can deliver for the many, albeit unequally and unevenly (Piketty, 2016, 347).

The success of a capitalist transformation is largely a function of the degree of market integration. The challenge in Egypt and other economies in the Global South that ended up with economies dominated by the private sector, compared to the Asian cases, is that market integration has never successfully taken place on a large scale. The outcome was the marginalization and exclusion of the majority from the production of economic value rather than their exploitation in the classical Marxian sense. Since so few actors assumed the role of market actors in the first place, little surplus value was created for distribution or accumulation.

Neoclassical institutionalism, which constitutes the theoretical basis of neoliberalism, argued that the market requires institutional infrastructure—private property rights, rule of law, and contract enforcement—so as to encourage market actors to engage in production and exchange at low transaction costs. Practically, however, it requires more than just the distribution of "rights" to create market actors that can meaningfully engage in the production of economic value, because constitution of the market is a sociopolitical process. The issue here is not only how economic freedom is upheld by continuous state intervention in the areas of private property protection and contract enforcement, but also about the kind of intervention that shapes the quality and quantity of market actors. These require the creation of an institutional framework that provides access to capital, financial and nonfinancial, as well as skills, education, training, and other forms of human capital.

This book explores the institutional disadvantages in peripheral capitalist orders that underwent liberalization without much development in a way that departs from the focus of the existing literature on describing things that have been absent and move to describing the things that exist in order to link the country's institutional settings with its nondevelopmental outcome and political economic crises.

The central argument is that failing to integrate more people into the market could perhaps explain Egypt's failed capitalist transformation during the past four decades. This study traces this failure to a lack of vibrancy and an unrealized potential to grow on the part of the vast majority of private sector enterprises. This is the essence of cleft capitalism as the institutional explanation for the lack of market integration and underdevelopment, which goes beyond Egypt into other economies in the Global South, primarily among non-oil Arab countries.

What defines cleft capitalism is a pluralism of the rules and norms governing a segmented and unevenly developed private sector that is composed of many separate and largely unintegrated groups of private enterprises organized according to their capital size at the moment of market entry. Each enterprise population operates according to a distinct set of rules that differentially govern access to inputs (finance, land, technology, labor, and information), as well as to market outlets, and hence overdetermines the opportunities for growth. Under such a setting, the large majority of private enterprises have been denied access to inputs and, consequently, their chance for growth.

The key to market integration is allowing the most entrepreneurial and market oriented among the majority of private sector enterprises to fulfill their potential to grow and scale up. This is directly dependent on the existence, efficiency, and inclusiveness of the institutions and organizations governing access to factors of production: physical and financial capital.[4] Contrary to neoclassical institutionalism, capitalization precedes and even preconditions the emergence of formal market institutions rather than vice versa.

The problem of market integration in Egypt was not the absence of the Weberian spirit for exchange and the profit-making mentality among a majority of economically active people. Rather, it was the hard constraint of accessing capital. Indeed, social relations, networks, and norms have enabled many enterprises to become market actors in the sense of producing for exchange in view of repetitive profit making. They have created a condition of market-oriented embeddedness in which the private social and cultural capital of microenterprises and household businesses could be used to access and process information, raise initial capital, and acquire basic entrepreneurial skills, as well as lower the cost of exchange despite weak formal contract enforcement and poor public information (Khan and Jomo, 2000, 21). However, market-oriented embeddedness was not enough to achieve market integration due to restrained access to capital. It barely enabled business entry and survival, let alone growth and expansion.

The central mechanism behind cleft capitalism has been the outcome of a sociopolitical coalition—primarily state bureaucratic actors who made direct use of financial and physical capital. This coalition of multiple and diverse bureaucratic actors remained disproportionately in charge of defining the uses of state authority in the economic sphere, though not always in a harmonious, coherent, or coordinated manner. It led to the perpetuation of centralized, hierarchical, and authoritarian organizations and institutions that raised the cost of accessing finance and land for the majority of market actors in Egypt throughout the decades that followed infitāḥ.

CLEFT CAPITALISM: A SEGMENTED PRIVATE SECTOR

The launch of infitāḥ in 1974 marked a period of private sector growth. The resultant private sector was by no means uniform or homogeneous, as Egyptian private enterprises came in a great variety of sizes and legal statuses. According to a census conducted by Egypt's Central Authority for Public Mobilization and Statistics (CAPMAS, 2014, cited in ʻAbdel-Wahāb, 2014), the country had 2.1 million privately owned enterprises in 2014, the vast majority of them operating on a very small scale and seldom formally registered. Altogether, these small-scale enterprises employed 2.8 million workers, excluding employers and self-employed entrepreneurs.

These small-scale establishments (SSEs) are the main focus of this book. The term *establishment* itself is borrowed from F. Schumacher's seminal work, *Small Is Beautiful* (2011 [1973]), and is intended to be broader than the terms *enterprise* or *firm*. It accommodates the many different forms that small-scale economic activity take, ranging from household businesses, sole proprietorships, and workshops all the way to legally registered firms. These are small, usually labor-intensive social units that undertake production- and distribution-related tasks, regardless of their legal status, and also transcend the technically unnecessary distinction between microenterprises and small enterprises that is usually superimposed on them by creditors, donors, and development agencies and government bodies. Moreover, rampant informality, where a large portion of economic activity is not caught on official records, provides a limited basis for distinguishing between small-scale establishments based on metrics such as employment, turnover, or capital as data are often largely inaccurate or missing altogether.

In contrast to the few large enterprises at the helm of the economy that ultimately carry out value creation, the broad base of SSEs has shown little capacity to grow, generate good-quality jobs, invest, or be competitive in national or export markets. In this sense, the Egyptian private sector has demonstrated persistent signs of the missing-middle syndrome: the virtual absence of SMEs after decades of private sector development. In contrast there are the few very large, primarily Egyptian,[5] enterprises that held the greatest share of output and investment, as well as the more than 2 million microenterprises that employed fewer than five workers in low-capital, low-skill, and low-productivity activities (Stevenson, 2011, 81).

Indeed, the missing-middle syndrome has been a structural expression of cleft capitalism and a long-standing trait of the Egyptian private sector since its inception. According to the CAPMAS census of 1996, SMEs, defined as those hiring more than ten workers, constituted 1.4 percent of all private Egyptian enterprises, a percentage that remained largely unchanged from 1.3 percent in 1986. The 2006 census depicted a similar picture, with microenterprises (defined as employing fewer than five workers) constituting 94 percent of all Egyptian private enterprises and medium-sized enterprises only 0.8 percent. "Relative to the total stock of enterprises in the country, there are very few that grow beyond 10 employees. Of the 1.79 million private sector companies registered with the Social Insurance Fund in 2007, less than one percent (0.75 percent) had more than 20 employees" (Stevenson and Abdel Aziz, 2008, 1).

The missing middle is an acute manifestation of a market integration problem. The issue is not that Egypt has had a very large number of SSEs but that it has been the general inability of these establishments to grow into units that produce value and exploit resources, including workers. In other words, Egypt's middle void is not so much a result of the challenges SMEs face in accessing finance or markets, which has served as the favorite topic for much neoliberal development literature since the 1990s (Beck, Demirgüç-Kunt, and Martinez Peria, 2008; Beck, Demirgüç-Kunt, Laeven, and Levine, 2008; Nasr, 2008; De la Campa, 2011; el-Kabbani and Kalhoefer, 2011; Rocha, Farazi, Khouri, and Pearce, 2011; Hendy and Zaki, 2013). Rather, it has been derived from the challenges facing SSEs to gain the capacity to grow into SMEs.

Crucially, the missing middle has lowered the prospects for market integration and hence has largely precluded any chance of developing vibrant, labor-intensive industries capable of linking with big business to create jobs and make use of Egypt's large pool of unskilled and semiskilled labor. In contrast, it marks a private sector that is largely made of tiny units that suffer from low productivity, undercapitalization, and an inability to scale up.

The extent of Egypt's missing-middle syndrome becomes much clearer by comparing the structure of its private sector with that of the more successful cases of market-based development, primarily in Asia. Whereas SMEs made up around 4 percent of all enterprises in Egypt in 2006, they constituted 51.7 percent in Malaysia. Medium-sized enterprises (hiring between 51 and 150 workers) represented 9.1 percent of Malaysian firms based on a 2002 survey (Saleh and Ndubisi, 2006, 4), while overall SMEs accounted for 25.8 percent of all value-added production and approximately 20 percent of exports. These substantial numbers, however, remained "lower than [in] many other countries, such as the Philippines, Hong Kong [and] Taiwan" (Saleh and Ndubisi, 2006, 1).

In Taiwan, the share of SMEs began expanding steadily in the 1950s, with small enterprises increasing from 8.02 percent in 1954 to 22.38 percent in 1966 and 25.20 percent by 1996 (Wu and Huang, 2003, 3). Such an increase occurred at the expense of microenterprises (hiring fewer than nine workers in the Taiwanese definition) whose total share dropped from 90.7 percent in 1954 to 70 percent in 1996 (Wu and Huang, 2003, 11). These figures demonstrate the broad-based capacity of private sector enterprises to scale up and become competitive at a national or even global scale. Indeed, by the mid-1990s, Taiwanese SMEs contributed around half of total exports (Wu and Huang, 2003, 14).

China also possesses a vibrant, broad base of private sector SMEs. According to Zhu and Sanderson (2009, 23–24), "SMEs contribute more than 60 percent of the nation's GDP, 50 percent of tax revenues, 70 percent of import and export trade and 80 percent of urban employment." Anderson, Li, Harrison, and Robson (2003) estimated that officially registered SMEs account for 60 percent of China's GNP, 40 percent of profits and taxes, and nearly 68 percent of exports in some sectors.

Thus, a missing middle is not a structural feature of all economies in the Global South. It reflects certain institutional conditions in the capitalist transformation that in the Egyptian case, stifled the access of the majority of private enterprises to inputs and market outlets critical for their growth. Indeed, the vast majority of SSEs have been subject to a great variety of constraints and barriers to growth. According to Stevenson (2011, 84):

> The literature seeking to explain the greater predominance of micro and very small enterprises in developing countries suggests that the following can all be factors acting to constrain the emergence of medium-sized and larger firms: the low education and skill levels of micro- and small-enterprise owners; a high level of uncertainty or insecurity in the economy (which leads to the minimization of investment and risk); weak property rights; the inability to exploit economies of scale due to liquidity constraints and lack of transport infrastructure and services; rigid labor restrictions that make hiring of formal workers difficult and expensive; imperfect information; high transaction costs and insufficient access to and use of technology.

All of these features have been endemic to the Egyptian private sector since before the infitāḥ of the mid-1970s. However, as the previous examples of success attest to, such features are not inherent in economies in the Global South, but are themselves the result of enduring institutional arrangements that determined the actual access of private sector firms to production inputs (land, finance, technology, and skilled labor) as well as market outlets. These are the institutional rules and norms that restrain the choices of market actors and define their strategic behavior in relation to environmental constraints (Steinmo, Thelen, and Longstreth, 1992).

The few private sector enterprises that could meaningfully engage with the production and exchange of economic value were either politically connected or able to take advantage of their initial large size to play an intermediary role between the Egyptian market and the world economy. The others, made up of hundreds of thousands of private SSEs, were born tiny and remained so. This economic apartheid reflects an uneven institutional arrangement that this book calls "cleft capitalism" that has stood as the main characteristic of the capitalist order that emerged in Egypt over the past four decades. I present the concept of cleft capitalism as an institutional explanation for the lack of dynamism and vibrancy of the Egyptian private sector (GEM, 2008, 2010, 2012; Stevenson, 2011), an economy that has been overwhelmingly made up of tiny establishments incapable of scaling up and creating highly productive and high-wage employment opportunities.

The state of cleft capitalism does more than determines the way enterprises interact with the institutions surrounding their operation, which naturally differs by firm size, economic sector, and legal status; it also implies the existence of several different subsystems of business rules and norms with different codes and mechanisms of enforcement. The perpetuation of initial size differences (once small, always small) is largely mediated through the interaction of different subsystems of enterprises with each other. In addition, larger firms are not attracted to dealing with the broad base of private sector enterprises due to their limited productivity and lack of competitiveness. This in turn contributes to the inability of most SSEs to reach out to national or international markets and instead resign themselves to serving very local markets to sell their goods and services (al-Mahdi and Rashed, 2010, 110).

In addition, the lack of capital, skills, and technology required to produce high-value goods and services has precluded SSEs from creating backward and forward linkages with larger producers. These linkages usually require the existence of SMEs that specialize in the production of inputs demanded by bigger producers and distributors. A Ministry of Finance report (2004, 16) held that the missing-middle syndrome "results in weak linkages between the large and the SME sector, and hence in unduly high import content of products [and] lack of efficiency due to the weakness of local competition." Semifinished and intermediate goods made up 40.3 percent of total Egyptian imports in 2013–2014 according to the CAPMAS (cited in ʿAbdel-Bāri, 2015). These imports are more than double the value of exports, resulting in a huge and chronic trade deficit that is a constant burden on official reserves as well as the national currency.

The absence of backward and forward linkages meant that large businesses could not exploit SSEs, especially in labor-intensive industries and services.[6] In more successful cases of transformation, such as Turkey since the 1980s, large businesses, often with strong ties to the state, based their expansion in manufactured exports on extensive ties with small sweatshops that could produce inputs and final products to be marketed abroad by trading companies run by large business groups (Öniș, 1999; Adly, 2012a). This model originated in Japan in the 1950s and 1960s and was picked up by South Korea in the 1970s where the broad base of the private sector was well integrated into the chains of production and distribution of large firms. In Egypt, this never happened because SSEs were caught in a spiral of undercapitalization and lack of access to basic inputs and information that could have made them tempting targets for exploitation by big business—Egyptian or foreign.

This can partly explain Egypt's inability to diversify its role in the global division of labor, which remained dependent on selling cheap energy even when it became a net energy importer itself between 2006 and 2011 (Adly, 2012a, 110–112). Diversifying out of crude energy dependency required boosting labor-intensive manufacturing and service sectors, which in turn necessitated well-educated and skilled laborers, as well as dynamic private enterprises that could tap into such resources. However, given the institutional arrangements that marked Egypt's capitalist order, these ingredients were absent despite some attempts by the state, especially during Mubārak's last decade in power, to develop them. As Figure 1.1 indicates, the structure of Egyptian exports has not changed much since 1989, Note, for example, a general inability to diversify away from selling crude oil and natural gas, which are by definition capital intensive and confined to enclaves largely disconnected from the rest of the economy.

In general, the Egyptian state was not able to invest much in capital formation beginning in the 1990s due to a combination of fiscal crises and austerity under the auspices of international financial institutions. The gross capital formation of the public sector averaged only 11.13 percent of GDP between 1989 and 2010 (World Bank, 2017a), while the private sector, where the bulk of investment had progressively passed, failed to compensate for state withdrawal. Overall, the resultant pattern was that of a low capital formation ratio to GDP and stagnant, or even declining, rates of capital formation growth. Indeed, the Egyptian ratio of gross capital formation to GDP has been low in comparison to other countries with lower per capita incomes, such as India and Vietnam. According to the World Bank, Egypt's ratio of gross capital formation to GDP averaged 19.6 percent between 1989 and 2012, compared to 29.89, 31.21, and 41.74 percent for India, Vietnam, and China, respectively (World Bank, 2017a). Not only has Egypt's average ratio been low, it has also shown a stagnant or even declining trend throughout the 1990s and 2000s.

Throughout this period, the Egyptian private sector did expand, and it did so significantly. The problem was not the high barriers to entry, as mainstream neoclassical literature on development has long held; rather, it was the high

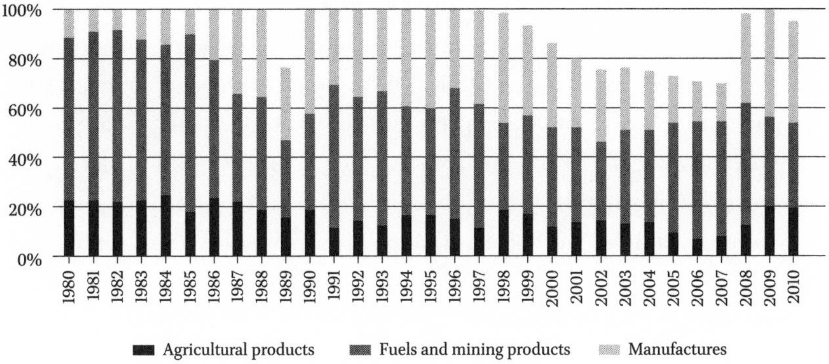

FIGURE 1.1. Egypt's Export Composition, 1980–2010 (in percent).
Source: World Trade Organization, *Time Series, Egypt* (1980–2012), http://stat.wto.org/StatisticalProgram/WSDBStatProgramYear.aspx?Language=E.

barriers to growth. Indeed, many could enter and start new enterprises—though usually from a very low point in terms of capital, productivity, and skill—which may explain the expansion in the private sector's share of total employment. However, as the market has expanded due to a combination of state withdrawal under the pressure of chronic fiscal crises and international conditionality, on the one hand, and population growth and continuing urbanization, on the other, the system of institutions that emerged excluded the large majority of the private sector from any meaningful engagement with the production of economic value. This was not the result of deliberate or premeditated state policies that sought the marginalization of these thousands of small entrepreneurs; rather it was the precise opposite: the inability to develop institutional arrangements that could have better integrated these small-scale market actors. This dismal economic situation, however, did have political repercussions.

POLITICS: THE DELEGITIMIZING EFFECT OF CLEFT CAPITALISM

Economic liberalization and the departure from state socialism was a response to the fiscal crises that hit Egypt in the 1970s and 1980s. The (economically) liberalizing authoritarian regimes of Anwar al-Sadāt and Ḥosni Mubārak sought to create a vibrant private sector that could deliver higher growth rates, attract foreign and other Arab investments, and increase state revenues (King, 2009; Soliman, 2011; Adly, 2012a). The plan was to tailor economic liberalization to the requirements of authoritarian survival and reproduction, or, as Roccu (2013, 28) put it, "the attempt to reconstruct hegemony on new foundations." Liberalization and the growth of the private sector were seen as a means to emerge from the recession that hit in the late 1960s through growth generation and job creation. However, trade liberalization, deregulation, and the divestiture of state-owned companies were to be gradual, if not sluggish, so as to avoid any large-scale social disruption like the riots witnessed in January 1977.

The ruling incumbents in Egypt were consumed with managing the contradictions that unfolded between the paternalistic authoritarian ethos of the postindependence state they inherited and the internal and external pressures and incentives to undertake liberalization measures. The Mubārak regime in particular had to adopt economic liberalization and privatization throughout the 1980s and 1990s under the growing pressure of fiscal crises, hard currency shortages, recession, and foreign conditionality, in the process alienating the social constituencies that originally depended on an exchange of political rights for economic entitlements—mainly to labor and the middle classes.

Politically, cleft capitalism and its structural manifestation, the missing-middle syndrome, deprived the Mubārak regime of the ability to develop a solid base of a small or middle bourgeoisie (i.e., owners and managers of small and medium businesses) that could have stood as support blocks in favor of economic liberalization and market reforms. These groups could have functioned as alternative social bases to mobilize against those who lost out from the liberalization process: the public sector workers and employees who constituted the core constituencies of the postindependence state (King, 2009; Soliman, 2011).

Cleft capitalism created a spiraling situation where the regime became increasingly dependent on a few large businesses and business families in order to face increasingly dissatisfied, and disenfranchised, social groups. However, the integration of these new "economic elites" did not replace the need for an alternative social base of support for the ruling regime. Despite the attempts to outsource patronage networks to private capital holders via the ruling National Democratic Party (NDP) and parliamentary membership during the last decade of Mubārak's rule (see Soliman, 2011), the negative impacts of liberalization and privatization could not be offset.

It is noteworthy that the literature on cronyism and state capture on Egypt has almost solely concentrated on the role state incumbents played in enriching handpicked businesspeople and business families through the misuse of public authority rather than the role these politically connected businesses played in sustaining and legitimizing the ruling regime. However, the work of the late Samer Soliman (2006, 2011), which focuses on the rising stars of NDP-linked businessmen in the ruling party–dominated parliament as well as the not-so-competitive presidential elections, was exceptional in its investigation into how the regime attempted to preserve its power through patronage rather than simply resorting to repression.

Ultimately, over three decades of capitalist transformation failed to produce winners that were large and organized enough to extend the support that their authoritarian patrons needed. Such a development, or nondevelopment, stands in contrast to other nations, such as Turkey, China, and Malaysia, where economic liberalization created a broad base of SMEs with the capacity to grow and compete in national and international markets that provided support for liberalizing incumbents.

The practical outcome in the Egyptian case was the continuous erosion of the economic and social privileges once enjoyed by the middle classes and unionized labor. Because Mubārak and his regime could not easily or quickly undo the old social coalition (Bayat, 1993; Posusney, 1997), the only option was to hold together some sort of coexistence between features of the old order and those of the new. For instance, the state remained a major, if not the largest, single employer through the creation of low-paid and often redundant jobs in the bureaucracy. The state also largely retained its distributive role in providing large food and energy subsidy programs. Indeed, the deficit and public debt through the 1990s hardly suggest that the Egyptian state had grown smaller or that liberalizing incumbents could finally free themselves of the old-order commitments.

The limited resource base available to the ruling regime compounded the challenges. The overall share of external rent in GDP (defined to include extractive industries, geopolitical rents, and foreign aid) has been small and consistently declining since the 1990s. The total share of oil and natural gas production, together with revenue from the Suez Canal, averaged a mere 11.3 percent of GDP between 1991 and 2006 (Central Bank of Egypt, 2018d). In fact, Suez Canal revenue actually declined from 3.2 percent of the total GDP in the period between 1991 and 2001 to 2.9 percent from 2001 to 2006. Similarly, Egypt's total energy production remained constant in absolute terms between 1992 and 2001, yet it became a net oil importer in 2006 when consumption overtook production for the first time. The country would nevertheless re-emerge as a net energy producer thanks to a temporary surge in natural gas production in 2005/2006. However, this proved to be short-lived: Egypt became a net energy importer once more in 2011/2012 as local consumption of natural gas exceeded production.

The same trend applies to foreign aid and grants. Soliman (2006, 62) marked the decline in the ratio of foreign aid to GDP from 5 percent in 1994 to a mere 1 percent in 2000. According to the Central Bank of Egypt (2018d), the ratio of foreign grants to total state revenue maintained a consistent downward trend between 2001 and 2012, with the ratio decreasing from 5.45 percent in 2001 to 1.57 percent in 2005 and 0.86 in 2012. This decline significantly narrowed the base of external rents and rendered economic performance increasingly dependent on export expansion and the attraction of foreign investment, an exceedingly difficult—and ultimately unattainable—task given the stagnation of the broad base of private sector enterprises.

The ultimate result was the slow but persistent unraveling of the old distributional alliances, which inaugurated the eventual unmaking of the social populist coalition on which the very foundations of the postindependence state stood since the time of Gamāl ʿAbdel-Nāṣer (Kandil, 2012).

All this suggests that the failed market making and unraveling of the sociopolitical and economic orders in 2011 under the pressure of rising discontent goes beyond the mere self-enrichment, cronyism, and corruption of the incumbent regime. Whereas some writers and scholars prefer to view the previous few decades as a melodrama with the former dictator's family and their cronies starring as villains, a deeper reading would suggest that it was more of a tragedy. Egypt's security-oriented regime had to struggle with a plethora of structural and institutional restraints that they hoped to overcome, or at least paper over, so as to retain and reproduce their authority—a task that ultimately proved impossible. This of course does not relieve them of their historical responsibility; however, their repression, corruption, and long series of wrongheaded policy choices did not occur in a void. Rather, they were restrained by a number of factors that led to the rise and perpetuation of cleft capitalism.

In sum, this chapter has shown that despite the successive waves of liberalization, deregulation, and privatization that led to the creation of a private sector–dominated economy in Egypt, the capitalist order that resulted proved to be neither developmental nor politically sustainable in the long term. Economically, it was a low-growth model that failed to generate sufficient investments or jobs to provide a long-term, sustainable improvement in living conditions. Socially and politically, it failed to deliver for an increasingly youthful population that expected decent employment and better standards of living. The capitalist transformation instead contributed to the slow yet sure erosion of the socioeconomic base of the authoritarian postindependence state that once relied on a broad coalition of unionized labor and urban and rural middle classes (Roccu, 2013, 99). In short, those who won from the capitalist transformation were too few to outnumber and outweigh those who lost, setting the stage for alienation, discontent, and, finally, revolt.

Given the detrimental economic effects that cleft capitalism and an unintegrated economy have had on Egypt, this book aims to answer the question of how this suboptimal institutional arrangement came about and what political-economic factors produced and reproduced it.

BOOK STRUCTURE

Chapter 2 engages critically with the conventional wisdom, largely informed by neoclassical institutionalism, on market making in Egypt and MENA. Chapter 3 then presents the key concept of cleft capitalism that describes and explains Egypt's failed capitalist transformation and its political-economic repercussions. A primary argument is that cleft capitalism encourages an economic sociological turn in the study of market making in Egypt, while maintaining that the economy cannot be understood away from broader social and political contexts.

Chapter 4 turns to demonstrating the exact institutional mechanisms through which cleft capitalism was produced and reproduced through time. It traces the core problem to the perpetual undercapitalization of SSEs due to the high barriers associated with accessing financial and physical capital—bank credit and desert land, respectively. In turn, this condition is explained in terms of the dominant sociopolitical coalition that has reigned since the advent of infitāḥ. The power relations within this ruling coalition have produced and reproduced hierarchical and centralized capital-regulating organizations that maintain a high cost of access to land and bank credit for the majority of private sector enterprises. Only those with large initial private capital or strong political ties, or both, could adapt to these barriers and grew to comprise the country's big business class, while most SSEs were excluded from the system.

Chapter 5 addresses the question of where the institutional condition of cleft capitalism came from. It examines at length the multiple political-economic factors since Egypt's infitāḥ in the mid-1970s that shaped the role of the state amid the process of market making and why they led to the production and perpetuation of cleft capitalism.

Chapters 6 and 7 give a detailed, dynamic, and diachronic analysis of how access to financial and physical capital has been governed in Egypt since infitāḥ. They provide thorough descriptions of the institutional framework regulating access to capital and why they have sustained high barriers to accessing capital, and hence to growth, for the broad base of private sector SSEs despite progressive marketization.

The final two chapters explore in detail two of the three business subsystems that constitute Egypt's cleft capitalist order. Chapter 8 offers a detailed and vivid picture of Egypt's *baladi* capitalism, the label given to the first component of cleft capitalism and that comprises most SSEs. Informed by extensive field research conducted in mid-2013, the chapter depicts a lively portrayal of how Egypt's private SSEs evolved and the diverse and often complex modes of articulation between what is formal and informal and what is economic and social. Chapter 9 subsequently studies the other subsystem, labeled "dandy capitalism," in the same manner by showing how coordination problems were dealt with. The book concludes by drawing on the main findings and offering some insights into the future of capitalist development in Egypt and the MENA more generally.

Chapter Two

BEYOND CRONYISM

IN J. R. R. TOLKIEN'S *LORD OF THE RINGS*, ONE RING RULES OVER all else. As carved on the mythical object: "one ring to rule them all, one ring to find them, one ring to bring them all and in the darkness, bind them." As Tolkien imagined one magical item as the key to controlling everything, neoclassical institutionalism came to explain underdevelopment across the world in a single idea: the absence of functioning property rights capable of upholding free markets. From their view, the world is divided into two camps, the "West and the rest," with institutions ensuring property rights explaining the "mystery" of capital, markets, and development (De Soto, 2000). Little focus, however, is directed toward the variation that exists among the residual category of "the rest," and even less effort is made to illuminate the institutional developments that may produce these varying outcomes.

As outlined in Chapter 1, this book argues that Egypt's failed market making since the mid-1970s has been due to more than just cronyism or the general lack of the functioning formal market institutions of private property rights and the rule of law. Rather, a deeper cause traces back to a condition of weak market integration due to the predominance of cleft capitalism as an institutional condition governing Egypt's transformation. This is not confined to Egypt by any means and is applicable to other countries in the Global South, namely, other non-oil North African nations and others in South Asia and possibly Latin America.

This argument stands to critique the underlying assumption of neoclassical institutionalism: that capitalism cannot exist, let alone function, in the absence of the set of political-economic institutions that historically evolved in northwestern Europe and North America between the sixteenth and nineteenth centuries (Fahmi, 2010, 59). Here, there is a hidden element of what Alfred Stepan (2000) once called the "fallacy of unique founding conditions," where the only road toward capitalism is presumed to pass through a market democracy that combines universal political rights with private property protection (Haber, North, and Weingast, 2008; Robinson and Acemoglu, 2012).

This assumption of neoclassical institutionalism conjures up strong, albeit implicit, elements of both Eurocentrism and ahistoricism. History suggests in fact that capitalism initially developed in the absence of such political and institutional conditions, largely forming through a number of "private order institutions"—that is, "situations in which order prevails despite the lack of a third-party enforcer of that order [i.e., the state]." As Greif (2006) notes, "In such situations, the prevalence of order or its absence reflects the behavior of the interacting individuals rather than what transpires between them and a third party" (8). Indeed, the rise of the notion of the rule of law in late eighteenth- and early nineteenth-century Europe was, according to Foucault, Davidson, and Burchell (2008, 168), ultimately concerned with the limiting of state power in relation to civil society and market actors rather than bringing the state in to serve as a third party in social and economic interactions.

Throughout the past four decades, a number of economies in Asia, Latin America, and East and Central Europe have demonstrated how countries can achieve significant success in generating growth, boosting global competitiveness, raising investment rates, and improving standards of living without a priori having functioning formal market institutions and clearly defined private property rights. Rather, they have relied on different modes of governance that combine elements of market, hierarchy, community, and a mix of formal and informal rules and norms that could nonetheless perform the task of coordinating economic activity to generate growth and competitiveness. For instance, Stark (1996) observed in his authoritative article on postsocialist Hungary that property transformation "involves the decentralized reorganization of assets and the centralized management of liabilities. Together they blur the boundaries of public and private, the boundaries of enterprises, and the boundedness of justificatory principles." Walder (1995) noted that China's strong growth in output and productivity was attributed to the clear redefinition of government ownership rather than private property rights. Hence, there is little reason to maintain the notion that capitalist transformations in the Global South have to start where another historical experience ended.

While it is true that the prevailing socioeconomic institutions in Egypt, and the MENA region more generally, have failed to overcome the restraints on their developmental potential (Achcar, 2013), this cannot be simply subsumed under the question of why they failed to create functioning formal markets like those that developed in late-nineteenth-century North America and Western Europe (Greif 2006, 347; Foucault et al., 2008, 168–169; Panitch and Gindin, 2012, 4). A more accurate way of posing the question would be why the existing modes of economic governance—be they formal or informal, public or private, or combinations of these—failed to play a developmental role in the case of Egypt in contrast to other economic success stories, primarily in East and Southeast Asia.

Successive waves of liberalization, deregulation, and privatization in Egypt from the mid-1970s served to pull more and more social groups and individuals into the orbit of market exchange (Farsoun, 1988, 165; Hopkins, 1992, 15). With massive urbanization, the retreating share of agriculture in total employment, and the shrinking role of the public sector, more and more Egyptians became increasingly dependent on the market for their livelihoods (Assaad, 2010, 34–37; al-Mahdi and Rashed, 2010, 94). However, the emerging capitalist order was deeply divided into several parallel business subsystems that over time created a number of structural chasms between different groups of private sector enterprises (cleft capitalism). Under such an arrangement, the broad base of private sector enterprises and entrepreneurs was systematically denied any credible chance to access the production inputs and market outlets that were necessary for growth.

The most acute structural expression of cleft capitalism has been the missing-middle syndrome wherein the private sector is divided between a few large enterprises on the top and a vast ocean of microenterprises on the bottom, with the virtual absence of any stratum of SMEs. Those that could grow into the ranks of large, private enterprises were the ones endowed with large initial private capital, strong external linkages, or some salient political connection. Those that started small remained so in perpetuity, demonstrating the stagnant and disabling character of the prevailing institutional order.

Studies of Egypt's lackluster development performance have largely focused on the issue of crony capitalism, particularly the routes through which big business emerged since infitāḥ (Imām, 1986; Zaalouk, 1989; Heydemann, 2004; Adly, 2009, 2012b; King, 2009; Roll, 2013; Diwan, 2013; Chekir and Diwan, 2014; el-Tarouty, 2016). They stressed the uneven distribution of private property rights between different market actors, as well as the fact that favorable access to resources (e.g., allocated state-owned land, divested SOEs, public procurement, bank credit), information, and economic opportunities went to a small number of actors by virtue of their strong political ties.

It is undeniable that politics has played a significant, if not a central, role in the rise of big business in Egypt since the mid-1970s. This is hardly surprising, let alone unique; history shows that the rise of big private capital has usually been driven to some degree by political dynamics. This is true even in the freest and most market oriented of advanced capitalist economies, England (Deane, 1965) and the United States (Bairoch, 1995; Panitch and Gindin, 2012, 26, 31–33), as well as the cases of late industrialization such as Germany, Japan, and Italy, where the state assumed a crucial role in the allocation of resources in partnership with large, private businesses (Gerschenkron, 1962). Indeed, rent generated by public policies has often been such a pervasive element of primitive accumulation that it becomes very difficult to separate market making from rent seeking. However, as Khan and Jomo (2000, 79) note:

> It makes no sense to ask what the total rent-seeking cost in a society is, or what the structure of rights would be in the absence of all rent seeking. That is a bit like asking what the world would look like in the absence of all friction. None of the structures or activities, which we know, might be viable in the absence of all friction, and, similarly no institutions and rights might survive if all rent-seeking expenditures really disappeared.

This literature on cronyism and rent seeking suffers from a blind spot in terms of assessing the problematic nature of Egypt's capitalist transformation. Where Egypt's large enterprises came from does not explain the missing-middle syndrome or the lack of vibrancy and dynamism in the rest of the private sector. The issue with Egypt's private sector, as well as other cases of failed market transformation, seems to lie more with its inability to engender a robust stratum of SMEs rather than the existence of large enterprises that are politically connected. Indeed, in other instances throughout the Global South, the emergence of large businesses, even along crony lines, went hand in hand with the development of a robust stratum of SMEs in the private sector (examples are the cases of China, South Korea, Taiwan, Malaysia, the Philippines, and Turkey in the 2000s and a number of Central European countries that joined the EU in 2004). This did not occur in Egypt, where the capitalist order remained cleft.

This chapter proceeds by first critiquing the literature on crony capitalism together with its neoclassical institutionalist foundations. It then moves on to developing an alternative explanatory model for Egypt's failure to achieve market-based development and the manifestation of cleft capitalism.

OVERSTATING CRONY CAPITALISM

The literature has drawn a strong correlation between cronyism and predation, on the one hand, and the authoritarian dynamics of ruling regimes, on the other (Haddad, 2011). In the MENA, it focused primarily on the predatory economic practices of ruling presidential families and their cronies, who used state power to pursue their own narrow private interests at the expense of the public good (Erdle, 2010; Owen, 2014; Rijkers et al., 2014). The lack of accountability and democracy provided a ripe political context for an unholy alliance between wealth and power.

Not only was the capitalism in MENA and Egypt, as well as many other parts of the Global South, best described as cronyism; it also provided an explanation for the problems in these countries of economic underperformance, social marginalization, inequality, and the eventual political legitimacy crises that afflicted their ruling regimes. They maintain that in the absence of an even distribution of property rights, there are scant incentives for the broader base of society to engage in exchange or investment. Hence, subsistence, not capital accumulation, has become the driving motivation of the majority of entrepreneurs in the Global South (De Soto, 2000). This stands in contrast to the West, where accumulation and investment thrive under the firm establishment of private property rights (North, 1990; Acemoglu and Robinson, 2012).

This book's argument regarding the explanatory power of cleft capitalism stands on the claim that crony capitalism, as rampant as it was in Egypt, cannot be the sole the reason that market integration failed.

In the decade that preceded the January revolution of 2011, Egypt witnessed the simultaneous intensification of various forms of cronyism, on the one hand (Adly, 2012b; Diwan, 2013; el-Tarouty, 2016), and economic growth and expansion on the other. The accelerating pace of privatization (Hanieh, 2013, 50–52), deregulation of key economic sectors, and an expansion in the allocation of state-owned land for real estate, tourism, and agricultural projects all fed into an extensive network of cronies tied to the Mubārak regime. At the same time, all of these ills coexisted with high growth rates (the highest since the 1980s), unprecedented levels of foreign direct investments (FDI), and successful export expansion and upgrading. These parallel developments stand as paradoxical to the neoclassical assumption: the weakness of formal market institutions and the prevalence of crony practices did not deter investment and growth; rather, the opposite seemed to occur.

According to World Bank indicators, net foreign direct inflows to Egypt rose from an annual average of $746 million between 1990 and 1999 to $4.86 billion between 2000 and 2010, an increase of 552 percent (World Bank, 2017e, calculated by the author; see Figure 2.1). These figures compare favorably with other emerging economies: Egypt's average percentage of net FDI inflows stood at 4.74 percent between 2003 and 2011 compared to 2.77, 7.66, 3.87, 1.99, 2.62, 2.08, and 5.06 percent for Brazil, Chile, China, India, Mexico, Turkey, and the Czech Republic respectively (World Bank, 2017e).

Foreign and Arab investors did not seem vulnerable to, or at least significantly fearful of, risks of predation by the state or other market actors despite the weak status of the rule of law. Indeed, the FDI breakdown reveals that greenfield expansion stood at 43.4 percent of the total FDI inflows between 2005 and 2010, followed by 12.8 percent for privatization and 41.4 percent in the traditional oil and gas sector (Hanafy, 2015, 21). During the same time period (2005–2009), "manufacturing received real FDI of almost 13 billion EGP [Egyptian pounds] at 1992 prices, that is roughly double the inflows in 2000–2004 (7 billion Egyptian pounds) and more than triple the inflows in 1995–1999

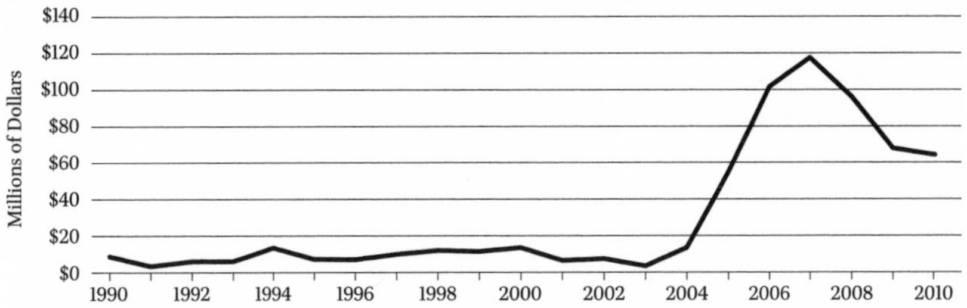

FIGURE 2.1. Foreign Direct Investment, Net Inflows.
Source: World Bank data, Egypt, 1990–2010, https://data.worldbank.org/indicator/BX.KLT.DINV.CD.WD?locations=EG.

(4 billion pounds)" (Hanafy, 2015, 21). This sheer increase in FDI net inflows in the 2000s occurred despite reports of rampant cronyism and corruption.

Exports also witnessed impressive expansion during this same period, with growth averaging 21.58 percent from 2001 to 2012, a significant increase from -2.94 percent during the 1990s and 8.8 percent in the 1980s (World Trade Organization, 2017). This export increase took place through closely knit state-business networks that were often opaque, informal, and self-serving (Roccu, 2013, 69, 97). However, favored businessmen were able to deliver positive macroeconomic results (Abdel-Latif and Schmitz, 2010). It is no surprise, then, that many international financial institutions regarded the years directly preceding the 2011 revolution as a model success story of growth, progressive liberalization, and economic opening.

This suggests that cronyism was not exclusively predatory or necessarily a drag on growth, as these rents were not solely delivered to unproductive actors or withdrawn from the market entirely. To the contrary, state rents in Egypt did contribute to the rise of market actors bent on using the rents to create economic value and expand exchange on the market. This was the case with construction, real estate, tourism, energy-intensive industries, and assembly manufacturing. Of course, extensive rent seeking and cronyism did not prove transformative for Egypt's economy, unlike in South Korea, for instance; the Egyptian state has had a limited capacity to create and manage rents for learning, which could have led to technological upgrading and value enhancement (Khan and Jomo, 2000, 88). It was not enough to push Egypt's economy into higher value-added niches in the global division of labor, a task that falls to the state rather than private market actors, who naturally focus on maximizing profits instead of designing and pursuing development strategies.

Strong challenges to some of the basic assumptions of neoclassical institutionalism have come from East and Southeast Asian capitalisms. In these examples, rampant cronyism persisted in the form of unequal access to productive assets, information, and market positions without proving inimical to overall economic growth or global competitiveness (Khan and Jomo, 2000; Kang, 2002). In fact, since the 1960s and through the 1990s, many East and Southeast Asian economies recorded impressive rates of growth, job creation, export expansion, and investment while lacking the institutional underpinnings of free market capitalism that historically evolved in the West or, more precisely, some areas given the great variety of capitalist institutions within Western Europe itself (Crozier 1964, 272). There is also little evidence that any of these success stories resulted from the broad emulation—or what Evans (2003) once called "institutional monocropping"—of Western, primarily Anglo-American, capitalist institutions.

South Korea, for instance, has operated under a notoriously cronyistic political economic structure since the 1960s (Krueger, 1987; Oh and Varcin, 2003). Here, the state has clearly picked winners (Amsden, 1992, 1997; Evans, 2012) and allocated resources on a nonmarket basis in favor of a politically selected few. Yet this cronyism did not impede export expansion or the industrial upgrading of the South Korean economy throughout the 1970s and 1980s. Evans and other statists have attempted to explain this seemingly odd development by emphasizing the bureaucratic characteristics of the South Korean state. By possessing qualities of embedded autonomy, they posit, the Korean bureaucracy was able to formulate and implement coherent and long-term public policies according to a well-defined conception of the public good. In short, the Korean state could distort price signals and discriminate in favor of handpicked big businesses without succumbing to rent seeking. In Alice Amsden's (1997) words, these states got institutions right while getting prices wrong.

Many scholars have critiqued this view of state bureaucracies that could seemingly perform miracles as a "Weberian idealization of state administrative offices [that was] neither very realistic nor theoretically plausible" (Goldberg, 2004, 67). Indeed, state bureaucracies are not simple implementation instruments in the hands of political leaders who instead face inherent principal-agent problems as bureaucrats develop interests of their own that may or may not align with those of politicians or the general public (Selznick, 1943, 50–51; Crozier, 1964, 6; Kaufman, 2015, 23). Moreover, there is no guarantee that state intervention would deliver the intended outcomes, as Kaufman (2015, 54) notes in the case of the US federal government: "Some government efforts have not been effective, some even exacerbated what was meant to improve or produced side effects as painful as the social ailments they were meant to cure."

Thus, while cronyism may not be overstated in the sense that it occurred (and still does), it certainly leaves much to be desired as a monocausal explanation for stunted development. "Even in Korea, corruption was far greater than the conventional wisdom allows—so rampant was corruption that we cannot dismiss it; rather, we need to explain it" (Kang, 2002, 3). Despite the centrality ascribed to state bureaucratic qualities in cases like South Korea (Amsden, 1992, 1997; Evans, 2012), Taiwan (Wade, 1990), and postwar Japan (Johnson, 1982), cronyism and development have also been demonstrated to have gone hand in hand in cases where state bureaucracies had considerably less capacity and autonomy, such as Turkey, Indonesia, Thailand, and Malaysia in the 1980s and 1990s. While these latter cases showed less impressive developmental records in comparison to South Korea, there is little evidence that rampant cronyism precluded their opportunities for growth and development.

China presents a challenging case to both neoclassical and statist institutionalisms: it has grown at an impressive average rate of 10 percent per year since the late 1970s, while showing poor records on property rights protection, rule of law, and formal contract enforcement (Worldwide Governance Indicators, 2017).

Nevertheless, it is not the case that the Chinese or East Asian "economic miracles" have had no institutional basis. Rather, the transformation to capitalism could rely on a set of institutional settings that shared little with the ones that evolved in the Western experience since the nineteenth century.

Table 2.1 displays two principal governance indicators, as well as a number of corresponding macroeconomic measurements that can be taken as proxies to general economic performance. The rule-of-law indicator reflects the confidence of agents in the rule of law, particularly the quality of contract enforcement, property rights, the police, and the courts, as well as the likelihood of

Country/ Indicator	*Rule of Law (Percentage)*	*Regulatory Quality (Percentage)*	*Average Gross Capital Formation to GDP (1989–2012)*	*Annual Average GDP Growth Rate (1990–2011)*
Egypt	52.07	37.39	19.16	4.50
Tunisia	53.89	52.23	24.53	4.54
China	40.41	44.43	41.74	9.92
Vietnam	39.54	28.03	31.21	6.96
Indonesia	28.88	40.33	26.58	5.09
Brazil	44.46	58.24	17.89	2.75
Turkey	54.4	60.5	20.63	4.35
India	55.86	40.51	29.89	6.14
OECD (2003, 2008, 2013)	87.33	88.33	—	—

TABLE 2.1. Governance and Macroeconomic Indicators in a Selected Group of Countries.
Source: Rule of law and regulatory quality indicators for the years 1996, 1998, 2000, and 2001–2011 were calculated from World Bank worldwide governance indicators, interactive database available online: http://info.worldbank.org/governance/wgi/#reports. Average GDP growth and gross capital formation ratio to GDP were obtained from World Bank data (1989–2012): https://data.worldbank.org/indicator/NY.GDP.MKTP.KD.ZG?locations=BR-CN-EG-IN-ID-TN-TR-OE-VN and https://data.worldbank.org/indicator/NE.GDI.TOTL.ZS?locations=BR-CN-EG-IN-ID-TN-TR-OE-VN, respectively.

crime and violence. Regulatory quality measures entrepreneurs' perceptions of the government's ability to formulate and implement sound policies and regulations that permit and promote private sector development (Worldwide Governance Indicators, 2017).

According to conventional neoclassical wisdom, higher rule of law and regulatory quality indicators should translate into higher investment rates (operationalized here as the ratio of gross capital formation to gross domestic product, GDP), as well as higher rates of growth. However, as the figures in

Table 2.1 indicate, there is not much of a straightforward relationship between the two. Countries such as Egypt, Tunisia, and Turkey possessed better rule of law and regulatory-quality indicators than China and Vietnam, yet their respective investment and growth rates were significantly lower.

According to neoclassical orthodoxy, weak protections for private property generally lead to state predation on businesses that either dissuades capital holders from investing or precludes their opportunities to grow out of small-scale enterprises. It also renders interbusiness transactions difficult due to the absence of a reliable third party, the state, to enforce agreements. However, despite a weak formal rule of law, an imperfect market sphere did emerge in Egypt, as well as in many other transforming economies in the Global South (Yāsīn, 2015). This was primarily due to two main sociopolitical factors: restrained state predation and market-enabling social norms and practices.

RESTRAINED STATE PREDATION

Since the infitāḥ, there have been few cases of egregious predatory acts of expropriation by the state against private market actors. Almost all cases occurred against actors whom the regime considered political adversaries rather than a generalized practice against private market actors. Prime examples were the expropriation of Muslim Brotherhood–related businesses and assets, in both 2006 and the aftermath of the 2013 coup. Aside from this, the state has refrained from any serious reversals of earlier guarantees against nationalization or sequestration that were given by the al-Sadāt regime at the outset of infitāḥ (see Moustafa, 2007). This was hardly exceptional to Egypt, however; it applies to the Global South more generally. According to Minor (1994, 180), "By the 1980s the expropriations would largely have become a thing of the past. Having already declined from 83 in 1975 to 17 in 1979, they fell to five in 1980, four in 1981, one in 1982, three in 1983, one each year from 1984 to 1986 and zero for the rest of the decade."

Although private property rights have been uncertain in Egypt even for economically powerful actors, this should not be confused or conflated with state predation over private property. For example, the en masse failure of Islamic-leaning capital investment companies (CICs) in the late 1980s was the result of a huge regulatory failure throughout the 1980s to protect depositors' private savings. State regulatory agencies like the Central Bank were too weak to intervene, so throughout the 1980s, CICs could wield significant political power to keep their sector unregulated. When they ran into deep trouble, probably because of the lack of regulation in the first place (Shuhayb, 1989, 35–36, 39), the state drove them out of business only after they had internally crumbled. This result was not the sequestration of privately owned assets but rather the loss of billions of savings of middle-class Egyptians.

The same logic would apply to cases where the state, usually through court rulings, could take back public land allocated to investors (the example of Talaat Moustafa Group's Madinaty project in 2009, when a court annulled the government decree allocating millions of acres to the giant developer after the project had already been launched [for more details, see Adly, 2012b, 9) or annul the privatization contracts of state-owned enterprises. Occasionally the regime has also used state-owned banks to put pressure on businesspeople for political purposes. As much as these cases involved the disruption of private property, they did not involve state predation over the private property of investors; rather, the contested publicly owned assets were usually transferred to private hands at below-market rates and in shady deals of privatization.

Of course, informal payments in the form of bribery and extortion have been widely reported in Egypt, yet fieldwork does not indicate that these were enough to drive market actors out of business altogether. Rather, they were factored in as an informal cost of doing business in Egypt, costs that were easy to absorb given the negligible tax burden on private sector enterprises (Sadowski, 1991, 122).

This restrained, or politically guided, predation can be explained by a number of international and domestic political factors. The international factors came principally from the influence and conditionality of the ever-present International Monetary Fund and the World Bank, but also from the United States, which sought the universal protection of property rights in third world countries through bilateral investment agreements (Vandevelde, 2009). External actors used conditionality to push for the liberalization of trade and capital movement, strong budget constraints, public sector privatization, and incentives for foreign investments. Domestic factors were related to the old and continuous history of private property in modern Egypt, even during the heyday of Nasserist state-led development that never fully extended its policies downward into the realm of micro and small businesses. Indeed, especially in the sectors of retail trade and construction, the private sector always remained dominant despite state socialism ('Abdel-Faḍīl, 1980; Morsi, 1980; Shukri, 1987; el-Kadi, 2009, 133).

MARKET-ENABLING SOCIAL PRACTICES AND NORMS

A number of other crucial market-sustaining factors were predominantly social in origin. In this sense, this book maintains that the story of capitalist transformation is more Polanyian than Hayekian, arguing that markets in the Global South have sprung out of existing social relations with a broad variety of private institutions, mechanisms of social and self-enforcement of agreements, and complex modes of articulation between formal and informal rules. In other words, individual entrepreneurs and enterprises are eminently embedded in social relations, which is how they mobilize resources, access inputs, and circulate and process information. These Polanyian traits ultimately constitute the market by lowering transaction costs and channeling resources for exchange.

As an example, the growth of the Chinese economy has occurred in the absence of any significant developments in terms of regulatory quality or formal property rights protection. Hence, China has not shown the characteristics of a developmental state or a market-preserving one (Tsai, 2004). Its progressive economic liberalization and impressive growth record took place without full-blown privatization or any substantial introduction of private property rights (Walder, 1995; Dong and Putterman, 1996).

To make sense of this puzzle, scholars have employed network analysis, social capital, and enterprise organization to explain the Chinese economy's impeccable performance in the absence of universally enforced property rights or the rule of law (Chen and Chen, 2004; Chen and Peng, 2008). A body of literature has emerged that analyzes the concept of *guanxi* as the building block of Chinese burgeoning capitalism. Chen and Peng (2008) and Chen and Chen (2004) presented guanxi as the medium through which family and collectively owned businesses become congenial to a symbiotic relationship between the interests of the individual and those of the organization. Unlike formal market settings, where the very evolution of capitalism was characterized by the rise of impersonal exchange (Greif, 2006), Chen and Chen (2004, 321) maintain that "*guanxi* personalized human relationships even in formal business organizations," as "it is difficult if not impossible to be impersonal in China."

This implies the existence of an institutional basis—essentially informal and deeply embedded in social and political relations—that is quite different from that of the Western experience with capitalism or that, at the very least, offered functional equivalents to property rights and third-party contract enforcement. As Alff (2018, 176) notes, "In changing historical contexts, the primary economic features of capitalism—free wage labor, production for the market, private ownership over means of production and the extraction of surplus value for the purpose of capital accumulation—depended on certain cultural and political factors and social relations, many of which scholars continue to consider as pre-capitalist, non-capitalist or anti-capitalist." Either way, the presence or absence of the rule of law and property rights does not explain much of the divergence between countries like Egypt, Vietnam and China, as they largely lack in all of them.

The inability of the concept of crony capitalism to fully account for these developments largely derives from the fact that it is more often used to describe the lack of certain institutions—property rights, contract enforcement, and the rule of law—than to engage with the existing institutional rules and norms that regulate economic transactions among actors. This lack can be traced to the neoclassical origins of crony capitalism as a concept, based on the assumed presence of an ideal market-upholding institutional setting that serves as the criterion against which all capitalisms have been judged. Hence, describing capitalism in non-Western contexts often becomes a simple statement of missing institutional features rather than a description of the actual institutions that govern economic transactions, as divergent as they may be from formal Western-style private property rights and the rule of law (Xin and Pearce, 1996; Peng, 2004; Peck and Zhang, 2013).

Aside from contemporary Asian capitalisms, there is a long list of non-state institutions that harbored capitalist exchange in pre-nineteenth-century Europe–-for example, cities, guilds and corporations, private clubs, and authorized monopolies like the East India Company. As Greif (2006, 347) notes, "This history calls into question the conventional wisdom that the rise of the European state was a precondition for the rise of markets. The community responsibility system suggests the importance of the opposite line of causation:

the institutional demand created by the market influenced the development of state-governed, law-based institutions." Hence, it may be more accurate to say that markets make states rather than that states make markets.

Indeed, capitalism developed in Europe over two or three centuries before the establishment of the rule of law by the second half of the nineteenth century. It would be ahistorical, and indeed inaccurate, to identify these institutions as the precondition for any capitalist transformation in the Global South. Moreover, in these cases, property rights emerged only after a property-holding class had consolidated its economic and political position over that of the state. This resonates more with the classical Marxian account of the emergence of the bourgeois state than with that of neoclassical institutionalism as in Haber, North and Weingast (2008) or Robinson and Acemoglu (2012).

The fact that a number of recent cases of capitalist transformation in the Global South were able to achieve developmental breakthroughs without the initial possession of the institutional underpinnings of the West (as of the late nineteenth century) has made it necessary to search for alternative institutional explanations. However, this theoretical and empirical effort has thus far been largely confined to the successful cases of market making. No similar efforts have been undertaken to study the socioeconomic features of the capitalist order in regions like the MENA, including Egypt, and the institutional disadvantages that have contributed to its underperformance. Those have remained subject to the usual explanation given by the neoclassicals regarding the absence of strong property rights and the prevalence of nonmarket-based capitalism, cronyism, and state capture.

BEYOND NEOCLASSICAL INSTITUTIONALISM: A FIRM-CENTERED APPROACH

Studying capitalism in the Global South requires looking for alternative conceptual and theoretical tools. The challenge lies in developing an analytical lens through which to view the broad base of private, small-scale establishments (SSEs) that are responsible for most of the production, exchange, and employment in a country like Egypt. The focus here should be on the rules and norms that govern how they operate, as well as whether they are granted access to the production inputs and market outlets that would lead to growth opportunities. This requires a shift in research from the formal supply of private property rights by the state (or lack thereof), to the institutional rules—

formal, informal, and semiformal—governing access to inputs and markets on the ground.

Small-scale establishments constitute almost 98 percent of all Egyptian enterprises and employ the largest proportion of the labor force by far. The number of micro and small enterprises in Egypt is estimated to be around 2.34 million firms, or 4.3 million if the informal sector is included (Stevenson, 2011, 80–81). An analysis of the potential of these establishments to grow and scale up into larger enterprises would reveal the potential dynamism of the Egyptian economy. From a sociopolitical perspective, the owners and managers of these SSEs constitute a sizable stratum of small capital holders, self-employed persons, and small employers. Indeed, according to data from the Central Agency for Public Mobilization and Statistics, Egypt had around 3 million employers in 2007, most of them owners of micro and small establishments (cited in al-Merghany, 2010, 144).

The bigger picture of this private sector, mainly its diversity and sheer magnitude, eludes analyses anchored around cronyism, or neoclassical institutionalism more generally, which lack a comprehensive approach that could tackle all the interrelated institutional features of a capitalist order. For instance, they have nothing to say about labor or industrial relations, education and vocational training, skill formation, taxation and subsidy policies, or administration and public investment. Such aspects are crucial for a deeper understanding of how a capitalist order functions, as well as its resulting macroeconomic and developmental outcomes (Hall and Soskice, 2001). Furthermore, they are central to understanding the production and distribution issues associated with the Egyptian economy. The ways in which skills form, as well as how labor and capital relations are managed, must be integrated into any comprehensive analysis of Egypt's capitalist order.

Accordingly, this book adopts a firm-centered approach that focuses on the strategies that enterprises employ to pursue growth and investment within their institutional environments. My approach thus builds on but departs from the varieties of capitalism (VoC) approach.

VoC provides a dynamic angle for viewing capitalism as a system of economic units (i.e., firms) operating in reaction to institutional restraints. It is a more comprehensive approach than neoclassical institutionalism because it transcends the near exclusive and highly formalistic focus on property rights and contract enforcement to explore other areas that heavily shape and influence the competitive advantages of capitalist economies--for example, labor and industrial relations, education and training, social protection, finance, and corporate governance. VoC views the interaction of these different institutional settings as the institutional complementarities that define the features of the overall national economy, indicate its overall coherence, and explain its macroeconomic performance.

Thus, this book's firm-centered approach shares the theoretical underpinning of VoC that capitalism is a set of institutional rules that govern the behavior of market actors. These rules are established and observed in order to overcome the coordination problems that market actors face in accessing essential production inputs, such as land, capital, labor, information, and technology. The institutional solutions to these coordination problems may be numerous, and they often give rise to varying modes of governance depending on the sociohistorical paths that different countries have taken. Hence, capitalism can exist within a great variety of institutional arrangements according to particular national contexts, as well as sociohistorical and political restraints. The way economic institutions develop across countries affects, if not shapes, the macroeconomic and development outcomes of a specific economic system while also determining its competitiveness and specialization within the global division of labor.

The VoC literature has traditionally distinguished two Weberian ideal types of national capitalism that reflect two modes of governance. The first is liberal market capitalism, which primarily bases coordination between economic actors on market mechanisms. The United States and the United Kingdom are its prototypes. The other mode is that of coordinated market economies, primarily represented by Germany and the northern European countries that depend less on market mechanisms and more on hierarchical structures like workers' and employers' unions to coordinate economic agents. In addition, a number of combinations and hybrids exist between these two extremes, such as in Japan and other countries across Europe.

VoC, however, demonstrate a strong North Atlantic bias and therefore do not lend themselves easily to scholars studying the Global South. Indeed, according to VoC scholars, the approach has been designed to primarily study the developed market democracies of North America and Western Europe, the economies in which the problems of coordination have been efficiently solved. As it turns out, these also happen to be cases with functioning private property systems and the universal rule of law. However, this did not prevent some scholars from employing the approach to study capitalist orders in the Global South.

Ben Ross Schneider's (2009) attempt to apply VoC to Latin America led him to present the label of "hierarchical capitalism," wherein coordination problems are managed by giant economic groups and multinational corporations that operate through vertically integrated processes of production and distribution. These firms dominate these economies, while labor relations are atomized due to weak unionization and high levels of informality. Schneider's approach suffers from a number of shortcomings. Because he focuses solely on multinational corporations or large, multisector holdings, he neglects the broad base of micro, small, and medium-sized enterprises that serve as the economy's main employers and retain a significant share of output. He also neglects the issue of private business informality that represents between one-third and half of all GDP in most regions in the Global South (see Table 2.2).

This one dominant institutional feature suggests that many, if not most, transactions in the Global South economies are conducted according to informal rules and social norms that are enforced by private-order institutions, or self-enforced in the absence of any third party (Greif, 2006). The focus of VoC on formal institutional rules, be they market based or hierarchical, lends little regard to the often informal social institutions and organizations that are embedded within the social relations of communities. Focusing on how economic transactions are actually conducted on the ground requires a modification of the neoclassical definition of institutions as rules (North, 1990) that the VoC approach implicitly adopts. VoC is also insensitive to power relations within the economic sphere, which are often critical in the Global South (as well as the North, though in a more differentiated way given the functional rule of law). There is not much room in the traditional VoC framework for key factors like rent derived from the state via subsidization, transfer of public property, and anticompetitive practices tolerated or even enforced by state action. In addition, labor is incorporated as a mere factor of production like any other without problematizing its social character and how it has been related to class conflict with capital.

Region	*Share of Informal Sector (% of GDP)*
East Asia	32.3
Europe (excluding OECD countries)	38.9
Central Asia	38.9
Latin America	41.1
South Asia	33.0
Sub-Saharan Africa	40.0

TABLE 2.2. Share of the Informal Sector in Total GDP: Comparative Figures.
Source: Schneider, Buehn, and Montenegro (2010, 19).

This book adopts an alternative definition of institutions. As Greif (2006) maintained, institutions do not just imply rules that are enforceable by a third party, but also comprise "rules, beliefs and norms as well as their manifestation as organizations." In short, he holds that "an institution is a system of rules, beliefs, norms and organizations that together generate a regularity of social behavior" (Greif, 2006, 30). This definition allows us to capture the great variety of institutional arrangements that govern business transactions among private enterprises, as well as between these enterprises and the state. This includes the actual invocation of formal rules, as well as the interplay with informal norms and practices in what this research identifies as a broad gray area of semiformality and semipublic and semiprivate arrangements. In this broad realm, rules that are established and enforced by the state are combined and rearticulated within informal political and social rules and norms. Hence, such a conceptualization allows us to discuss different modes of coordination that represent various articulations that have emerged through the interaction of markets, hierarchies, and communities.

Many successful Asian economies depended on sui generis institutional arrangements that combine private and public ownership and management--for example, township and village enterprises (TVEs) in China. Wang (2005, 177) noted how Chinese TVEs fell between the categories of private and public, and of state and enterprise, as they were de facto sociopolitical units that resulted from China's fiscal decentralization in the late 1970s. Lacking formal legal status during their years of expansion, TVEs were essentially countryside collectives that combined the public ownership of assets with local social relations based on kinship and community dynamics. They proved to be, according to Wang, one of the most dynamic sectors in the Chinese economy in the 1980s and 1990s.

Nan Lin (1995) described how the institutional basis of China's economic expansion relied on the incorporation of both market and collective mechanisms. Robust local networks led to enduring institutions, while the interaction of markets, bureaucracies, and indigenous social institutions created and sustained a viable and competitive economy (Lin, 1995, 344–345). He concludes that "the local coordination perspective allows us to understand how and why locally-embedded socio-cultural institutions coordinate rather than compete with each other in order to compete more efficiently in the external or global market."

Other scholars underlined the role that economy- or sector-encompassing associations could play in macroeconomic performance by developing and implementing policies in partnership with the state (Maxfield and Schneider, 1997). Schneider's (2004) examination of Latin American economies such as Brazil, Colombia, Mexico, and Argentina observed how sectoral or economy-wide business associations were key coordination channels both within the economy and between the private sector and state bureaucracy. Others have also evoked the developmental role that business associations can play by gathering and disseminating information, coordinating upgrading and marketing strategies, and pooling resources and delivering services (Stark and Bruszt, 1998; Riddle and Gillespie, 2003; Neidik and Gereffi, 2006).

These examples suggest that markets can be incubated within a great variety of social and political institutions. Indeed, as Peck and Zhang (2013, 21) concluded in the case of China, its variety of network capitalism emerged

> in an environment characterized by weak legal infrastructures, limited property-rights protections, deficient capital-market structures and extreme institutional uncertainty (none of which, it should be noted, are conditions remotely typical of mainstream varieties of capitalism), social-network ties have effectively filled some of the attendant institutional voids, working around some of the obstacles of the old command system in making critical information, resources and opportunities accessible to firms and entrepreneurs.

Market-oriented embeddedness in turn imbues strong Polanyian undertones to market making in the Global South, where social relations come to uphold and constitute the opportunities (as well as limitations) for exchange, accumulation, and exploitation. In many cases, capitalist relations become embedded in broader social and political networks, institutions, and organizations, all the while lacking the precondition of the Hayekian state that upholds formal property rights and enforces contracts. While markets certainly require institutions, they need not be only of the formal, state-enforced variety.

The aim of this book is to develop the conceptual and analytical tools to describe the various institutional configurations that arose during the past four decades of Egypt's transformation into a capitalist economy. The ultimate goal is to link the institutional dynamics that effectively govern business operations with macroeconomic, social, and political outcomes. Employing a firm-centered approach, the next chapter describes the economic subsystems that have emerged throughout Egypt's capitalist transformation, as well as the institutional configurations that characterize, and ultimately constrain, their operations.

Chapter Three

EGYPT'S CLEFT CAPITALISM

SINCE THE LAUNCH OF ECONOMIC LIBERALIZATION IN 1974, SIZable segments of Egyptian society have been drawn into the market as workers, the self-employed, shopkeepers, merchants, and brokers and entrepreneurs. Some were driven by the zeal to make profits and accumulate capital through systematic exchange, while others were pushed into the market for lack of secure employment, especially with the contraction of the public sector and massive rural exodus.[1]

Given the combination of low-entry barriers and weak growth potential, it is difficult to distinguish the least from the most entrepreneurial among this population, and the small-scale establishments (SSEs) they initiated, without succumbing to teleology by focusing on those that actually grew. The question becomes how to distinguish those that had the potential to grow but could not because of systemic factors from those that never entertained such thoughts of expansion in the first place, seeking instead mere subsistence.

On one end of this question, we have what I call the underestimators: those who have dismissed almost any semblance of entrepreneurialism among millions of private sector enterprises and entrepreneurs. At the other extreme stand the overestimators, who have counted nearly all of them as entrepreneurial. This book argues that both answers are static and uncritical. and therefore simply wrong.

One of the overestimators is renowned economist Hernando de Soto (2012), who cited the case of a Tunisian fruit peddler Moḥamed Bouazizi [Būʿazizi], whose self-immolation inadvertently triggered the popular uprisings of 2011, to show that "entrepreneurs not meeting their potential" ignited the Arab revolts. Confusing the subsistence efforts of the urban poor with entrepreneurship is quite problematic, as it dilutes the very concept of entrepreneurship and questions its relevance in such contexts of high unemployment and extreme socioeconomic marginality.

The underestimators have dismissed almost all private SSEs in the economies of the Global South as unentrepreneurial due to their inability to grow beyond their initial small size. For instance, many indexes of entrepreneurship, such as the Global Entrepreneurship Monitor (GEM), have excluded necessity-driven, or subsistence-oriented, microenterprises from the realm of entrepreneurship (Evans and Leighton, 1989, 1990; Reynolds et al., 1994). This broad dismissal largely rests on the view that necessity-driven entrepreneurship is the reason that micro and small enterprises are neither productive nor growth generating in the Global South, a rather tautological argument. It is similar to explaining underdevelopment in terms of rampant poverty, though the latter often is an effect of the former rather than a cause. Instead, the question that should be asked is why most private sector entrepreneurship has been driven by necessity while being marked by low productivity and low growth potential. This implies that the focus of study should be on the system of institutional rules and norms that governs the broad base of private enterprises rather than the psychology of individual entrepreneurs.

This blindness toward any semblance of entrepreneurialism in economies of the Global South has also been the result of the superimposition of a very narrow concept of entrepreneurship that led to the biased notion that genuinely entrepreneurial enterprises exist only in isolated enclaves of high-technology, high-skill activities. This perspective has ignored the broader private sector in search for replicas or extensions of Silicon Valley–like businesses in countries where traditional industrial, service, and agricultural sectors actually dominate (Schumacher, 2011).

If entrepreneurship is essentially about the creation of economic value and exchange, it is safest to search for these proxies for value creation and, in turn, the extent of entrepreneurship by distinguishing the self-employed from employers. Small-scale establishments that hire wage workers, regardless of their legal status or eventual success or failure (Smith, 2009), are a good indicator of entrepreneurship in the Weberian sense of seeking to engage in the creation and exchange of economic value in view of profit making. It may also serve as the best criterion for the extent of entrepreneurialism in Egypt's private sector, given the dearth of accurate information about capital and turnover due to rampant informality compared to labor. In contrast, the self-employed are usually "refugee" or "forced" entrepreneurs who temporarily set out to work on their own until they can find a paid job (Van Stel and Storey, 2004; Myant, 2007, 18).

According to the Central Agency for Public Mobilization and Statistics economic census of 1996, almost twenty years after infitāḥ, 372,000 micro and small enterprises (around 23 percent of total private enterprise population) were owned and operated by employers rather than the self-employed (those hiring no workers).[2] These businesses were not simple household enterprises, where workers are unpaid family members and consumption and production are shared jointly within the household; rather, they have been established for more than mere self-employment and subsistence. As such, this book's primary population of interest is market-oriented SSEs.[3]

Extensive fieldwork has revealed some quite colorful expressions of entrepreneurship in sectors that are often deemed traditional, if not marginal, by the mainstream business literature (Adly and Khatib, 2014, 55). From a mechanic in the poor Cairene neighborhood of Imbāba who was able to generate a small taxi business, to an illiterate garbage collector in the shantytown of the *Zabālīn* (literally meaning "garbage people" in Egyptian Arabic) who was able to develop a plastic and paper exporting business worth hundreds of thousands of dollars, a substantial number of Egyptian enterprises have demonstrated an unmistakable entrepreneurial spirit despite undercapitalization, high risk, and the occasionally hostile formal institutional environment.

These cases are added to a host of other examples that have generated a long trail of novels, movies, and urban legends that have captured the dramatic rise of people who made it from nothing to everything in the artisanal and commercial quarters of Egypt's large cities. Of course, only this exceptional few, worthy of becoming subject matters of novels and legends, could make it against all odds. Nevertheless, their existence suggests that there is not necessarily a lack of entrepreneurial values in the Egyptian culture or worldview.

Focused on this category of hidden entrepreneurs, this book maintains that social relations in Egypt have been generally conducive to market-based relations because the country has had no lack of people looking to become market actors with profit making and accumulation in mind. While most of the relations, institutions, and norms that sustained market making were socially embedded—that is, they were dependent on family, friendship, and other personal ties—they functioned relatively efficiently in facilitating exchange and lowering transaction costs in an economy that has lacked a strong rule of law, contract enforcement, and credible public information.

Contrary to the expectations of neoclassical institutionalism, the weakness of formal property rights neither impeded the expansion of market exchange nor deterred thousands of Egyptians from engaging with this expanding market since the mid-1970s. Alternative private economic orders have retained the capacity for sustained market creation and expansion, albeit imperfectly (Yāsīn, 2015).

In Egypt, this market expansion was not conducive to market integration, the element of development that is crucial for job creation and widely shared gains. The resultant capitalist order was cleft. In order to grow, private enterprises must have access to inputs and market outlets that go beyond what is immediately available via their direct private social capital (François, 2004, 4). Indeed, cheap and efficient access to capital, both physical and financial, is a prerequisite for any functioning and integrated capitalist order. While markets do require institutions, the vast majority of individuals and households cannot become market actors and thus make use of the private property protection and contract enforcement that these institutions bestow if they are deprived of minimum levels of physical, financial, and human capital.

Throughout Egypt's capitalist transformation, access to capital, namely, finance and land, remained quite restrained for the vast majority of private market actors. This was due to politico-historical factors that were continually perpetuated, eventually leading to the rise of institutional arrangements that were exclusionary for the broad base of private sector enterprises and entrepreneurs. At the same time, this cleft situation deprived the few that could grow from establishing the type of robust forward and backward linkages with a solid base of SSEs that have powered the labor-intensive industries of Southeast Asia and China (Goldberg, 2004, 19).

CLEFT CAPITALISM: DESCRIPTION AND EXPLANATION OF A FAILED MARKET MAKING

Cleft capitalism builds on, but decisively departs from, the varieties of capitalism (VoC) approach. It does not seek the depiction of any broad institutional features of an "Egyptian" capitalism. The VoC approach assumes that capitalism exists in different institutional guises on national bases. However, once it is taken on a tour outside the universe of advanced market democracies, this limitation of VoC, or what Peck and Theodore (2007, 56) call its "methodological nationalism," becomes quite apparent. In many parts of the Global South, Egypt included, there may well be a variety of economic subsystems within a single nation-state. This was captured in Peck and Theodore's (2007, 57) work on China, whose capitalism they described as variegated, referring to its "spatially uneven development and polymorphic capitalism(s)." Other scholars (McNally and Chu, 2006; Peck and Zhang, 2013) also underlined how China's economic liberalization led to the rise of differentiated systems of "indigenous" capitalism(s).

Cleft capitalism is hence not a national variety of capitalism that may place Egypt on the VoC spectrum of coordinated-to-liberal market systems. It is more of an institutional condition of multiple coexisting business systems in which market actors play by different sets of rules. This multiplicity differentially and decisively affects the ability of enterprises to access inputs and grow. Under these parallel arrangements, only those with a large initial or acquired endowment of private capital—financial, physical, human, political, and social—could grow alongside a further set of politically connected cronies. This took place on top of an ocean of small-scale establishments doomed to stagnation.

Those who started big could grow bigger, including many who did not develop organic and constant ties with the state and its crony network. Thus, contrary to the expectations of the cronyism literature, Egypt's economic problem did not lie in the inability of some private enterprises to grow into the ranks of big business without possessing political connections. The real issue was in the disabling institutional framework that prevented the rise of a medium-sized capitalist stratum—the missing middle. Economic liberalization led to the coevolution of various business subsystems that implied the variance in access to inputs and market outlets. Both the performance of those in each business subsystem and the interaction (or lack thereof) among them is what defined macroeconomic performance at the national scale.

Three Business Subsystems: Baladi, Dandy, and Crony Capitalisms

A business subsystem is a complex adaptive system of coordination and control exercised in three domains (Whitley, 1999; Redding, 2005):

1. Intrabusiness, or within the enterprises, which stand as the integrated survival units held together under a form of ownership
2. Interbusiness, in reference to transactions between market actors across the economy in a way that decides how they access inputs, mainly land, capital, and labor, as well as skills, technology, information, and market outlets
3. Transactions that involve the state, defined in Weberian terms as the sole organization with a credible claim over public authority that regulates private economic activity in its name. Private enterprises deal with the state in many capacities: as the regulator of market entry and exit via business registration, permits, and bankruptcy rules; as a party to economic transactions in the form of subsidies, distribution of tender and procurement, taxation, and even informal payments via corruption and extortion; as well as the regulator of access to certain inputs like publicly owned land, banks, and the stock market.

As the case of Egypt reveals, cleft capitalism comprises three business subsystems: baladi, dandy, and crony capitalisms. The coevolution of these three business subsystems in Egypt's four-decade transformation implied differential rules and norms governing each of these three areas: access to inputs, primarily capital; access to market outlets; and the interaction among the enterprises themselves, as well as their relations with the state. It also has implied an uneven development of private sector enterprises and the subsequent unintegrated or trifurcated structure of the productive economy exemplified by the missing-middle syndrome.

Baladi Capitalism

Baladi capitalism has governed the broad base of the Egyptian private sector, made up of tens of thousands of micro and small enterprises.[4] Baladi capitalism captures the dynamics of a deeply rooted Egyptian entrepreneurialism that has expanded over the past decades as a result of various push and pull factors, ranging from state withdrawal to market enlargement due to population growth, urbanization, and inflows of remittances from workers abroad (Pagès-El Karoui, 2012, 3–4). The term *baladi* has multiple meanings in the Egyptian colloquial language, roughly denoting "folksy" or "of the common people." It is used in this sense to refer to preexisting social relations and structures within which business transactions are deeply embedded, facilitated, and conditioned. It is worth noting that *baladi* is not used here in the sense of rural or the sense of autochthonous or indigenous. It overlaps with "economic informality," but it usually implies a mix of formal and informal rather than being strictly illegal or extralegal.

The defining feature of baladi capitalism is the low degree of differentiation between the social and the economic; that is, the social life of an individual or group (e.g., family, friends, neighbors, community) is deeply intertwined with their economic activity. This has generally confined the large majority of enterprises to tightly knit social networks in order to access production inputs and market outlets. Low differentiation makes most transactions rooted in private knowledge, interpersonal trust, and social sanctions. Hence, it is directly contingent on the concrete social identity of the respective SSE owners and managers.

Dandy Capitalism

In contrast to baladi capitalism, dandy capitalism refers to the realm wherein a few thousand Egyptian private enterprises have functioned, internally as well as externally, along rules that implied a higher degree of relative differentiation. The word *dandy*—*shiyāka* in the Egyptian dialect—was chosen to metaphorically label this system of rules as the antonym of baladi.[5] Due to their large initial endowment of private financial and social capital, these market actors evolved into corporate market actors by the 1980s and 1990s.

This higher degree of differentiation implied a relative separation between the enterprise as a market actor, on the one hand, and the concrete social identity of those who own and manage it, on the other. Social ties of family, friendship, and community (or religious group in the case of Coptic or Salafi businesspeople) of course remain relevant, though they are internalized into the complex organizational forms of the enterprises—*sharika*—that separate control and senior management from conducting routine transactions in order to access inputs and final markets.[6] This higher degree of differentiation granted these enterprises a greater ability to conduct impersonal transactions that were less contingent on their social relations—for example, accessing inputs such as finance, land, skilled labor and technology, as well as final product markets.

The rebirth of the Egyptian private sharika since the mid-1970s was the outcome of a sociohistorical process that allowed for the parallel differentiation of the economic from both the social and the political. The institution of rules—formal, informal, and semiformal—enabled the rise of a few corporate market actors that grew into the ranks of large private capital and, to a lesser extent, the very thin stratum of medium-sized enterprises. (This point is covered extensively in Chapter 8.)

Crony Capitalism

Aside from the scale of social-economic differentiation, the degree of differentiation between the political and the economic accounts for the third subsystem, the all-too-familiar crony capitalism. Crony capitalism implies a low degree of differentiation between political power and economic action. Preferential access to state rule making and implementation, as well as to public resources such as state-owned land and divested public assets, natural resources, and monopolistic positions in the market, all distinguish cronyism from the two other subsystems, where access to state power is less essential for conducting business, making profits, or accumulating capital (Heydemann, 2004; Haddad, 2011; el-Tarouty, 2016).

Crony capitalism, narrowly defined, refers to a special relation between power and wealth where uneven access to political authority, usually taking the form of controlling or heavily influencing the supply and implementation of laws and regulations, enables a politically connected few to generate unnatural and nonmarket-based profits (Diwan, 2013; Chekir and Diwan, 2014). In light of this narrow definition, many of those who fared well in Egypt's transformation toward capitalism were not strictly cronies. This leads us to the fact that there were indeed other routes to capital accumulation than politically generated rent. Three main features distinguish these paths and underline the relative differentiation between the political and the economic that has distinguished dandy from crony capitalisms.

First, under dandy capitalism, private enterprises are generally rule takers rather than rule makers. Unlike cronies and captors, they have no systematic capacity to formulate state actions in order to serve their private interests.

Second, there exist private sources of capital accumulation other than the state. Contrary to cronies, dandy capitalists can accumulate capital without relying primarily or exclusively on access to public assets or privileged market positions enabled by state regulation (or the lack thereof).

Third, the many private businesses that do owe a great deal of their growth to rents accruing from state policies like protectionism, subsidies, incentives, and tax exemptions do so in the absence of any larger contractual relation with the state. This is reflected in the many instances of rent without cronyism, where those who benefit from state-facilitated rents play no explicit or implicit role in the reproduction of political power (Sadowski, 1991, 102). In other words, rent was politically free and generally untargeted in the sense that it was not tied to the two principal functions that cronies perform: enriching their patrons in office and maintaining their political power. A typical example of this politically untargeted rent is the domestic automotive industry, which developed in the 1980s and 1990s under heavy state protection, where many of the business families that reaped rewards from this industrial policy, like the Ghabbour, Kastor, Hāshem, and al-Wahāb, were never explicitly tied to the Mubārak regime through National Democratic Party (NDP) membership or other forms of regime support. All four family businesses benefited handsomely from protective inwardly oriented policies in the automotive sector, though nearly all shied away from any explicit political role and avoided any substantial financial ties to the security establishment, military, or presidential family.

As will be shown in more detail in the coming chapters, quite a few private enterprises could grow and expand in this way since the infitāḥ of the 1970s. Tracing the sources of capital accumulation that had relatively little to do with access to political power or the illicit takeover of public funds reveals that many firms remained as market actors and were not mere facades of forces within the state apparatus. This held even for many private businesses that lived on state rent through tariff protection, public land allocation, or energy subsidies.

Indeed, many business families that could progressively grow since the 1970s, like the Sawiris (diversified group in telecommunications, construction, and tourism), Elsewedy (electric cables), Mansour [Manṣūr] (diversified group in retail, manufacturing and financial services), Diāb (agriculture), and Elaraby [al-ʿArabī] (electronics and home appliances), cannot be reduced to mere facades or middle people for the political leadership or networks of agencies within the state bureaucracy by making business deals for them and sharing the rent that accrues from their asymmetrical access to power and information. Most of these business families did not emerge from the public sector or any security or military body, and they were not organically related to the ruling presidential family. Some were relatively large capital holders (financial as well as social and cultural) from the period that preceded the 1952 military takeover, while others came from the retail trade and construction sectors that survived state socialism in the 1960s. These entities were described historically as the traditional capitalist stripe that resurfaced after the infitāḥ. Imām (1986) distinguished these outsiders from the bureaucratic bourgeoisie of the time that was made up of former generals and public sector managers who started private businesses and capitalized on their connections to and expertise in the state bureaucracy.

In fact, the market opening since the 1970s even allowed entrepreneurs who were by no means regime sympathizers to grow based on their external market linkages, provided that they played no active role against the ruling regime. This is how Muslim Brotherhood–related businesspeople (e.g., ʿAbdel-ʿAẓīm Loqma and ʿAbdel-Raḥmān Seʿūdi) have been able to expand their businesses since the 1970s. In fact, the Brotherhood organization itself invested in a number of trade- and service-based activities since the 1980s despite the impending risk of expropriation by the authorities (ʿAbdel-Ḥay et al., 2006; Adly, 2016). Other examples include the old Wafd-related families (e.g., Badrāwī, ʿAbdel-Nūr, and Serāg al-Dīn) who expanded their businesses despite the tension around the resurrection of the Wafd party in the 1970s and 1980s. While they may have been politically co-opted to an extent, it would be far-fetched to describe these families as regime cronies back at these early stages.

In some instances, the intermarriage between old bourgeois families, on the one hand, and military officials and high bureaucrats, on the other, provided a degree of social capital that was critical to evading state predation and navigating what was still a state-dominated economy. However, this could hardly apply to everyone. For instance, the Coptic business families, such as the Sawirises (construction, telecommunications, and tourism), the Ghabbours (automotive), Beshāy (steel industry), Berzy (textiles and then food staffs), Magued Sāmi's Wādi Degla group (construction, housing and sports clubs), and Sāmi Sa'd's trading group, to name a few, were able to make their way mostly successfully despite having little opportunity to marry into the predominantly Muslim families of the bureaucratic elite. These examples, along with many others, demonstrate that not all benefits deriving from the liberalization process were kept inside the regime circuit (Roccu, 2013, 101).

These cases created a different pattern from those of post-Soviet Eastern and Central Europe, where there was no formal private sector under Communist rule and the private sector that did emerge was born out of the previously divested public sector (see Stark and Bruszt, 1998; Windolf, 1998; Fischer, 2001).

In Egypt, conversely, the small private sector in cities and the countryside was never completely crushed by the state under Nāṣer. Retail trade, construction, personal services, and agriculture remained strongholds of private sector activities even during the heyday of state socialism. By the mid-1970s, after almost fifteen years of state-led development, the private sector still supplied 56.18 percent of total output compared to 43.8 percent for the public sector. Small, private producers dominated agriculture (98 percent), trade (60 percent), and housing (88.2 percent) and had a significant presence in light manufacturing and services (O'Brien, 1966, cited in Waterbury, 1983, 160; Zaki 1999, 74). This created a relatively large pool of private capital to the extent that the al-Sadāt regime targeted their mobilization via the 1977 investment law amendments, which extended the same incentives, exclusive to foreign investors under Investment Law 43 of 1974, to Egyptians.

Moreover, Egypt has been among the countries with a slow public sector privatization drive, which formally took off only in the early 1990s. Privatization occurred mainly in the manufacturing sector, while public utilities, extractive industry, and infrastructure were largely shielded. Between 1988 and 2008, the total value of privatized state-owned enterprises stood at $15.7 billion dollars (Hanieh, 2013, 52). By 1997, only 134 companies were privatized out of 314 companies initially deemed eligible for privatization in 1991. According to World Bank data (2015a), Egypt privatized 10.4 companies a year between 1989 and 1999, compared to 444, 100, and 26.3 in Poland, Hungary, and Mexico, respectively. The same trend could be noticed, with the proceedings accruing to the government from privatized state-owned enterprises (SOEs). Whereas the Egyptian government received an annual average of $417 million during the period 1989 to 1999, the proceedings averaged $3,664, $1,217, $6,986, and $1,449 million in Mexico, Poland, Brazil, and Hungary, respectively, during the same period

The privatization of SOEs did not pick up in earnest until 2004: 70 percent of all privatization-generated revenue since 1991 was realized between 2004 and 2008 (Hanieh, 2013, 52). By this time, private sector firms had already established dominant market shares in the key sectors, including manufacturing, construction, tourism, retail, and wholesale trade and agriculture (Central Bank, 2017, cited in Adly, 2017, 6).

Although the privatization process did catapult some private businesses into the ranks of dominant enterprises, it was hardly essential to the creation of the private sector in Egypt. Before the intensification of the privatization drive, Egypt already had a well-developed class of big capitalists, who depended on alternative means of capital accumulation. While some large businesses entered the regime's networks at a relatively late stage, such as Moḥamed Mansour's brief stint as the minister of transportation and Aḥmed al-Maghrabi and Rachīd [Rashīd] Moḥamed Rachīd's occupancy of economic posts under Aḥmed Nazīf (2004–2011), they were chosen for these posts because they were large businesspeople, and not vice versa; that is, most of their enterprises were fairly large before they took office.

Table 3.1 portrays the three business subsystems that together make up cleft capitalism.

THE TRIANGLE OF DIFFERENTIATION

Cleft capitalism aims to explain in institutional terms why small-scale establishments in Egypt have failed through decades of market making to grow into a stratum of medium-sized firms, a development (or nondevelopment) that has led to the macroeconomic feature of the missing middle. Cleft capitalism

Business Subsystem	*Baladi Capitalism*	*Dandy Capitalism*	*Crony Capitalism*
1 **Enterprise (intrabusiness organization)**	Social market actors. Low differentiation between the social and the economic.	Corporate market actors. High differentiation of the economic from the social and the political.	Political market actors. Low differentiation between the economic and the political.
2 **Rules governing access to inputs and market outlets**	Private social capital (i.e., networks of family and friends, interpersonal trust, and social relations); instrumental in accessing inputs (skills, information, capital, and labor). Private social capital substitutes imperfectly for inaccessibility to land and finance on an impersonal basis.	Private social capital internalized within corporate organization for control rather than accessing inputs and markets. Accessing inputs on nonmarket basis: intrabusiness by creating business groups through vertical integration and unrelated diversification or through interbusiness alliances with suppliers, distributors, and banks. Access to market outlets through branding and trade names.	Asymmetrical access to political power is instrumental in accessing inputs (land and capital) and market shares.
3 **Dealing with the state**	Low adaptation. Private social capital helps in navigating through bureaucracy, lowering transaction costs and risks of predation. Contract enforcement happens through social mechanisms amid occasional and partial invocation of formal rules with the growth in business operation.	High adaptation. State predation is unsystematic and politically targeted; raises costs of doing business rather than preventing it altogether. Private social capital enables access to state-controlled and state-regulated finance and land using large initial capital, both financial and social.	Favorable access to state power generates unnatural profitswith the possibility of predatory actions on other market actors (consumers, competitors, and Treasury). Preferential access to the supply of laws and regulations for private uses or influencing their implementation.

TABLE 3.1. Cleft Capitalism Business Subsystems

differences, discrete markings of different colors on leaves

is a sort of variegation on the national level. However, this variegation is not based on regional discrepancies, as Peck and Theodore (2007) suggested in their study of China. Rather, this book focuses on the varieties of business subsystems coexisting within the same geographic market in Egypt. The differentiation among these business subsystems is derived from the different modes of articulation between the political, the social, and the economic, as well as the uneven impact this has had on different groups of enterprises and entrepreneurs. In turn, the size of an enterprise is viewed as a long-term consequence of the system of institutions rather than a static feature.

In this sense, cleft capitalism builds on but is distinct from the classical literature on dual economies (Hirschman, 1957; Baumol, 1969; Lewis, 1979; Frank, 2004) or locational development discrepancies (Krugman, 1991; Rauch, 1993). However, it is not about a modern urban sector that is developing side by side with a premodern, largely rural sector, as these spatial or sectoral distinctions (urban versus rural or industry versus agriculture) become irrelevant.

The concept of cleft capitalism is also an attempt at transcending the dichotomy of formal versus informal sectors of the economy. Under cleft capitalism, all three subsystems are made up of rules, norms, and relations that combine formal and informal elements. Between economic formality and informality exists a continuum rather than a distinct dividing line between two separate economic sectors (Chen, 2005).

Under cleft capitalism, the differentiation of the economic, the social, and the political that distinguishes each business subsystem remains relative. Contrary to neoclassical conventional wisdom, market making in Egypt did not imply the disembeddedness of economic actors from their social and political relations. In all three subsystems, social relations like family and friendship ties, interpersonal trust, and community play some role. However, the question becomes how the modes of articulation that determine what is social and what is economic, as well as what is economic and what is political, developed. The literature on Egypt's capitalist transformation that draws on neoliberal precepts largely dismisses the economic element of most market actors, as scholars of cronyism and state capture consider economic actors to be mere extensions of political power. Many sociologists and anthropologists also dismiss the presence of the economic as they consider market actors involved in micro and small enterprises, household businesses, and the informal sector as mere extensions of social entities and relations of people (Kharoufi, 1991; Hoodfar, 1997; Bayat, 2010, p. 1997).

In contrast, this book asserts that Egypt's capitalist transformation produced a genuine economic sphere, albeit limited, that was relatively differentiated from the social (survival- and subsistence-driven activities) and the political (cronyism and capture). This economic space has hosted a population of small-scale entrepreneurs who have been oriented toward market exchange, repetitive profit making, and accumulation—what this book refers to as baladi capitalism and a population of dandy enterprises that could grow into the ranks of medium-sized and large firms.

Egypt's imperfect market sphere emerged in the absence of strong formal institutions (i.e., the rule of law, property rights, and contract enforcement) via two main sociopolitical factors: restrained state predation and market-enabling social norms and practices. As noted, there have been a limited number of cases where egregious predatory acts of expropriation took place against private market actors after infitāḥ, as almost all were limited to actors considered political adversaries of the regime.

In addition, this book invokes the Polanyian view that markets emerge out of existing social relations; in other words, economic relations are largely embedded within social ones. This market-oriented embeddedness implies a mode of articulation between the community and market wherein modes of economic governance emerge to create a socially institutionalized area that may be labeled "familiarized markets." Whereas price signals are considered in any exchange decision, community networks serve as a social interface to safely navigate markets and deal with parties who lie beyond immediate high-trust circles.

Contrary to the view of neoclassical institutionalism, these embedded networks do not always impede the expansion of market exchange via the creation of isolated islands of socially closed-off groups; rather, they often serve to provide information about opportunities that lie beyond the safe circles of preexisting social ties and may even offer the means to mitigate the risks of less-personalized transactions. This is the way in which networks of family and friends may serve to familiarize market actors and transactions.

Although market-oriented embeddedness enabled a market to emerge and expand despite weak formal institutions, it nonetheless failed to offer the broad base of SSEs systematic and low-cost access to the capital that is necessary for the type of growth and market integration that empowered the East and Southeast Asian economies. It remains to be explored how this relatively differentiated economic sphere arose and why it remained so limited throughout Egypt's transformation, but there is no doubt it exists

Figure 3.1 roughly depicts the three axes—political, economic, and social—and the relative differentiation among them. The main criterion distinguishing the modes is the mechanism through which the allocation of economic value occurs: price, power, and reciprocity for the economic, political, and social spheres, respectively.

The triangle in Figure 3.1 is composed of three continua between three Weberian-like ideal spheres of economic exchange where value is allocated according to three different mechanisms. (The shaded part indicates roughly the area of market-oriented embeddedness, be that socially or politically embedded. The practical objective of this exercise is to map the different activities that have involved the creation, exchange, and distribution of economic value in Egypt since the initiation of market making in the mid-1970s.

The economic pole is meant to represent the ideal sphere of pure market exchange: price-oriented anonymous transactions. The social pole is where economic value is supposedly allocated on a strictly nonprofit basis and directed for social integration purposes. The political pole represents where authority governs the allocation of economic value. Between the three poles exist areas where the political, the economic, and the social combine or mix to different degrees.

The Economic-Social Axis: Between Dandy and Baladi Capitalisms

This book focuses primarily on how the economic has been articulated within, and hence relatively differentiated from, the other two spheres: the political and the social. The closer the mode of articulation is to the economic pole, the more market oriented it is, and vice versa. This area hence includes a broad variety of practices and norms that are politically as well socially embedded through which production for exchange may take place in the absence of strong formal institutions and information symmetry.

In its extreme, the social pole implies that the units, which undertake production and distribution of economic value, are completely inseparable from

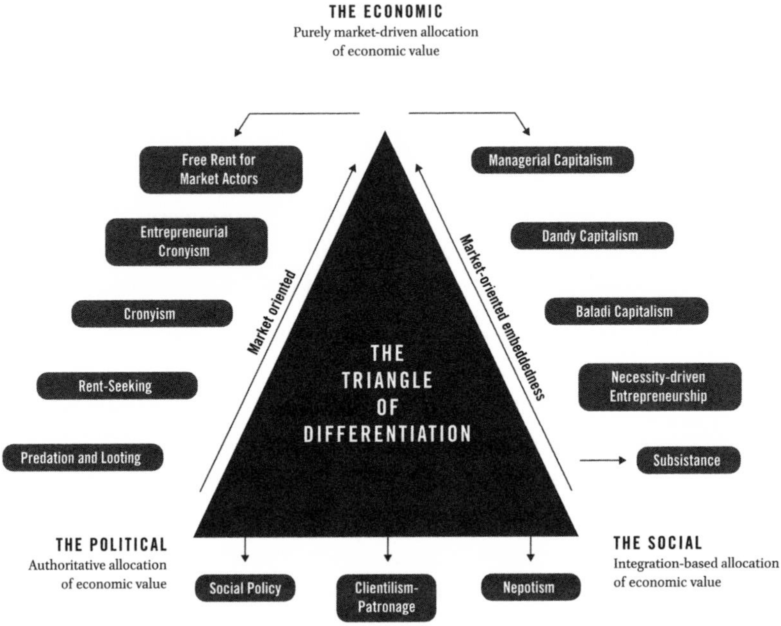

FIGURE 3.1. The Triangle of Differentiation. The graph shows the different modes of articulation between the political, the social, and the economic.

their social functions. This is the case when production and distribution take place on a nonmarket basis and are primarily driven by subsistence (e.g., nonwage family labor in agriculture and menial and marginal activities in cities). In accordance with Adam Smith's classical definition, this is a form of noncapitalist economic activity, as it is not based on production for exchange. At the opposite (economic) pole, there lies a fully differentiated capitalist system where enterprises are ideally disembedded from any Polanyian social context. Such is the case with managerial capitalism, for instance (Chandler, 1993).

In between these two extremes is a broad range of modes of articulation between the social and the economic where we can find both baladi and dandy capitalisms. Differentiation may be high or low depending on the extent to which economic activity is embedded in broader social relations. However, unlike Polanyi's definition of embeddedness as an inherently nonmarket mode for value production and distribution (where exchange happens on the basis of reciprocity, that is, gift giving), there are cases of market-oriented embeddedness where social relations play a role in the production and distribution of commodities and services that are ultimately produced for exchange on the market. Moving one degree away from the social pole toward the economic, we encounter what some call "necessity-driven entrepreneurship." This characterizes the self-employed and household businesses that produce goods and services for exchange on the market; however, they are hardly considered capitalist as they seek income rather than regular profit making and accumulation (Hopkins 1992, 15). In this sense, they are much more like proletarians, yet without employers, than entrepreneurs (Elyachar, 2004, 30).

In sum, economic activity along this axis implies that the production, exchange, and consumption of value are part and parcel of broader social relations (Polanyi, 1957; Granovetter, 1990). This is especially the case in countries where formal market institutions are either virtually absent or considerably underdeveloped. In Egypt, as in many other transforming economies, the private sector emerged out of existing social relations that in almost all instances created a situation of deep embeddedness. The mode of articulation between the social and the economic has been crucial for the growth potential of private enterprises; however, in most cases, the low differentiation between the economic and the social functions that characterizes baladi capitalism was inimical to conducting impersonal transactions, and hence limited market access to either inputs or outlets.

Conversely, dandy capitalism implies a higher degree of differentiation between the social and the economic and a greater ability to conduct impersonal transactions in accessing inputs and final market outlets. Yet both subsystems are capitalist and market oriented as production is geared toward exchange and repetitive profit making rather than subsistence. Dandy capitalism is merely another manifestation of market-oriented embeddedness; however, it is closer to the ideal economic sphere for having enabled the development of corporate identities or enterprises that are relatively independent of the concrete social identities of their owners.

The Economic-Political Axis: Between Captors, Cronies, and Capitalists

On the economic-political axis, the closer the mode of articulation is to the political, the more the allocation of economic value is dictated by power rather than markets. In the extreme, there exist the purely predatory activities of state incumbents (Hellman, Jones, and Kaufmann, 2000; Evans, 2012). These cases of predation and looting are where economic value flows to those in power and is intended for immediate self-enrichment rather than engaging in future exchange. Further along the scale we find rent seeking, where power is used to extract unnatural profits for those politically connected. This again usually involves short-term exchange (hit and run) for the purpose of self-enrichment as opposed to regular market exchange. In Egypt, these rents went out of market circulation and into the private nonmarket accumulation of state captors, namely, within top state institutions like the military andthe intelligence community, and the Mubārak family (Sfakianakis, 2004; Adly, 2012b; Roll, 2013; el-Tarouty, 2016).

State captors are mainly concerned with self-enrichment (and the enrichment of their patrons) or the continuous reaping of rent while maintaining no motive to expand or become genuine market actors. The most notorious examples were seen in middle people, such as Ḥusein Sālem, who have hovered around as moneymen for the general intelligence agency since the 1980s. They possess little market presence distinct from their real functions as middle people for those in power. For instance, Sālem's involvement in looting Egypt's natural resources through the exporting of underpriced gas to Israel (Adly and Paluelo, 2013) was motivated by self-enrichment together with filling the coffers of his principals at the general intelligence agency, and possibly for the Mubāraks. He was involved twice with the Israelis in oil and natural gas–related business in the 1990s and 2000s, all the while never becoming a businessman with work separate from that of his principals.

As we continue to move toward the economic end of the axis, the entanglement between political power and economic value allocation begins to be clear. In terms of cronyism, it indeed exists at a place on the spectrum where political power plays a role in making profits, though this usually occurs through preferential access to markets, information, and inputs with the ultimate objective of repetitive profit making, usually in a context of restricted competition. Nonetheless, some cronies have shown a more entrepreneurial spirit by moving into market-oriented activities at later stages, giving themselves a new life as market actors and reducing their reliance on political power to generate profits. This stage, which could be called "entrepreneurial cronyism," shifts the focus from the origin of productive assets and capital to the manner in which they are directed.

Indeed, some cronies developed clear entrepreneurial traits over time as they directed politically targeted rents toward investment and value creation with the ultimate goal of exchange. The elements of repetitive profit making and capital accumulation separate these actors from mere rent seekers or looters despite their political connections and the source of their initial capital. As Khan and Jomo (2000, 126) noted in reference to the role of rents in spurring entrepreneurial growth, "Since transfers can be the basis of primitive accumulation, they can play an essential role in the transition to capitalism."

The Sawiris family is a case in point. While there is little doubt that their capacity to develop Egypt's largest private business relied on their not-always-transparent access to state-owned assets (Sfakianakis, 2004; Roll, 2013), their entrepreneurial zeal was demonstrated by expanding their business into frontier markets in the 2000s—Algeria, Iraq, Myanmar, Pakistan, and even North Korea. This is in no way to deny the political dimension of their success (e.g., allegations of having special ties with the US government); nevertheless, their ultimate motives of capital accumulation and market expansion serve to set them apart from mere rent seekers. Another prominent example is Moḥamed Farīd Khamīs, the owner and manager of Oriental Weavers with close ties to the Mubārak regime. Despite these political connections, Khamīs invested heavily to integrate his business group vertically and ultimately expand it to global markets.

The resultant pattern has been increasing differentiation between these private enterprises and state power as the former have retained corporate identities as market actors. This stands in contrast to cronies, who remain indistinguishable from the bodies and groups within the state from which they receive support. This distinction is crucial for disentangling market actors from state power and rent seekers from entrepreneurs, which always prove to be conceptually difficult tasks in transforming economies such as Egypt. Whether in the instances of cronies-turned-entrepreneurs or in the case of untargeted rents in the form of energy subsidies or import substitution policies that were unrelated to any particular cronyistic dynamic (Adly, 2012a), market actors emerge and operate under capitalist impulses at many places along the economic-political axis.

The Political-Social Axis

The third axis between the political and the social poles, which lies beyond the direct scope of this book, refers to the different modes of articulation between power and social integration concerns in allocating economic resources. The closest case in which political power allocates resources for social purposes is social policy that targets entire classes, regions, or groups in return for political support, national integration, or some notion of social justice. The other extreme is where political power is used to allocate resources for private rather than public social purposes, such as nepotism and favoritism toward particular groups, usually to those in which incumbents belong. These are the least political due to the fact that the allocation occurs for the private good of narrowly selected individuals or groups. Between these two modes, we may encounter patronage and clientelism where specific social groups are allocated economic resources using public authority, though this is directed toward power perpetuation rather than a desire to please the relatives or acquaintances of incumbents.

A DYNAMIC OUTLOOK TO THE MISSING MIDDLE SYNDROME

Cleft capitalism as an institutional condition has produced a small number of large, concentrated enterprises on top, hundreds of thousands of micro and small units at the bottom, and almost nothing in between. The economic-political axis conceptually describes the nature of those powerful actors at the top: captors, pure cronies, entrepreneurial cronies, and other actors who play by the rules of dandy or crony capitalisms. In turn, the economic-social axis houses the subsystem of baladi capitalism that describes the broad sector of small and medium enterprises at the bottom. Both the performance of the enterprises within each business subsystem and the interaction (or lack thereof) among them defined the macroeconomic underperformance witnessed on the national scale.

Since infitāḥ in 1974, differentiated rules governing access to capital evolved in a way that made capital, specifically bank credit and desert land, accessible and affordable to only a few market actors, to the exclusion of the vast majority. The cause of this lack of access to capital for (potentially) entrepreneurial populations has been institutional. In Egypt, the institutional rules—formal, informal, and more often a mix of both—that govern the distribution of opportunities for accessing capital have shown a sustained bias in favor of market actors with large initial and acquired capital. This has been the underpinning of the institutional conditions for the production and reproduction of cleft capitalism. Those with large initial and acquired capital (derived from private wealth, political connections, or partnerships with foreign enterprises) maintained their access to more capital, while those who started small remained so, with no credible chance to grow.

The inability of this broad base of SSEs to grow accounts for Egypt's missing-middle syndrome and the overall stagnant character of its capitalist order. There is considerable field evidence that a substantial amount of entrepreneurial potential has been wasted throughout the transformation toward a private sector–dominated economy, which is a reflection of the systemic and institutionalized denial of capital that could have enabled these small establishments, and in turn the overall economy, to expand into more efficient and more competitive forms.

Indeed, the raw organic material was present in the form of predominant social practices, norms, and institutions. What was needed was better access to capital that could have pushed more SSEs toward conducting more impersonal transactions, or what I call "familiarized markets," where social ties play a role in facilitating market transactions in the absence of functional contract enforcement and private property protection. This was the route taken by vibrant and competitive private sector firms in Taiwan, China, Malaysia, and Turkey, for example (Chen and Rozelle, 1999; Demir, Acar, and Toprak, 2004; Hashim, 2005; Siu, 2005; Yeh and Yi-Ching Chen, 2007; Wright et al., 2008; Zulkifli-Muhammad, Char, bin Yasoa, and Hassan, 2009).

The perpetual undercapitalization of SSEs also hindered organic formality, where growing micro and small enterprises increasingly invoke state-set rules and regulations in ingenious combinations, with social, and hence informal, mechanisms of enforcement and process- rather than person-based trust. Indeed, field evidence suggests that Egyptian enterprises with higher levels of capitalization, and hence greater capacity to produce and exchange value, move gradually beyond their immediate and narrow social circles while invoking formal rules as measures of last resort against potential opportunism and defection. This reveals a considerable amount of unrealized potential, as this trend toward organic formality occurred on a small scale even among the largest Egyptian SSEs, despite the persistently high costs, low return, and low trust in formal institutions.

Ultimately, baladi capitalism granted survival rather than growth to those who played by its rules, a state of low adaptation. According to GEM (2008,

21; 2010, 34), the Egyptian private sector showed low discontinuance rates: only 3.8 percent of adult Egyptian enterprise owners were no longer active, of whom 1.3 percent quit their work and the remaining 2.5 reported shutting down their business. These extremely low ratios of enterprise churning may serve as an indicator of not only weak entrepreneurial dynamism but also of survival, an important feature to bear in mind when considering how failure is penalized and how difficult it is to restart or restructure a business.

Conversely, the institutional rules that make up dandy capitalism represented a relatively successful high adaptation to the institutional and political constraints of weak property rights, contract enforcement, and rule of law. These rules have made it possible for a few thousand private sector enterprises to gain better access to production inputs and market outlets via a higher degree of differentiation between the social and the economic, and thus a greater capacity to conduct impersonal transactions.

Ultimately, cleft capitalism has perpetuated a suboptimal state in Egypt's political-economic system. Larger firms rarely interacted with the broad base of private sector enterprises due to their limited productivity, lack of competitiveness, and overconcentration in labor-intensive and low-skill sectors. As the subsystem of dandy capitalism in which most of these large firms found themselves was an adaptive response to a political and economic setting that was largely disabling, it could not pass on its capacities for growth or expansion to the lower strata of the economy, and thus overcome the ills of cleft capitalism, described at length in Chapter 1. As later chapters explain, the roots of this failure are political rather than economic.

Chapter Four

THE ORIGINS OF CLEFT CAPITALISM

IN AN OLD NORSE BALLAD, THE HERO SVIPDAG SETS OUT ON A quest to save his fated bride, the goddess Mengloo, from a fortified stronghold never before reached by any human. Before his seemingly impossible task, Svipdag converses with the watchman who guards the entrance to the fortress. The watchman informs him that two great hounds stand guard at the entrance, one sleeping by day and the other by night, so that no one may ever pass unseen. Svipdag asks the watchman about the possibility of throwing meat toward the beasts, then darting past while they are distracted. The watchman answers that only the two wings of a specific cock can be fed to them. Only a special sword can kill this cock, he continues, but a great giant guards the sword. When asking about the possibility of stealing the sword from the giant, Svipdag learns that only the tail feather of this very cock can lure the sword away (Crossley-Holland, 1980, 123–124). Svipdag is caught in a vicious circle: the sword needed to kill the cock can be obtained by only taking the tail feather of that very cock, which is impossible.

Like Svipdag, small-scale establishments in Egypt have faced an impossible dilemma: the need to be rich in capital in order to access capital. In order to produce, and hence become market actors, entrepreneurs need capital in the form of money (credit or equity) and physical assets (e.g., land, machinery). The focus here is on physical and financial capital. In terms of human capital,

I consider this a separate, sociopolitical matter deriving from capital-labor relations as opposed to an additional factor of production as neoclassical theory asserts. Here, human capital is narrowly defined to include the skills and knowledge of the owners and managers of enterprises rather than the skills that workers obtain; thus, employers cannot be considered owners of human capital in the way they are of land, machines, or cash unless they directly own their skilled workers as slaves (Pickety, 2016, 52–53). The education, training, and skill acquisition by workers in a given economy is of prime importance, though it is subject to processes separate from those that mediate the access of entrepreneurs to tangible capital.

This chapter explores the specific institutional mechanisms through which Egypt's unintegrated system and thus its cleft capitalist order came about. The main argument is that the capital-regulating organizations, such as banks and public land management agencies, that govern the allocation of capital to market actors have been hierarchical and centralized. These institutional features created a general discomplementarity between capital-regulating organizations and the broad base of small-scale establishments (SSEs) that raised the barriers to capital access for the latter.

In turn, the need for congruence between the private sector and capital-regulating organizations highlights that institutional arrangements are vital not only for creating a playing field conducive to market exchange, as neoclassical institutionalism would maintain, but they also play a critical role in facilitating the creation of market actors (Khan and Jomo, 2000). The manner in which access to capital is distributed will determine whether an integrated market emerges or a situation of cleft capitalism takes hold. An additional argument here is that this distribution, or redistribution, of capital access is itself a result of sociopolitical processes that either create, or do not create, the institutional intermediaries capable of mediating between capital-regulating institutions and the broad base of private sector SSEs. As the final section argues, SSEs in Egypt were never part of the sociopolitical coalition whose vested interests determined the institutional nature of capital access.

PRIMITIVE ACCUMULATION: FROM KARL POLANYI TO KARL MARX

Neoclassical institutionalists have held state institutions capable of upholding private property rights and enforcing contracts as crucial for successful market making (North, 1990; World Bank, 1997). However, if the vast majority of individuals and households are deprived of minimal physical, financial, and human capital, how could they become market actors capable of making use of private property protection and contract enforcement? Asian economies, such as China, Vietnam, and Malaysia, as well as the earlier development models of South Korea and Taiwan, all fared much better than Egypt in achieving market integration despite the lack of robust formal private property protection. The ability to produce such actors presupposes some redistribution of assets and capital, whether it is physical (e.g., land), financial, or human (defined strictly as education, training, and skills for the owners and managers of capital). Indeed, this initial redistribution of capital is essential for market integration and the creation of a market society.

In Egypt, as well as many other economies in the Global South, market-oriented embeddedness has created conditions in which the private social and cultural capital of microenterprises and household businesses could be used to access and process information, raise initial capital, acquire basic entrepreneurial skills, and lower the cost of exchange despite weak formal contract enforcement and poor public information (Khan and Jomo, 2000, 21). However, in the case of Egypt, this market-oriented embeddedness has not been enough to achieve market integration in the form of a dynamic, competitive, and interlinked base of private sector enterprises. This limitation is derived from the fact that accessing capital requires dealing with public institutions and organizations rather than just private networks of family and friends, which was prohibitively costly for most SSEs.

Today, capital provision is the domain of public rather than private institutions and organizations. Private order institutions that have their own rules and norms and mechanisms of self-enforcement, like family, friends, neighborhoods, clans, and community, can no longer perfectly or efficiently substitute for public ones. Since the nineteenth century, Egypt's modernization process has resulted in the weakening or even dismantling of non-state (and largely premodern) intermediate institutions and organizations like guilds, sects, religious orders, and clans and tribes, which progressively led the emergence of a direct relationship between individual citizens and the state with no intermediate organizations in between (Hourani, 1981, 40; Ayubi, 1995, 100; Ghazaleh, 2010, 201; Menza, 2012, 35). This was especially the case in urban areas, though even in the countryside, the progressive transition into commercial agriculture since the mid-nineteenth century has led to the decline of the tribal and kinship-based collectivities that performed productive tasks. This trend was accelerated by rapid rural-to-urban migration beginning in the 1920s and 1930s (Khafaji, 2013, 203).

In such a setting, private savings, wealth, and property have had to pass through public organizations that go beyond familiar social circles. Thus, the presence of some form of complementarity between the private and public spheres is of crucial importance for accessing financial and nonfinancial capital and is decisive as well in determining whether private social capital hinders or helps market actors interact with public institutions. In turn, these interactions often require the presence of intermediate institutions that are capable of bridging the gap between public and private socioeconomic institutions; however, such arrangements have been missing from Egypt's capitalist transformation. As a result, there has been no complementarity between capital-regulating organizations and most SSEs, and it is this lack that has produced Egypt's cleft capitalist order and missing-middle syndrome.

Here, the story of capitalist transformation shifts from Karl Polanyi to Karl Marx, who addressed the question of primitive accumulation at the early stages of capitalism. Primitive accumulation occurred through sociopolitical rather than economic (i.e., market-based) means—for example, the bestowing of private property rights of land to the first generations of capitalists, as well as acts of colonial accumulation via expropriation, dispossession, and enslavement. Neo-Marxists believe that politics has always been so central to capital accumulation that primitive accumulation continues to persist, and contrary to classical Marxism, it is not an initial phase that has passed (see Glassman, 2006; Harvey, 2007; Bonefield, 2011). Primitive accumulation is an arbitrary process that transfers public resources to private hands, contributing immensely to the rise of capitalist classes capable of and willing to produce for market exchange. Indeed, at some point, "all developing countries had substantial transfers supporting primitive accumulation" (Khan and Jomo, 2000, 25). The predominant forms were transfers from the state to certain private actors in a process in which public resources were converted into private ones.

In this process, political dynamics mattered greatly in shaping the details of the capitalist transformation and the interaction between the state and private sector. These usually depended on institutional arrangements that reflected sociopolitical coalitions pushing to shape the transformation and determine, intentionally or unintentionally, the form and degree of market integration. In some instances, institutional rules governing capital access allowed a deeper and broader form of market integration by engendering a large base of vibrant and competitive small and medium enterprises (SMEs) alongside large businesses (domestic as well as multinational corporations). In others, capitalization was available only to those few who were already large or politically connected, denying the broad base of private SSEs any serious opportunity to scale up.

Conventional neoclassical wisdom, like that found in Hernando de Soto's writings (2002), sought the market integration of the broad and largely informal private sector through legal and procedural formalization. This formalization process was the way in which de Soto and others maintained that assets could be turned into capital and informal activities brought into market circulation. However, the results of legalistic formalization fell well short in achieving financial inclusion and market integration. As Niall Ferguson (2008, 278–279) holds:

> There seems to be a flaw in the theory. . . . In de Soto's native Peru, too, ownership alone doesn't seem to be enough to resuscitate dead capital. True, after the Peruvian government in 1988 accepted his initial recommendations, there was a drastic reduction in the time it took to register a property (to just one month) and an even steeper 99 percent cut in the cost of the transaction. . . . Yet, economic progress of the sort de Soto promised has been disappointingly slow. Out of more than 200,000 Lima households awarded land titles in 1998 and 1999, only around one quarter had secured any kind of loans by 2002.

According to Ferguson, this flaw could be explained in the fact that credit, including mortgage, is extended to households that have income rather than just registered property, which is typically made up of houses and hence is largely of no productive use. This was not the case in Peru or any other Latin American country where the majority of owners of the newly formalized property remained poor and active in the informal economy. Market integration hence requires the making of real market actors who are interested in producing for exchange with the aim of repetitive profit making. This is achieved through capitalization and is shaped by the institutions governing access to physical and financial capital.

The literature on such primitive accumulation amid market transformations in the Global South focused almost exclusively on relations between the state and the capitalist classes. The state began moving away from delivering welfare services to the poor and the middle classes while doing whatever it took to sustain the market through tax cuts and subsidies to large businesses. Meanwhile, income and wealth flowed up to a limited clique of businesspeople and corrupt officials in the name of market making and private sector development (Mitchell, 1999; Achcar, 2013; Hanieh, 2013). It was a case of market making by dispossession (Elyachar, 2005).

Alternatively, state developmentalists focused on how states could pick winners among market actors as part of their larger pursuit of national development without succumbing to rent seeking (Amsden, 1992; Evans, 2012). For instance, Khan and Jomo (2000, 25) discussed the ability of the state to discipline rent recipients by monitoring their performance and maintaining the capacity to wean infant industries away from protection and subsidies as they grew. In turn, a related body of literature directed focus toward the private sector, specifically in its ability to collectively organize, allowing for self-regulation and self-discipline, usually through developmental associations on the sectoral or national levels (Streak and Schmitter, 1985; Schneider, 2004). However, very little has been said about the interaction between the state and SSEs, particularly in the successful cases of market integration where the middle was present.

In Egypt, public policies enabled primitive accumulation by a limited number of private sector actors as well as political clients and cronies. Of course, pure looting and asset stripping took place, and overwhelmingly in some sectors; however, as mentioned in Chapter 3,a capitalist class did take root in Egypt by the 1980s and 1990s that was interested in market exchange and repetitive profit making rather than pure rent seeking or asset stripping. Hence, the problem did not ultimately lie in the inability to engender a capitalist class capable of owning and running big enterprises, but rather in the fact that this capitalist transformation was too shallow to produce SMEs.

Cherchez l'État

In order to understand the ordeal of accessing capital in Egypt, a focus on the state is crucial. Access to capital, especially finance and land, has been heavily governed—formally, informally, and semiformally—by state action in a way that makes this a particularly interesting area of interaction between the political (the state) and the economic (the market).

It must be stated, however, that the state, especially in the Egyptian context, has never been a monolithic actor or even a single coherent bureaucratic unit. There has always been some disparity and tension, or even conflict and competition, within and among various organizations and agencies. Moreover, the use of state authority in pursuit of some alleged public interest has never been easily separated from the private interests of various bureaucratic actors and their allies. Indeed, the private interests of parties within the state were not always easily distinguishable from their claimed pursuit of the public good (Selznick, 1943, 54; Crozier, 1964, 156–157). Problematizing the concept of unitary state action is central to a deep understanding of the political determinants of access to financial and nonfinancial capital.

In Egypt, finance can be equated with access to bank credit, as the country has maintained a bank-based financial system since colonial times (Issawi, 1947, 163; Tignor, 1984, 35; Vitalis, 1995, 32–34). Although capital markets were historically vibrant before independence, including futures markets (Goldberg, 2004), they lost almost all relevance by the early 1960s with the advent of nationalization and the firm installation of state-led development programs that expanded the public sector (Waterbury, 1983, 68, 69, 73).

Despite the rejuvenation of the stock market in 1992 after four decades of morbidity, it never assumed a central financial role except for a short-lived boom between 2004 and 2008. The only internationally comparable data, offered by the World Bank, date back to 2006. Between 2006 and 2011, the stock market capitalization as a percentage of GDP, a traditional indicator of the weight of the stock market in an economy, shows that the median in Egypt was 42.18 percent. This was similar to lower-middle-income countries (41 percent), but well behind East Asia and the Pacific (111.34 percent) and the member countries of the Organization for Economic Cooperation and Development(132.24 percent; World Bank, 2017g). Moreover, it is not clear whether this temporary surge in stock market valuation occurred due to inflation or the enhanced value of the underlying assets. Nonetheless, this stock market activity was largely confined to a few very large companies that could afford to issue stock for public trading.

Accordingly, Egypt seems to fall in line with the conventional wisdom regarding financial systems in many parts of the Global South: "At low levels of economic development commercial banks tend to dominate the financial system, while at higher levels domestic stock markets tend to become more active and efficient relative to domestic banks" (World Bank, 2017g).

Other nontraditional financing tools like venture capital, leasing, mortgaging, and private equity emerged quite recently, as late as the mid-2000s, but have remained underdeveloped, with only small shares in capital markets (Nasr, 2008, 68–72; Ismail, 2009, 83). Again, most have been confined to certain sectors, mainly high tech, with occasional interest in traditional sectors such as industry, tourism, or agriculture even though they constitute the greatest part of the economy (al-Sa'īd, 2013; Wahba, 2013).

The banking sector has been substantial in capital provision, while at the same time remaining under the heavy influence of the state in a variety of ways, especially since political independence in mid-1950s. First, the state has been the formal and informal regulator of the sector through the Central Bank, established in 1961. The setting and enforcement (or lack thereof) of rules governing credit extension were always the domain of state incumbents, ranging from the political leadership to technocrats (e.g., central bankers and chairmen of state-owned banks), bureaucrats, ruling party officials, and security and military officials (Adly, 2009; Roccu, 2013; Roll, 2013). In many instances, state incumbents chose to either not enforce or otherwise twist some formal rules in favor of informal arrangements along the lines of patronage, nepotism, or populist economic policies, supporting the earlier problematization of state authoritative action.

Second, since the full nationalization of the banking sector in the early 1960s, the state has been a major owner of commercial banks (Waterbury, 1983, 149). Despite rounds of privatization and internationalization since the mid-1970s, state-owned and -controlled banks continue to hold a sizable share of total banking sector assets, deposits, and loans (Ikram, 2007, 182; Roccu, 2013, 45, based on Central Bank and World Bank data).

Finally, the state has been one of the biggest debtors to the banking sector, either for the financing of public debt or through the solicitation of credit for state agencies, state-owned enterprises (SOEs), or politically connected businesspeople (Barth, Caprio, and Levine, 2001; Nasr, 2008, 23–24).

In terms of access to land, a virtually infinite supply of desert has stood out as a main feature of Egypt's political economy since infitāḥ. If the country were abundant in any factor of production beside cheap unskilled labor, it would be the desert (World Bank, 2006; Sims, 2014, 2). The hundreds of thousands of square meters of arid and uninhabited space have become critical for urban and, to a lesser extent, rural expansion in the past four decades. As the outright legal owner and ultimate allocator of desert land, the state has taken on a major investment and development role in this area since the late 1970s through a variety of development agencies, state-owned enterprises, megaproject authorities, and the military.

Access to this desert land was supposed to be cheap, because it should cost only the infrastructure needed to make it usable for investment in industry, services, agriculture, and housing. However, like access to bank credit, it has been subject to high administrative and economic barriers for the majority of SSEs. This restrictive access to the land, despite its abundance, fed into the inaccessibility of bank credit that was predicated on the heavy demands of banks for collateral (Mohieldin and Wright, 2000, 664–667; Rocha et al., 2011, 9, 27–28; Adly and Khatib, 2014, 34, 75) with a special preference for real estate, to create an impossible obstacle for SSEs.

Thus, over the past four decades, the increase in the absolute and relative size of the private sector in output, employment, and investment has not translated into easier access to finance and property for the majority of private enterprises and entrepreneurs. Granted, the private sector, as an aggregated category, did increase its share considerably in bank credit and desert land (Shawkat, 2012; World Bank, 2017i); however, this access has been concentrated in a limited number of firms that either already possessed a relatively large initial endowment of capital or were otherwise politically connected. The continuous barring of the vast majority of SSEs from accessing capital in the form of bank-based financing and desert land stands as the causal institutional and material mechanism behind Egypt's cleft capitalism and the missing-middle syndrome.

Capital-Regulating Organizations

The institutional bias against SSEs has resulted from the hierarchical, authoritarian, and centralized character of Egypt's capital-regulating organizations, which refer to banks in the case of finance and governmental land-managing organizations with regard to desert land. Since the late 1970s, centralized civilian and military bureaucracies have been responsible for planning, allocating, and directing the development of desert land for economic purposes, while the banking sector has remained closely regulated by the central government, either directly through the Central Bank or indirectly through state-owned banks.

In both instances, capital-regulating organizations were centralized in terms of administration, politics, and geography. Administratively, they followed a hierarchical structure wherein the flow of information and decision-making processes was strictly top-down. Politically, these central organizations were closely tied to the helm of state authority, be it the military and security agencies, the presidency, or the leadership of the former ruling party (Waterbury, 1983, 80; Adly, 2009; Roll, 2013). Finally, these organizations were geographically centralized as they regulated access to capital on a national scale with little penetration to the local level. For instance, the Egyptian banking sector suffers from the problem of under-branching compared to many middle-income economies. The ratio of bank branches per 100,000 between 2004 and 2014 averaged 4.8 in Egypt versus 11.73, 9.93, 12.5, 17.57, 19.15, and 46.55 in India, Indonesia, Thailand, Tunisia, Turkey, and Brazil, respectively, during the same interval (World Bank, 2017h).

For these reasons, the capital-regulating organizations often lacked the institutional capacities, incentives, and channels to collect, process, and coordinate information flows with local and socially embedded SSEs. The institutional result was that dealing with such organizations raised the transaction costs of accessing capital, as well as the premiums for accessing capital on a market basis—collaterals in the case of bank credit and the high price for land. Given these high administrative barriers and high premiums, capital became accessible and affordable only to those who already enjoyed a relatively large endowment of initial or acquired private capital, which resulted in the perpetual undercapitalization of the broad base of private sector enterprises.

This restrictive access to capital resulted from a general lack of complementarity between the state-regulated organizations charged with setting public policies governing access to credit and land on the one hand, and the broad base of private SSEs on the other. The notion of institutional complementarities is borrowed from the VoC literature, in which Soskice and Hall (2001, 17) highlighted areas of interdependence among various institutional arrangements.

"Complementarity" here refers to the degree to which the private capital that market actors possess enables them to access more capital by lowering the transaction costs of dealing with state-controlled and state-regulated capital providers such as banks and public land development agencies. In other words, public-private complementarity indicates the presence of mechanisms through which local, socially embedded, and personalized-knowledge and networks can translate into access to financial and physical capital from public institutions.

Throughout Egypt's capitalist transformation, high degrees of complementarity existed only between capital-regulating organizations and a small number of market actors, most of them already well capitalized from the outset of market making in the 1970s and 1980s. The few with this relatively large initial or acquired capital, be it in the form of cash and assets or sociocultural capital through social ties, education, and experience with business or the bureaucracy, or both, enjoyed lowered transaction costs of accessing capital beyond the direct social circles of entrepreneurs and entrepreneurial families (Imām, 1986, 55–56). The great majority of SSEs, however, lacked enough capital to lower the transaction costs of accessing the capital necessary for their growth.

The Missing Intermediaries

Intermediary institutions are arrangements of rules and structures that small-scale establishments can use to access production inputs, including land, technology, and skilled labor, and are crucial in creating complementarities between public and private institutions. While Frederick Schumacher (2011, 149) originally coined a similar concept in his discussion of intermediary technology that could lend itself to small-scale and often labor-intensive establishments and enable them to become more productive and capable of growth, this chapter applies the concept to a broader range of inputs, particularly land and finance.

Such intermediaries have existed in the more successful cases of capitalist transformation in the Global South that achieved a more integrated market, namely, the Asian capitalisms where vibrant and competitive strata of SSEs burgeoned and showed an ability to scale up. While these intermediaries existed in a variety of forms, a simplified typology suggests they can be either top-down or bottom-up.

Top-down intermediaries extend public or semipublic channels to local and socially embedded enterprises, allowing the emergence of complementarity between the two. They collect, transmit, and process information, as well as monitor the behavior of private enterprises in order to lower the transaction costs of accessing capital. This is done in a myriad of ways depending on the level of formality.

First, formal intermediaries translate socially embedded private capital into formalized and standardized knowledge for use by capital-regulating organizations. Banks with extensive local branches, special funding schemes for micro and small and medium-sized enterprises, credit bureaus, and credit-guarantee companies may broaden the clientele. For example, the Malaysian government created the Credit Guarantee Corporation Malaysia Berhad, which established an SME credit bureau that operated as a comprehensive information center offering credit reports and credit ratings (Zulkifli-Muhammad et al., 2009, 70–71). The collective loans that microfinance institutions like Grameen banks use, where community solidarity serves as an enforcement mechanism for debt repayment, are another example (Dowla and Barua, 2006; Yunus, 2007). In a third example, China's rural credit cooperatives acted as local banks and capitalized on dense social networks to extend loans to 25 percent of domestic SMEs in the early 2000s (Wang, 2004, 39).

Second, semiformal intermediates imply mixed property rights between the public and private sectors at the local level. A typical example would be township and village enterprises (TVEs) in China, which served as the locomotive of growth and employment in the 1980s and 1990s (Wang, 2005).

Third, informal intermediates operate through the use of local patronage networks. Again, a salient example is found in China, where local governments have had access to productive assets such as land, credit, and state-owned enterprises (Lin, 1995; Walder, 1995; Peck and Zhang, 2013). These local governance structures were socially embedded within community networks of entrepreneurs and incumbents who were usually tied together through kinship and guanxi networks. As of the 1960s, they could use these local resources made available as a result of Mao's decentralization attempts (Gabriel, Resnick, and Wolff, 2011) and then under Deng Xiao-Ping's fiscal federalism (Tsai, 2004; Jin, Qian, and Weingast, 2005).

The second typology is that of the bottom-up intermediate institutions. These extend up from local groups and grassroots communities to the public organizations in charge of providing capital. In these settings, local and social collectivities are usually granted a public or a semipublic character so as to facilitate the process of accumulation for their members.

These relations can take place directly or indirectly. Examples of direct relations come in the form of cooperatives or associations that engage in resource pooling and allocation like the community cooperatives of nineteenth-century Germany (Prinz, 2002; Cull et al., 2006; Guinnane, 2011). More indirect cases typically involve semipublic associations that enter into partnerships with banks or government bodies. In these cases, associations could transmit information and build monitoring and enforcement capacities in addition to performing the tasks of interest aggregation and representation for their members while pooling and channeling resources (Stark and Bruszt, 1998; Riddle and Gillespie, 2003; Schneider, 2004; Neidik and Gereffi, 2006).

Where Intermediaries Come From

The presence of both types of intermediary institutions, top-down as well as bottom-up, may enable a sustainable expansion of a client base to include broader socioeconomic strata latent with entrepreneurial potential. However, such institutions are not easily fostered. Path-dependency theorists have noted that the creation or transforming of institutions is economically and politically costly (David, 1994; Karl, 1997). It requires overcoming restraints rooted in past institutional legacies and all the vested interests and stubborn worldviews that they harbor (Goldberg, 2004). Nonetheless, the issue of agency is quite important in answering the question as to why such institutional intermediaries sometimes do not emerge and why state incumbents or influential socioeconomic actors are either unwilling or unable to invest in establishing them, from the top or the bottom.

China provides good examples for the successful establishment of intermediary institutions. Land reform and the establishment of rural cooperatives under Mao (1949–1976) provided the basis for the robust rural industrialization that took place after the liberalization of 1978. Mixed forms of public-private ownership and the collective economy, institutionalized in the form of the township and village enterprises (TVEs), provided the institutional basis for the rapid national expansion that was largely based on rural industrialization throughout the 1980s and 1990s (Wang, 2004, 41). In addition, enterprises owned and operated by provincial governments were equally important throughout this period after economic and fiscal powers were delegated to these governments under Mao in the 1960s and in the late 1970s by Xiao Ping's fiscal federalism. This undoubtedly created a positive institutional environment for the emergence of a vibrant and competitive base of publicly owned SMEs (Walder, 1995). Even while the Chinese economy shifted toward greater dependence on private SMEs, they nevertheless enjoyed robust formal and informal intermediary institutions that secured them the capital they needed to grow (Wang, 2004).

In Malaysia, the cultivation of a broad base of SSEs was a deliberate state strategy beginning in 1971. The Malaysian government began to show a formal commitment to SME support under its New Economic Policy, which aimed "to improve people's welfare and restructure ethnic economic imbalances" (Fay and Jomo, 2000; Saleh and Ndubisi, 2006, 2). The policy was driven by ethnopolitical concerns, with the aim of making Malay Muslims more economically active and countering the commercial dominance of ethnic Chinese.

Another example is seen in the rise of Turkey's "green capital" or "Anatolian Tigers" in the 1990s and 2000s. The rise of the Tigers was organically tied to the arrival of Islamist and, later, post-Islamist, political parties into power (Demir, Acar, and Toprak, 2004, 172; Adly, 2012a, 192–197; Görmuş, 2017). While the central government in Turkey did not extend direct support to these rising SMEs in the 1980s and 1990s, it did provide an advantageous regulatory framework. A prime example was allowing interest-free banking as early as 1983, which was crucial in channeling workers' remittances and contributed to the capital accumulation of a growing number of Anatolian SMEs (Demir et al., 2004, 169–171). The situation changed dramatically after the rise of the Justice and Development Party to power in 2002. Ever since, state support for SMEs, both financial and otherwise, has expanded at increasingly accelerating rates (OECD, 2004; Adly, 2012a, 68, 191)

Taiwan's "black-hand bosses"(businesspeople who were once menial workers and apprentices) also represent an example of the power of top-down intermediary institutions. Since the 1950s and 1960s, these firms have risen to economic prominence by expanding from small workshops into exporting SMEs (Wu and Huang, 2003). This development can be explained in terms of a broader political compromise between the Kuomintang government and the indigenous Taiwanese population that allowed the emergence of a mixed economy with large public sector firms and small and medium-sized private enterprises.

INSTITUTIONS AS SOCIOPOLITICAL COALITIONS

The intermediate institutions that facilitated market integration across other capitalisms, particularly in Asia, did not emerge in Egypt. Conversely, the institutional system that evolved to regulate capital provision, and the sociopolitical coalition that upheld it, maintained a systematic bias against SSEs. Such a system has resulted from rules, norms, and practices that have been enacted and reenacted throughout Egypt's long march toward market making. In this sense, institutions are a reflection of certain sociopolitical coalitions that included "social groups bound together through institutions that affect implicit (and explicit) contractual relations, expectations and specific mechanisms for the collection and transmission of information" (Goldberg, 2004, 2; see also Greif, 2006, 526).

In Egypt, the hierarchical, centralized, and authoritarian capital-regulating organizations that have emerged are the outcome of such a sociopolitical coalition, made up primarily of bureaucratic actors who directly used financial and physical capital. Since infitāḥ, this coalition has remained largely in charge of defining public authority in the economic sphere, though not always in a harmonious, coherent, or coordinated manner. Market mechanisms did penetrate deeply to reach sizable social strata, probably for the first time in the country's contemporary history (Farsoun, 1988, 165; Hopkins, 1992, 15). However, accessing affordable financial and physical capital remained stifled in the service of certain bureaucratic constituencies.

Only a few private actors, some with connections to the state and others not, could use their large initial and acquired capital and strong ties to external markets to clear the high barriers and adapt to the rather ambivalent and sometimes unfriendly state economic institutions. These were the actors that came to comprise dandy capitalism. In addition, some political and bureaucratic insiders became increasingly entrepreneurial in their activities, representing the most entrepreneurial elements of the cronies. Meanwhile, private SSEs remained locked out; baladi capitalism would never realize its entrepreneurial potential.

A Coalition of Bureaucratic Actors

Capital-regulating organizations that emerged from the state-led development initiatives in the 1950s and 1960s significantly expanded the size and mandate of the state bureaucracy and SOEs in regard to the allocation of economic resources (Waterbury, 1983; Tignor, 1984). The sequestration of foreign and non-Muslim and non-Egyptian minorities' assets following the Suez War of 1956 was also part of the story (Beinin, 1998; Abdulhaq, 2016). Outright nationalization of large Egyptian enterprises soon followed in virtually all relevant industrial and service sectors, along with significant land reforms between 1952 and 1961.

Within this context, the state created bureaucratic, centralized, and hierarchical institutions that directly managed economic resources and regulated capital provision. Financial capital-regulating organizations, for example, were represented by an atrophied capital market and dominant state-owned banking and insurance sectors, with the Treasury and its SOEs standing as the main borrowers (Zaki, 1980, 378). It was also within this same context that desert lands were subjected to strict militarized regulations out of national security concerns. These institutional rules, structures, and norms came to bear significantly on the economic role the state was to play from the advent of infitāḥ in the mid-1970s, as it is important to remember that institutions are sticky, especially when they imply certain patterns of power and resource distribution (Steinmo, Thelen, and Longstreth, 1992; Karl, 1997).

These organizations outlived their original Nasserist purpose of facilitating accumulation for a state-led development model. After infitāḥ, they were reinforced by power dynamics within a broad coalition of bureaucratic actors, leading to the creation and perpetuation of prohibitively high barriers to accessing capital for private actors. Whereas large private businesses or those with political connections could break in and adapt to the high costs, most SSEs could not. This fundamentally resulted from the fact that none of the predominant bureaucratic actors, ranging from the top leadership in the presidency, the various security and military bodies, and the NDP, to different actors within the bureaucracy, were vested in the inclusion of SSEs and the realization of market integration.

The political leadership inherited large constituencies of state-dependent workers from Naṣer's years of import substitution and public sector expansion ('Abdel-Faḍīl, 1980, 123). Indeed, the feature of the state as the employer of last resort continued to persist throughout the decay and gradual dismantling of state-led development, and state workers in the bureaucracy and state-owned enterprises continued to be a crucial social constituency for political stability (Ayubi, 1995, 33). Under al-Sadāt and Mubārak, the regime leadership would use its enormously concentrated power to devise policies that would balance their sought-after economic liberalization while maintaining social and political stability (Soliman, 2011).

Within the bureaucracy was a bureaucratic bourgeoisie, defined by the use of public employment for private accumulation of wealth that would play a key role in maintaining the prevailing institutional arrangements. This bourgeoisie could be found staffing the higher echelons of important civilian, military, and security bureaucracies, with significant shares of public authority and crucial functions (for example, the military; security agencies; the judiciary; revenue-generating bodies in areas of taxation, oil and gas sales, and the central bank) in regime survival. In terms of sheer numbers, a 2006 census estimated that higher-echelon bureaucrats, including managers, directors, and top officers, constituted 4 percent of the workforce in the government bureaucracy (226,000 out of 5.4 million) (al-Merghani, 2010, 162).

However, the majority of the state-dependent workforce has been composed of poorer and more numerous employees, whose sustenance was nonetheless crucial for stability (around 3 million in the 1980s and currently around 6 million strong). In contrast to the bureaucratic bourgeoisie, this group was more closely representative of a bureaucratic or state proletariat (al-Merghani, 2010, 150). According to the census, roughly 56 percent of the bureaucratic workforce worked in these low-paying and often redundant jobs, mainly in local government (al-Merghani, 2010, 162).

In addition, relevant actors within the bureaucracy could access power and resources both formally and informally. For instance, the military's sweeping mandate over desert land management was an integral part of its role as a powerful actor within the ruling coalition following the 1973 October War. This also served their direct economic interests that were either institutional (e.g., revenues to the military) or privatized (e.g., subsidized housing units for officers). This was in turn integrated into the strategy of the top leadership as a requirement for depoliticizing the military and as a means to lighten the fiscal burden on the Treasury (Springborg, 1989, 95, 114–116).

However, Egypt's centralized and hierarchical institutions governing capital provision were not entirely rationally or strategically designed. At times, these institutions were in the hands of bottom-up forces of bureaucratic actors who were focused on preserving or extending their access to physical and financial capital, or what Crozier once called bureaucratic subalterns (1964, 202). In fact, many of these bottom-up attempts were contentious and often led to undermining the coherence of the strategies pursued by the leadership to attract investment or encourage private sector growth (Adly, 2015).

Overall, capital-regulating organizations were used to cater to the needs of various state-dependent constituencies throughout Egypt's market-making process. Despite the fact that the components of the prevailing bureaucratic coalition did witness some changes after infitāḥ, there remained strong elements within the state bureaucracy that reinforced an institutional setting that would make capital affordable and available to the state. The state increasingly abandoned its earlier Nasserist role as the center for accumulation and motor behind social and economic development (Bradley, 1983; Waterbury 1983, 17). Instead, it became a mechanism for the delivery of rents, under many forms, for dependent constituencies within the bureaucracy.

That state authority used to facilitate access to resources for various groups within the bureaucracy may tempt some to label this as state capture, but it is not. Hellman, Jones, and Kaufmann (2000) defined *capture* as systemic political corruption in which private interests significantly influence a state's decision-making process to their own advantage. Capture was clearly visible in Egypt, where the presidential family and top incumbents used state authority in order to reap personal gains (Adly, 2012b). However, it hardly applies to the catering for broad constituencies of state dependents and their families. This was the case with the expansion in public employment in the 1980s and 1990s and the subsequent growth of the government payroll that was primarily deficit-financed through bank borrowing. Despite the fact that these resources were spent to generate income for these dependents, this was dictated by political requirements for legitimacy or social peace and stability rather than the captors' lucrative ends. The same explanation applies to state uses of desert land for national megaprojects, which created niches for patronage distribution, rent seeking, and capture for certain individuals or groups. However, the bigger process has been tied to questions of dominance, coalition maintenance, and regime legitimation, all of which go beyond the simple utilitarian logic behind state capture (Evans, 2012; on Egypt not being a mere kleptocracy, see Sadowski, 1991, 128).

Private Big Business: A Coconut Octopus Story

Al-Sadāt's infitāḥ served as the starting point for Egypt's transformation in the direction of a private sector–dominated and market-based economy. The push came from the al-Sadāt regime's attempts to resolve its economic and fiscal crises, as well as a sign of its foreign policy realignment with the Western bloc (Hussein, 1982, 443).

Changes to formal rules were dictated by the political elite's interest in incentivizing private investment, either as a solution to macroeconomic problems or in order to furnish economic opportunities for aspiring elites within the state apparatus, resulting in the emergence of crony capitalists from the public sector (Imām, 1986; Zaalouk, 1989). Restrained state predation also created a space for different actors within the private sector, including some who were not politically connected to the regime, to move into more capital-intensive niches in the 1980s and 1990s.

These actors were largely Egyptian private investors who enjoyed large endowments of initial private capital, whether obtained from working abroad, retained from pre-1952 times, or emerging from linkages with the Arab Gulf after 1973 or through links to the state (Sadowski, 1991, 100–101). They came to benefit from the guarantees and incentives that the leadership under al-Sadāt established for foreign investors. In this way, they acted like the coconut or veined octopus, which uses the abandoned shells of snails on the ocean floor for shelter and hunting smaller crustaceans. While these shells were not made intentionally for the octopus, they nonetheless are a necessary condition for its survival. This is how stripes of Egyptian private actors came to invest and accumulate capital even in the absence of direct political ties.

Indeed, private businesses moved steadily from trade-related activities in the mid-1970s, when infitāḥ was launched, into more capital-intensive ones. By the late 1990s, Egypt had a consolidated class of big business owners in the key sectors of manufacturing, construction and real estate, tourist resorts and hotels, and agribusiness (Suleymān, 1999; Adly, 2017). Many of these businesses enjoyed favorable policies ranging from trade protection and fuel subsidies to accessing public procurement contracts and subsidized publicly owned land or the acquisition of privatized state-owned enterprises (Mitchell, 1999; Sfakianakis, 2004; Adly, 2012b).

However, despite their growing economic weight in the 1980s and 1990s, these big private businesses lacked significant political representation in the circles of power where decisions were made and implemented (Zaki, 1999, 121–123; ʿEzz al-dīn, 2003). Cabinets and the inner circle around the president, where most power was vested, were almost completely made up of bureaucrats with military, civilian security, and intelligence backgrounds, with little room for independent technocrats or businesspeople in the actual process of decision making. Nonetheless, with the advent of the twenty-first century, a few large enterprises did garner significant economic weight that led them to develop a greater stake in the policies affecting them (Soliman, 2011; Adly, 2017).

These incremental transformations would set the stage for a heightened political role for a few businesspeople and business families in the 2000s, especially with the advent of the Aḥmed Nazīf cabinet in 2004. This was the first time since the launch of infitāḥ that a team representative of the interests of big private business attempted to redefine the role of the state in relation to the market in accordance with the prevailing neoliberal ideology. Their project was aimed at liberating public assets, including bank credit and publicly owned land, from state administrative control. This was by no means easy; quarters within the vast state bureaucracy pushed back, resulting in a rather ragged and uneven reform track (Roccu, 2013; Adly, 2015).

Eventually these big business interests came to share power with the coalition of state dependents. These forces had to coexist, but now the operating environment within which this capitalist class had to work was difficult. They had to live with a state bureaucracy that was burdensome, incompetent, and sometimes resistant to marketization efforts. They also had to appease the still powerful military and look for areas of symbiosis (a practical solution was making the president the final arbiter on desert land uses, for instance). In turn, they faced turbulence from the State Council courts that managed to disrupt some of the key measures of marketization and the privatization of state-owned assets (Adly, 2012b).[1]

Despite the reforms of Nazīf's government, cleft capitalism remained an entrenched fact of socioeconomic and political life. Thus, the expansion of big business in capital- and technology-intensive sectors occurred with little backward or forward linkages with labor-intensive SSEs. Deepening capitalist relations and exploring the chances of exploiting Egypt's most abundant factor of production, cheap labor, did not seem to have been prioritized by the politically empowered businesspeople; whatever resources they had, they either kept to themselves or shared with the vast state workforce as a token of coexistence.

And Stay Out! The Historical Origins of SSEs' Exclusion

Whereas infitāḥ spread the seeds of a class of large businesses in Egypt, a middle capitalist stratum remained absent. This section traces the historical roots of the exclusion of SSEs, which may illuminate the lack of any significant intermediary institutions and complementarities.

Ironically, the rise of baladi capitalism—or entrepreneurship from below—was to a great extent an unintended consequence of some state actions in the 1950s and 1960s. One decisive factor was the waves of land reform between 1952 and 1961, which led to a massive rural migration to major urban centers (Khafaji, 2013, 202). This freed greater numbers of peasants to move into cities, a trend that began in earnest in the 1930s due to overpopulation and a limited supply of fertile land and led to the integration of millions of peasants and urban migrants into the cash economy rather than sharecropping ('Abdel-Faḍīl, 1980, 118; Khafaji, 2013, 329). However, this massive rural emigration was not absorbed by any dynamic industrial growth, as was the case historically in Western Europe, the United States, Japan, and, later, South Korea and Taiwan. In the absence of employment, many new urban arrivals were left with the option of self-employment, which meant that their subsistence would rely on the production of goods and services for market exchange. Thus, for the first time, millions of people became dependent on the market, though this was primarily geared toward making a living rather than making profits ('Abdel-Faḍīl, 1980, 76).

As early as the interwar period, Egypt had a mass of SSEs. Charles Issawi (1947, 111) cites the industrial and commercial census of 1937, when Egypt had 139,000 establishments, of which 74 percent employed no labor and only 3 percent employed over five persons. Robert Tignor's description of the state of Egypt's private sector in the interwar period includes the earliest available economic statistics:

> Despite some change in its activities, the small-scale manufacturing sector continued to be important in production and employment. Yet, with some notable exceptions, hardly any of the small operatives were able to break into the world of big business. The small businessmen in Egypt lacked capital and vision. They knew how to manage a small workshop, but could not contemplate administering a large factory. More importantly, they lacked the business and political contacts so essential for success in Pre-Nāṣer Egypt. In most cases, they had only a smattering of formal education, and if they lacked fluency in English and French they would have great difficulty entering the modern economic sector. (Tignor, 1984, 210; see also Beinin and Lockman, 1987, 263–265)

Had Tignor been writing in the 2000s, he likely would have diagnosed Egypt's private sector with a missing-middle problem dating back to the pre-1952 period.

One special feature of pre-independence Egypt that might have been consequential for SSEs under Naṣer was the heavy presence of foreigners and religious and ethnic minorities in nonagricultural and urban economic activities. Issawi (1947, 163–164) mentioned that Egyptians had a humble share in occupations in "modern" sectors (i.e., nonagricultural) in the late 1930s: whereas 59 percent of them worked in agriculture, just 10 percent could be found working in industry and transportation, 6 percent in commerce and finance, and 5 percent in services. Conversely, 24 percent of foreigners worked in industry and 22 and 20 percent in commerce and finance, respectively.

These figures were probably confined to large businesses due to the unavailability of such statistics about small and medium-size, let alone micro, enterprises during the same period of time (Abdulhaq, 2016). They may, however, suggest that foreigners or residents who belonged to ethnic and religious minorities—Jews, Greeks, Italians, Armenians, and Christian Levantines—dominated the biggest and most entrepreneurial among SSEs. They were better educated on average than Egyptians and probably had more opportunities to accumulate small amounts of capital given their enjoyment of consular protection and other privileges under the capitulations system (e.g., being exempt of taxes but also of potential extortion by local officials). Unfortunately, all of this remains in the realm of speculation for the lack of hard statistical data on SSEs, similar to the ones available on big business of the time.

The probable supposition that the most capitalized and most entrepreneurial SSEs before 1952 were foreign owned or belonged to minorities proved to be of consequence after the military takeover in 1952. Whereas big businesses were explicitly targeted by the state for Egyptianization, even before 1952 (Tignor, 1984; Abdulhaq, 2016), SSEs were Egyptianized in an unplanned manner. Minority populations diminished considerably and consistently in Egypt as of the end of World War II for a number of reasons. These ranged from sequestration of foreign assets in the aftermath of the 1956 war and rising nationalist sentiments among Egyptians after the creation of Israel to the expansion of the public sector after the nationalizations of 1961. The disappearance of non-Egyptian and non-Muslim minorities from economic life might have had two contradictory, and largely unintended, consequences for the political future of SSEs.

On the one hand, there has been an expansion of SSEs owned and run by Egyptians, especially those who managed to take over market niches and sometimes production assets that foreign and minority masters once owned. This could be referred to as some sort of silent encroachment that happened in the shadow of the Egyptianization and nationalization of large enterprises. It was not, however, a result of conscious state action by no means. Masters and entrepreneurs who belonged to religious and ethnic minorities or were foreign residents in Egypt would relinquish their property to their Egyptian apprentices (Elyachar, 2005, 111). Maḥmūd Elaraby [al-ʿArabī] (2015, 153), the owner of one of the biggest business groups today, specializing in electronics, gave a detailed account of how he and his brothers made their way into the ranks of wholesale merchants in the 1960s by acquiring the store of a prominent Jewish merchant, Ibrahīm Galaboh, who left Egypt (or was forced to leave) in the mid-1960s. Before that, Elaraby maintained that in the vibrant Moski neighborhood of Old Cairo, there were virtually no Muslim wholesale merchants. Big merchants were predominantly Jewish in this quarter, and Muslim (Egyptian) traders were retailers, including the Elarabys themselves. Elaraby's family-owned business was an exception that grew from a small enterprise in the 1960s to a medium-sized one in the 1970s and 1980s and then one of Egypt's biggest conglomerates in the twenty-first century.

Private SSEs were left not only to operate but to dominate key sectors like the wholesale and retail trade, as well as construction in the heyday of state-led development in the 1960s. In 1973, after almost fifteen years of state-led development, the private sector supplied 56.18 percent of total output compared to 43.8 percent for the public sector. Small private producers dominated agriculture (98 percent), trade (60 percent), and housing (88.2 percent) and had a significant presence in light manufacturing and services (O'Brien, 1966, cited in Waterbury, 1983, 160).

However, this unintended and largely uncoordinated Egyptianization weakened any chances of a political representation of SSEs or groups among them on a regional or sectoral basis, for instance, within the rising corporatist structure of the postindependence state. Small-scale establishments were never counted as an important part of the rising "Egyptian nation" at any decisive moment of the evolution of Egyptian nationalism. Unlike workers, peasants, middle-class professionals, and patriotic businesspeople, workshop owners were not part of the nationalist movement. Moreover, the fact that SSEs in urban areas were no extension of old guild-like organizations denied them organizational power or the ability to coordinate collective action on sectoral or regional basis at early stages of independence in the 1950s (Issawi, 1947, 95). Had they had such structures, they could have perhaps been included in the state corporatist deal under Naṣer in a way similar to what happened in Italy and Germany in the late nineteenth and early twentieth centuries.

Indeed, during the Nāṣer period, the de facto Egyptianization and expansion of the small, private sector did not coincide with the creation of any institutional complementarities between these emerging small firms and large capital. This boiled down to a quite paradoxical trap: their small size made them too "unmodern" to be included in state-led development industrialization, but if they were to grow, they became increasingly vulnerable to sequestration and nationalization, which remained a serious threat until the late 1960s (Waterbury, 1983, 167).

The way SSEs expanded under the Nasserist political economy had long-term consequences, even after infitāḥ and the relaxation of the nationalization and sequestration threats. It evolved largely into a nonstate sector; not only were a majority of them informal in legal status and operation, but they also developed no political linkages on the micro-, meso-, or macrolevels with capital-regulating organizations. Capital was accumulated through purely private and usually heavily socialized means for fear of state predation, and they remained concentrated in labor-intensive sectors because they possessed no institutionalized access to technology or capital. Ultimately, they were not part of any of the state development plans, and no forward or backward linkages were created between SOEs and privately owned SSEs (ʻAbdel-Faḍīl, 1980, 207).

The crucial political-economic point is that groups within the population of SSEs never wielded enough collective leverage on a sectoral or regional basis to push for easier and cheaper access to capital. While the mechanisms of rent and profit distribution, access to productive assets, and investment capacity varied over time (see Chapters 6 and 7), they nevertheless maintained the same exclusionary effect, and the institutional bias against the majority of SSEs persisted.

The broad base of privately owned SSEs was never party to the political processes that were largely responsible for the creation of market actors via capital redistribution (i.e., primitive accumulation). On the one hand, none of the owners of SSEs were part of the state corporatist legacy inherited from the Nāṣer times, and were hence excluded from the preexisting channels that might have acted as centers of capital access in such an authoritarian setting. This might have put them in a position similar to Chinese township and village enterprises or the semipublic-semiprivate forms of ownership and management that mushroomed in rural China throughout the 1980s and 1990s following the Chinese opening up of 1978.

On the other hand, the authoritarian dynamics of the ruling regime limited the collective mobilization of SSE groups that could have arisen on a sectoral, regional, or even political basis (e.g., supporting a political party, adhering to a certain ideology). Moreover, the utterly centralized configuration of the political regime significantly reduced the resources on the local level that could have allowed formal or informal channels of access to capital through patronage at the local government level (e.g., China's fiscal federalism). Indeed, the late Samer Soliman (2006, 111, 114) showed how the impoverishment of local governments in Egypt grew from the 1980s as assets and revenues were almost completely captured by the central government. Trivial amounts were then reallocated to local governments, subjecting local patronage networks to the powers at the center of the political system.

In sum, the intermediate institutions that facilitated market integration across other capitalisms in the Global South, particularly in East Asia, did not emerge in Egypt. Indeed, as the following chapters outline in detail, the crucial capital-regulating organizations that governed access to both financial credit and land, the essential inputs of growth, remained untethered from any meaningful connection to the broad base of SSEs. The institutional arrangements that mediated relations between these organizations and the private sector remained firmly biased in favor of large enterprises capable of capitalizing on their capital or political connections to acquire the inputs necessary for growth, while the broad base of SSEs remained cut off, undercapitalized, and perpetually small.

The following chapter discusses the historical and political factors that led to the production and reproduction of cleft capitalism after infitāḥ. A crucial question of analysis will be whether the emergence of cleft capitalism, and the ruling social coalition that produced and perpetuated it, was structurally inevitable or if there was room for change at certain critical junctures that was missed.

Chapter Five

HOW CLEFT CAPITALISM CAME ABOUT

THE SOCIOPOLITICAL FORCES THAT PRODUCED AND PERPETUATED the institutions underpinning cleft capitalism were the outcome of complex and interactive historical processes rather than the manifestation of a single, permanent, coordinated, and conscious force over the past forty years. Structural restraints, both natural and man-made, have shaped the institutional path along which this arrangement evolved, forming the stage where the different, and often regularly changing, actors interacted, and ultimately upheld Egypt's cleft economic order, both intentionally and unintentionally.

It was the predominance of a coalition of bureaucratic actors that maintained certain institutional arrangements for directly accessing land and bank credit. However, this was neither uniform nor always consciously pursued, as it did not always result from top-down decisions, strategic or myopic, by the top leadership of the executive, where most formal power resided. Rather, bottom-up forces from within a highly incoherent and fragmented bureaucracy solidified the same institutional arrangements of a centralized and hierarchical capital-regulating system.

The chapter distinguishes three crucial subperiods through which cleft capitalism evolved. These historical hinge periods were characterized by significant market-making measures—via liberalization, privatization, and private sector expansion—that failed to divert Egypt from the path of cleft capitalism.

The first period begins with the launch of al-Sadāt's open-door policy in 1974 and continues to Egypt's adoption of the Structural Adjustment Program (SAP) in 1990/1991. These were the years that witnessed the emergence of robust intrabureaucratic dynamics, as well as the diversification of the Egyptian private sector.

The second subperiod (1990–2004) starts with the SAP, which initiated Egypt's most comprehensive and consistent, albeit gradual, transformation toward market making under the auspices of the International Monetary Fund (IMF), the World Bank, and US Agency for International Development (USAID). This included the beginning of the privatization of state-owned enterprises (SOEs) and increased integration into the global division of labor through trade and capital movement liberalization. In turn, this represents the period of Egypt's transformation away from state capitalism under which the state assumed a direct role in production and accumulation of capital, to a model whereby the state served the function of sustaining the consumption of huge and diversified constituencies of state dependents. This transformation had major implications for the state's reliance on the domestic financial sector to sustain a huge workforce of ill-paid employees struggling to keep pace with rising inflation. The SAP created the opportunities through which large private business would emerge, setting the stage for the sociopolitical struggle between businessmen-turned-politicians, on the one hand, and bureaucratic forces, on the other, that would define the subsequent era.

Aḥmed Nazīf's cabinet initiated the third subperiod (2004–2011). Nazīf's tenure marked a qualitative change in the composition of the ruling coalition. For the first time since the military takeover of 1952, representatives of big private capital had a significant political weight in economic policymaking. The conflict over the role of the state in relation to market making intensified between the businessmen-turned-politicians and different bureaucratic actors, to the eventual demise of the former. The outcome of this struggle failed to produce a coalition committed to bringing in the broad base of the Egyptian private sector and thus ultimately reproduced the institutional underpinnings of cleft capitalism and Egypt's missing-middle syndrome.

INFIT–1990: INFITĀḤ: A MYTH CALLED POLITICAL WILL

In 1974, al-Sadāt launched infitāḥ: the starting point for Egypt's movement toward a private sector– dominated and market-based economy. Crucially, "the 'economic open-door policy' was not forced upon Egypt by domestic capitalist lobbies nor by Western creditors" (Waterbury, 1983, 123), but rather came from the al-Sadāt regime's desire to fix economic and fiscal crises, as well as a sign of its foreign policy realignment with the West. Al-Sadāt's plan, elaborated in 1974, was simple. Political and economic policy changes were meant to attract foreign capital inflows from oil-rich Arab countries that accumulated large dollar reserves in the wake of the first oil shock of 1973. In addition, the role of international financial institutions (IFI)—the IMF, the World Bank, and US-AID—in providing badly needed dollars in the 1970s through soft loans, trade facilitations, and grants (Ḥussein, 1982) further encouraged trade liberalization and private investment incentive schemes on the part of the government.

Initially, the Egyptian government targeted solely foreign and Arab investments (Law No. 143 of 1974). It appeared that the government either wanted to avoid any conflict with the still large public sector or did not see any great potential in the local private sector—or perhaps both. Because neither al-Sadāt nor any prominent members of his regime were particularly ideologically committed to economic liberalism, they ran liberalization on a largely pragmatic basis and in a piecemeal manner. Thus, rather than the leadership's political will, strategic vision, or long-term coherent action, a complex interaction between the top leadership and the different quarters within the bureaucracy, as well as other societal groups, including private businesses, shaped the subsequent transformation that derived from this liberalization process (Sadowski, 1991, 5–6, 11).

It was through this haphazard process that the winners of Egypt's post–state-capitalist phase would emerge. For instance, it was within this context that the seeds of the military's civilian economic empire were sown (Springborg, 1989, 98–124). In 1979, al-Sadāt issued Presidential Decree 32 establishing the National Service Project Organization (NSPO) to act as an economic arm for the military in predominantly civilian economic sectors, including agriculture, construction, and energy. The organization was authorized to run for-profit projects and establish joint ventures with private investors, including those from abroad. The military would soon convert its extensive regulatory mandate over desert land, largely a legacy from the Nāṣer period, into economic returns through extraction of rent from public and private developers (Barayez, 2016).

State-owned enterprises also initially stood to win out from infitāḥ. As John Waterbury (1983, 133) clearly demonstrated, rather than eliminating public enterprises, infitāḥ was initially meant to reinvigorate SOEs through the establishment of joint ventures with private capital in order to access finance and technology. Indeed, SOEs received 36 percent of all projects implemented after the launch of the open door policy in 1974, holding up to 38.9 percent in the spinning and weaving industry, 30.8 percent in food processing, 46.5 percent in mining, and 50 percent in building materials (Waterbury, 1983, 139).

SOEs constituted the second largest borrower from the banking sector during the 1970s (ranking just behind the Treasury), with a 15 percent share in total domestic credit (Zaki, 1980, 378). There were indeed many instances of state-owned banks having to extend loans to underperforming SOEs to save them from liquidity or insolvency given the inability of the state Treasury to offer the required funds. The political leadership remained adamant about preserving control over the banking sector, despite encouraging foreign banks to operate in Egypt (al-ʿAntarī, 2005, 25). The bailout of SOEs using bank credit would continue until the adoption of the SAP in 1990/1991 and the forced installation of hard-budget constraints that separated the state budget from SOEs.

Managing the State Proletariat

Containing the financial burden of the state workforce presented another issue to the leadership that was filtered through the liberalization process. Reversing earlier Nasserist policies, there was a de facto freeze on hiring new SOE workers as early as 1978. However, such a restriction could not work with the much larger workforce in the bureaucracy. Despite attempts at evading Naṣer-era commitments to extend public jobs to all university graduates, the al-Sadāt regime could only prolong the waiting period between graduation and hiring. The riots of 1977, occurring to protest the first austerity measures adopted under the auspices of the IMF, brought attempts to downsize the bureaucratic workforce to an effective halt (Sadowski, 1991, 156–157). This political context provided little room to apply a number of the clauses of the new law governing civilian employees (No. 43 of 1978) that aimed to professionalize the workforce and rationalize the wage structure (Gād, 2017, 7). Ultimately, graduates continued to swell the ranks of the bureaucracy while the wage bill continued to grow. This solidified the central government as the largest borrower from the banking sector between 1970 and 1977, with an overall share of 71.6 percent of total domestic credit (Zaki, 1980, 376).

Following al-Sadāt's assassination in 1981, Mubārak was reluctant to continue to push the same infitāḥ agenda throughout the 1980s. He chose instead to avoid any controversial liberalization or restructuring measures and made use of Egypt's access to oil-related rents following the 1979 oil shock, including foreign aid, workers' remittances, and Suez Canal fees. Mubārak continued to affirm the importance of SOEs, denying any intention to privatize them, and thus he kept the state atop the commanding heights of the economy in the name of national security and social justice. Nonetheless, restraining hiring in SOEs continued in the hope of lessening the financial burden on the Treasury. However, placing similar controls on hiring in the bureaucracy remained elusive, as the workforce continued to grow along with the payroll. Like al-Sadāt, the Mubārak regime could not rescind the Nāṣer-era commitment to university graduates regarding access to bureaucratic jobs. All the regime managed to implement the extension of the waiting period between graduation and hiring from three and a half years in 1984 to five years in 1987 (Gād, 2017, 8).

Despite these limits, the economy appeared sustainable until the oil glut of 1986, which denied the government access to critically needed revenues and forced Mubārak to negotiate a stabilization package with the IMF in 1987. This package, however, did not ultimately go into effect for fear of political turmoil, especially in the wake of the 1986 Central Security mutiny, when thousands of armed paramilitary soldiers rebelled against a rumored decree by the minister of the interior extending their conscription. It took the deployment of the army to subdue the mutiny. By 1989, Egypt was almost bankrupt. The government could not service its external debt, which hovered around $45 billion (Ikram, 2007, 150). Miraculously, Mubārak could secure a deal cancelling more than 50 percent of Egypt's external debt in return for Egypt's support for the US-led international coalition against Iraq in 1990 and the subsequent military liberation of Kuwait in 1991.

The Expansion of the Private Sector

In the decade that followed infitāḥ, many leftists tended to view Egypt's emerging domestic private sector as parasitic, serving new luxury import–dependent classes or, worse, as a comprador reintegrating Egypt's economy into the global capitalist division of labor at the expense of the national economic independence that was so hard won under Nāṣer (Morsi, 1980; Ḥussein, 1982; Shukri, 1987; Zalouk, 1989; Amin, 2009). This view was shaken by the subsequent developments in the private sector in the 1980s and 1990s. The early forms of intermediation via trade and brokerage gave way to more capital-intensive and higher value-added activities. Large domestic private enterprises began to engage in manufacturing, agriculture, tourism, construction, and importing technology, undercutting the private sector's characterization as simply parasitical or marginal.

Figure 5.1 shows the ratio of total goods and service imports to GDP in Egypt. Immediately following the launch of infitāḥ, the ratio soared. It jumped to 48, 43, and 49 percent in 1974, 1975, and 1976, respectively, representing the highest levels reached in fifty years (1960–2010). These were signs of an economic rebound after six years of warfare with Israel, as well as an indication of rising consumption, both public and private, thanks to the large oil-related rents that flowed to the Egyptian economy in the light of the oil boom of 1973 (Amin, 2009, 81–82).

The import surge would prove to be short-lived, however. Ever since, the ratio of imports to GDP has declined steadily and consistently, with the average share of imports falling from 39 percent of GDP during al-Sadāt's infitāḥ (1974–1981) to 30.6 percent in Mubārak's first decade in office (1982–1990). It declined further to an average of 27.66 percent in the interval between 1990 and 2003, and down again to 24.31 during the years of the Nazīf's cabinet (2004–2011).

Despite the steady and continuous decline in the share of imports, the private sector managed to increase its overall share in total GDP. "By 1985, one-third of industrial output, 60 percent of the gross domestic product (when the agricultural and service sectors are included) and 55–70 percent of industrial jobs were generated by private activity" (Gunter Meyer, 1988, cited in Sadowski, 1991, 132). Indeed, by the early 1990s, Egypt had a private sector–dominated economy, with a 72 percent share in the nonhydrocarbon GDP (CBE, 2017, cited in Adly, 2017, 6).

Much of this import decline and private sector growth can be traced to Mubārak's initial attempts to limit imports and redirect investment into more productive sectors— namely, manufacturing. In Mubārak's words, the government aimed to convert the earlier, consumption-driven infitāḥ into a

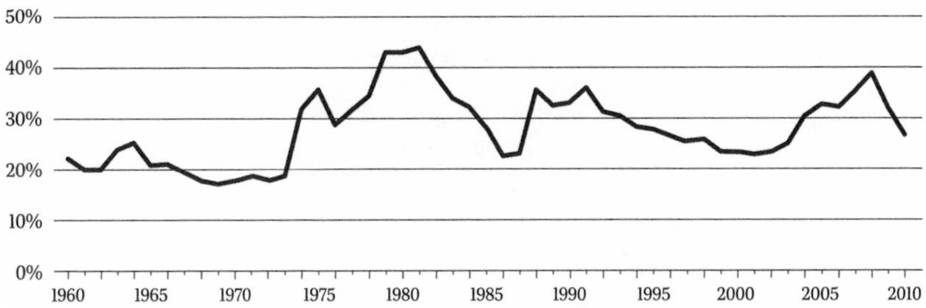

FIGURE 5.1. Imports of Goods and Services as a Percentage of GDP, 1960–2010. Source: World Bank data, Egypt (1960<->2010), https://data.worldbank.org/indicator/NE.IMP.GNFS.ZS?locations=EG.

productive one (Waterbury, 1983, 156). Throughout the 1980s, the state introduced protectionist measures, subsidies, and other investment incentives that amounted to public rents to private capital in the manufacturing, construction, and agricultural export sectors (Sadowski, 1991, 106–108). According to Sulaymān (1999), manufacturing was the fastest-growing sector in the entire economy throughout the 1980s and 1990s. Indeed, manufacturing extended its share in GDP from a low of 12 percent between 1982 and 1985, to 25 and 27 percent in 1997 and 1999, respectively (World Development reports, 1978–2000, cited in Adly, 2012a, 81; Figure 5.2):

> The industrial private sector [excluding extractive industries which remained the domain of foreign and publicly owned companies] was growing with an average annual rate of almost 7 percent in the same period (1980–2000), increasing its share in the total industrial labor force from 35 percent in 1980 to 55 percent in 1990 and reaching 76 percent in 2000. (Calculated from the Ministry of Industry data, cited in Adly, 2012a, 72.)

By the 1980s and into the 1990s, most manufactured imports were inputs of capital and semifinished goods for the domestic manufacturing sector. Chemicals, machinery, and equipment stood at a combined 35 percent of total imports and almost two-thirds of manufactured imports, while finished manufactured goods were mostly high-technology products that had no domestic producers, such as telecommunications equipment, which averaged 21 percent of total imports during the same period.

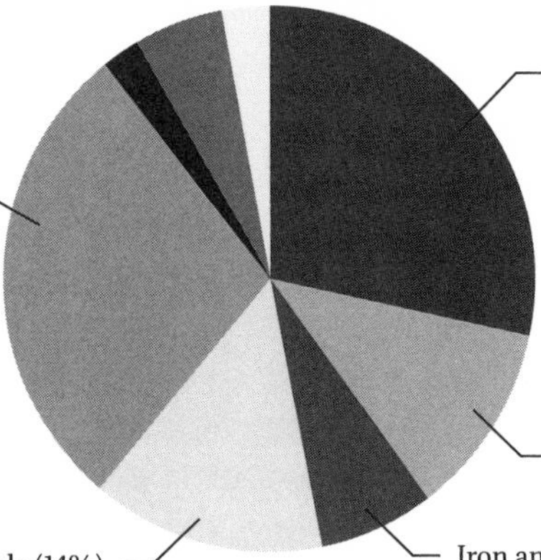

FIGURE 5.2. Goods Import Structure, 1990–2010.
Source: World Trade Organization, *Time Series: Egypt* (1990–2010). http://stat.wto.org/StatisticalProgram/WSDBStatProgramYear.aspx?Language=E.

However, this emergence of a stratum of large, concentrated, and robust private enterprises did not deliver any major development breakthroughs for Egypt. This was partly due to the lack of intermediate institutions that could have channeled capital to a broader base of micro and small private establishments, especially those in labor-intensive sectors. Cleft capitalism precluded that small stratum of large enterprises from exploring and exploiting backward and forward linkages and hence rendered the resultant market too segmented and unintegrated.

Existing prior to liberalization, Egypt's large base of small-scale establishments (SSEs) largely benefited from the rising levels of private consumption associated with infitāḥ, mainly due to inflows of foreign capital in the form of remittances, aid, and credit (Amin, 2009, 81). Moreover, the relative contraction of the public sector led to a visible increase in small-scale activities, not only in personal services but also in the more capitalized manufacturing and construction sectors.

However, most of the inflow of capital that helped fuel state and private consumption required financial mediation by capital-regulating organizations. Thus, private SSE owners in Egypt were required to establish workable linkages with state-controlled or state-regulated capital providers in order to access these savings in the form of credit or to access physical assets (i.e., desert land for productive purposes). The authoritarian and highly centralized dynamics of the ruling regime never allowed SSEs, collectively or individually, to break into this provisioning system. In turn, this disincentivized the politically powerful from bringing them in because the prevailing institutional arrangement preserved their direct access to physical and financial capital.

SUBPERIOD 2, 1991–2003: ECONOMIC LIBERALIZATION BACK ON TRACK

In the early 1990s, Egypt witnessed a serious resumption of the push toward trade liberalization, deregulation, and privatization in the wake of signing a new IMF stabilization package. Slashing the budget deficit, lowering inflation rates, and instilling hard budget constraints vis-à-vis SOEs, this stabilization package coincided with a structural adjustment program aimed at the gradual privatization of SOEs and deregulation.

As a result of the SAP, the bureaucratic coalition underwent a significant reconfiguration as the share of SOEs in output, investment, and employment witnessed a steep decline. Whereas many SOEs were either privatized, divested, or prepared for privatization, others suffered from low investment, obsolete technology, and overstaffing, leading to a decline of market shares in favor of privately owned enterprises. "By 1999, 137 out of the 314 companies declared eligible for privatization had been sold" (Hanieh, 2013, 52). However, even companies that were not sold or subject to divestment had seen a steady decline in investment and employment in absolute and relative terms between 1988 and 2006 (Assaad, 2010, xvi). By 1998, the share of SOE employment in the total labor force stood as a mere 7 percent, declining further to 5 percent by 2006 (Assaad, 2010, 35). The contraction of the SOE sector affirmed the transformation away from state capitalism to catering to the needs of sizable state-dependent constituencies. In turn, state actors, at the top executive level and various groups within the bureaucracy, showed a desire to access affordable and available capital for immediate use rather than accumulation for production.

In the meantime, big private enterprises began to break in economically. By demonstrating higher adaptation to the formal institutional milieu, they managed to move into more capital-intensive sectors. The contraction of the SOE sector and the state's chronic fiscal crisis supported this enlargement of the private sector (including SSEs) as more people, often younger and better educated, flocked into the market. The majority of these were driven by subsistence; however, a minority did have an entrepreneurial intent. Nonetheless, the delineations of the regulatory boundaries of capital-regulating organizations remained in the hands of the bureaucratic actors or representatives of their interests, including the top political leaders. Hence, the patronage networks that flowed from these organizations remained concentrated or targeted toward groups within the bureaucracy out of distributional concerns.

From State Capitalism to State Dependency

The situation in the state bureaucracy did not mirror this decline of SOEs. The Egyptian bureaucratic apparatus remained the employer of last resort for university and postsecondary graduates, with an annual growth rate of employment of 5.2 percent between 1988 and 1998, before decelerating to an average of 1.6 percent between 1998 and 2006 (Assaad, 2010, 16). In spite of government efforts to reduce the size of this bureaucratic workforce, government employees continued to constitute 32 percent of the total labor force in 1998 and 25 percent in 2006 (Assaad, 2010, 35).

According to Soliman (2011), these were mainly low-paid jobs created at the local government level as a mode of selective welfare distribution, usually as part of ruling party's patronage system. "Although real wages fell overall, they remained relatively higher in the public sector . . . . The fact that Mubārak's 2005 presidential campaign pledged a 100 percent increase in wage levels over a period of six years—is another indication of the state's commitment to maintaining support among [state-dependent] limited income groups" (el-Meehy, 2010, 61; Figure 5.3).

Cuts in public expenditure focused on subsidies, which the regime reduced continuously and considerably throughout the 1990s (el-Meehy, 2010, 13). For state dependents, efforts to keep their real wages above inflation offset this trend, revealing the Mubārak regime's conscious prioritization of this vast constituency compared to less concentrated segments of the labor force in urban and rural areas. In fact, the share of public employees' wage bill increased throughout the period from 17 percent of total expenditure in 1982/1983, to 19 percent in 1990/1991, 20.6 percent in 1996/1997, and 23.4 percent in 2000/2001 (Soliman, 2006, 74). Moreover, SAP measures that kept inflation rates below 10 percent largely enabled this maintenance of real wage levels.

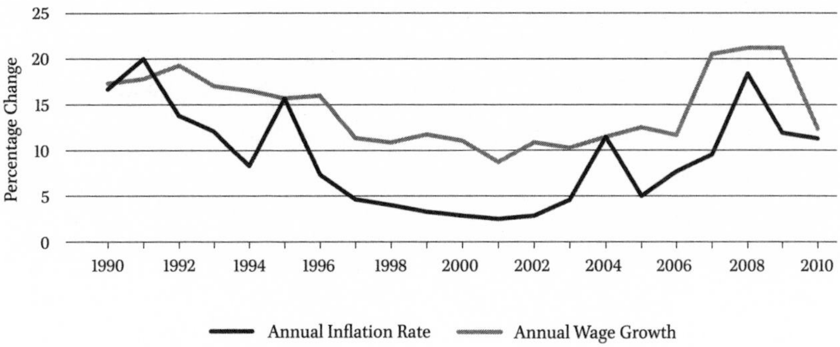

FIGURE 5.3. Annual Inflation Rates and Growth Rate in the Public Sector Payroll, Egypt, 1990–2003. The public sector payroll refers predominantly to employees in the state bureaucracy, excluding workers in economic and service agencies and state-owned enterprises, which were financially separated from the central government budget with the hard-budget constraints that began in the wake of the SAP in 1990/1991.

Source: Inflation rates are cited from World Bank Data: Inflation, consumer prices (annual %), Egypt, https://data.worldbank.org/indicator/FP.CPI.TOTL.ZG. The growth of public sector wages is cited in Gad (2017, 19), based on final accounts.

The real problem came from the revenue side. According to Soliman's calculations, state revenues fell sharply from around 45 percent of GDP in 1993 to a bit over 20 percent in 2001. Nonetheless, expenditures remained constant (around 30 percent of GDP), resulting in a steady increase in the budget deficit, which exceeded 10 percent of GDP in 1996/1997 and reached 18 percent in 2000 (Soliman, 2006, 229–230).

This state revenue contraction was largely a result of dwindling external rents from crude oil sales, Suez Canal fees, and foreign aid through the 1990s. Increasing tax revenues to compensate for these losses of rents was not an easy short-term solution. Historically, the Egyptian state suffered from a weak administrative and political capacity to collect taxes from the property and capital-holding classes. While the first ever income tax law was passed as late as 1949, the major expansion were of indirect taxation and customs, which proved to be less administratively and politically costly. Indeed, direct taxation on income and wealth stood barely at 16 to 19 percent of total tax revenues between 1957 and 1964, whereas indirect taxation accounted for as much as two-thirds (ʿAbdel-Faḍīl, 1980, 186, 189).

With the military takeover of 1952, income taxes became more progressive with the explicit aim of redistribution toward the poor. However, the sequestration of foreign private assets in the mid-1950s and the nationalizations of the early 1960s obliterated the large private sector, leading to a steep decline in direct tax revenues in 1961 and 1962 ('Abdel-Faḍīl, 1980, 186, 191). Meanwhile, surviving private sector activities in trade and services went unseen by the state authorities given their low capital intensiveness, rampant tax evasion, or economic informality ('Abdel-Faḍīl, 1980, 196). Ultimately, the shift to state-led development made the building of extractive institutional capacities from the private sector irrelevant.

Shifting forward to the historical context of the 1990s, it is clear why the shift to a private sector–dominated economic system was associated with a sheer decline in state revenues. In this instance, the Mubārak regime was caught between a rock and a hard place. On the one hand, international conditionality and the fiscal crisis translated into a shrinking SOE sector that could no longer act as an effective tax base for the state. On the other hand, with external rents declining, the state simply did not possess the required administrative, political, and economic capacities to directly collect taxes from the private sector—to which most of the productive output had passed. Building these capacities took time, money, human resources, and, above all, some sort of political arrangements for the legitimation and regulation of resource extraction and subsequent redistribution. Overall, the tax situation did not look much different from that of the late 1950s, with corporate taxes holding a humble share in total tax revenues, and indirect taxes in sales and customs standing for around two-thirds.

With this legacy of low extractive capacities, the state had to rely on borrowing from the domestic banking sector to support the rising deficit. Conscious of the hazards of foreign debt accumulation, the Mubārak regime relied heavily on domestic borrowing in the 1990s (Adly, 2012a, 220). The treasury first relied on the National Investment Bank (NIB), which came to hold around 40 percent of the domestic public debt stock by the mid-2000s. Originally established in 1980 with the aim of controlling all lending to SOEs, the changing role of the NIB revealed the shift from state capitalism to state dependency. By the mid-1990s, the NIB's central role became to finance the public debt, most of which went to recurrent expenditure rather than investment.

In turn, the government—this time the Treasury as opposed to the SOE sector—was becoming the largest single borrower from the banking sector, crowding out the productive private sector and raising the cost of credit. Compounding the issue, the government directed the bulk of these resources to supporting the consumption of constituencies deemed politically important rather than investment, public or private.

Nonetheless, there may have been a way out to free up capital for investment, though it would have required some strategic political action by the top leaders. The two possibilities would have been to redistribute or suppress consumption. Whereas the latter would have downsized the bloated and costly bureaucratic apparatus and sent redundant civil servants to swell the ranks of the informal labor pool, the former would have implied increasing tax revenues.

Neither would prove politically possible. The suppression of distribution by downsizing or maintaining the growth of the wage bill below inflation would have risked protest from a fairly concentrated labor force rooted in a Nasserist moral economy (which did eventually occur when inflation picked up in the mid-2000s). Alternatively, redistribution would have required some political arrangement with capital and wealth holders according to which they would pay taxes instead of the lucrative role of lending to the government to cover its deficit—which hardly seemed to be in their interests (Abdelkhalek, 2007, 12).

Big Private Business in the 1990s: An Economic Break-In

During the 1990s, many large, Egyptian private enterprises remained highly dependent on the state to make profits—be it through trade protection, access to public procurement contracts and state-owned land, or acquisition of privatized state-owned enterprises. However, these private businesses lacked autonomous and institutionalized representation within the circles of power where decisions were made and implemented (Zaki, 1999, 121, 123). Cabinets and the inner circle around the president, where most formal and informal power was vested, were almost completely composed of bureaucrats from military and civilian security and intelligence backgrounds, next to a few independent technocrats, in decision making (Kassem, 2004, 26).

Egypt's transformation into a private sector–dominated economy went hand in hand with the high concentration of capital and output in large family-owned conglomerates. For instance, in 2014, the annual turnover of ten of

Egypt's largest conglomerates stood at 4.45 percent of total GDP (Adly, 2017, 7). This is likely an underestimation of the real weight of these large businesses given that most are privately traded, and hence their financial reports are not disclosed. This trend became visible in the 1990s.

Despite the absence of public business information, personal net wealth may help reflect how some large business families have benefited from developments in the private sector. For example, in 2015, Forbes Middle East estimated the combined net wealth of two brothers of the Mansour family, Moḥamed and Yousef, both part owners of the multinational Mansour Group, at $5.7 billion. This was equivalent to roughly 2 percent of Egyptian GDP in 2014 (Forbes, 2015).

However, given the capital-intensive nature of these enterprises, their relative share in terms of total employment has not been as great. That said, some of the largest business conglomerates do hire tens of thousands of workers. For instance, the Elaraby [al-ʿArabī] Group, which dominates the electronics market in Egypt employs around 20,000 people (Elaraby, 2016). Qalaa [al-Qalʿa] Holdings, a leading investor in energy, mining, cement, agriculture, and transportation and logistics, employs around 39,000 people, according to its 2013 financial report (Qalaa, 2013).

Large Egyptian enterprises also came to play a significant role in the foreign currency–generating sectors of manufacturing and agriculture exports and tourism. Dominated by private enterprises, the manufacturing sector accounted for 40 percent of total Egyptian exports between 2004 and 2010, according to the World Trade Organization (2017). In addition, agricultural exports are almost entirely controlled by large private enterprises. This is also true of tourism, another capital-intensive sector (CBE, 2017, cited in Adly, 2017, 8).

Even as they expanded their activities in the Egyptian market during the first decade of this century, these conglomerates extended their operations abroad and became increasingly transnationalized, especially in the early 2000s. The activities of the Sawiris family, with its Orascom conglomerate, illustrated this tendency as it expanded into tens of frontier, emerging, and developed markets in the 2000s, including Iraq (2003), Bangladesh (2004), Pakistan (2004), Italy (2007), and even North Korea (2008). In addition, Elsewedy [al-Sewedy] Electric transnationalized its operations to Algeria, Ethiopia, Ghana, Italy, Nigeria, Qatar, Spain, Sudan, Syria, Yemen, and Zambia during the same period. According to the company's annual financial statements (Elsewedy Electric, 2010, 2014), 80 percent of its assets were located in Egypt in 2006, and 20 percent were outside. By 2015, this ratio had changed markedly, with 56 percent of its assets in Egypt and 44 percent elsewhere.

In sum, by the beginning of this century, Egypt had witnessed the emergence of a formidable class of large, private businesses that held a sizable share in capital-, skill-, and technology-intensive sectors. Some globalized their operations through exporting goods and services or by investing abroad, providing themselves a relative degree of autonomy from the Egyptian state. This was the context in which the Aḥmed Nazīf government took office in 2004, representing a political break-in for large businesses.

SUBPERIOD 3, 2004–2011: BIG BUSINESS'S BREAKING INTO POLITICS

In 2004, Aḥmed Nazīf, the minister of telecommunications, became prime minister. He would preside over the last, and probably most controversial, cabinet of Mubārak's long reign. Nazīf's government represented a marked shift in the composition of those in charge of economic governance in Egypt, as the economic team was made up almost entirely of businessmen heading family-owned conglomerates and neoliberal-oriented technocrats (Adly, 2017, 9). At the same time, powerful business figures came to play prominent roles in the ruling National Democratic Party NDP, pushing for a business-friendly (not to be confused with market-friendly) agenda in the legislature.

This phenomenon of big businessmen sharing power with Egypt's well-entrenched bureaucratic elite during the last decade of Mubārak's rule was closely tied to preparing the way for Gamāl Mubārak to succeed his aging father as president. The succession project—*mashrūʿ al-tawrīth*—forwarded an amalgam of sociopolitical and economic processes that aimed to alter the composition of the political elite while redefining the role of the state in the economy. The promotion of Gamāl Mubārak, as well as the changes in economic policy, unleashed considerable friction with other groups and organizations in the vast civilian and military bureaucracies (Adly, 2015). These actual and perceived changes endangered the interests of groups among the bureaucratic bourgeoisie as well as the bureaucratic proletariat.

As Roccu (2013) notes, these reforms led to the empowerment of certain elements of the large private sector. "Reforms aimed at downsizing the direct role of the state in the economy did unsurprisingly play in the hands of the Egyptian private sector" (2013, 59). Businessmen-turned-politicians were pushing for the protection of their privileged access to assets and market shares in a period when Egypt was becoming more capitalistic, though not necessarily on a free market basis (see el-Tarouty, 2016). Indeed, an increasing number of businessmen joined the NDP-dominated parliament between 2000 and 2010 (Soliman, 2006, 245–246).

The most notorious symbol of the advent of businessmen-turned-politicians was the steel tycoon Aḥmed ʻEzz. A central figure in the ruling party and head of the parliamentary budget committee, ʻEzz used his influence to amend the antitrust law in 2007 to preserve his monopolistic position in the steel market. He was by no means alone in this. Other businessmen who were personally close to or partners of the Mubārak family also gained from their positions.

These businessmen-turned-politicians cannot be simply reduced to a collection of thieves and corrupt officials. As Gamāl Mubārak's team pushed for the redefinition of the role of the state in the economy, they were able to deliver in terms of certain metrics of performance that were mainly inspired by the hegemonic neoliberal ideology of the time. The Egyptian economy generated high growth rates along with expanding fuel and nonfuel exports. Above all, FDI poured into the country in a manner unprecedented in Egypt's contemporary history.

The late Samer Soliman (2006, 248) was among the first to underline the class element at play in the big business rise to power throughout the 2000s. As private sector business figures became more vocal in the Mubārak regime, the NDP shifted toward serving the interests of the rising bourgeois class, a process that Soliman dubbed the *embourgeoisement* of the NDP. Although there was an undeniably strong element of cronyism and corruption, these businessmen-turned-politicians had a wide-ranging economic project that aimed at transforming Egypt's political economy.

Under the Neoliberal Sun

As a global hegemonic ideology for growth and development, neoliberalism informed this reform project. It provided their economic designs and schemes with some ideological coherence. It may also explain the rather long-term and comprehensive character of the program, which ranged from divesting or selling off SOEs, expanding the tax base by reducing tax rates, restructuring the regulatory role of the state in areas like banking and capital markets, and wide-ranging reforms in trade, exchange rates, and industry.

The businessmen-turned-politicians were there to stay. At one level, they have been described as bandits given their self-serving and conflicts of interest, though according to Olson's dichotomy (1993), they were "stationary bandits" rather than "roving bandits." They forged transnational alliances with IFIs along with international investment banks and equity funds, and were part of a broad ideational and normative network that subscribed to the neoliberal path toward development with growth. Their project was based on pulling more and more public resources into market circulation while providing themselves with the right of first access (Roccu, 2013, 101). In that sense, the Nazīf team was ultimately engaged in the creation of an imperfect market dominated by an oligopoly with asymmetric access to power and information.

Of course, there were international linkages at play as many of the rents (e.g., privatized SOE assets, state-owned land, energy subsidies, and monopolistic positions in the domestic market) were shared with foreign investors. This went hand in hand with growth in IFI-sanctioned exports and investments led by the FDI that the businessmen's cabinet subscribed to and had some successes in delivering. The cement sector stands as a key example wherein multinational corporations (MNCs) took over most privatized SOEs and enjoyed heavily subsidized fuels, all the while abusing the weakly regulated domestic market (Adly, 2012c, 8–9). LafargeHolcim, among other giant MNCs, was critical for increasing FDI and increasing cement production in the midst of a construction boom that pulled large segments of the economy forward through backward and forward linkages.

A similar story occurred in the export sector, where often politically connected manufacturing exporters enjoyed generous subsidies and direct access to political power via informal connections with the Ministry of Industry and Trade (Abdel-Latif and Schmitz, 2010). Despite these elements of cronyism, there was a remarkable increase in manufactured exports during the period, with an impressive annual growth rate of 24.5 percent between 2001 and 2010, compared to 5 percent between 1990 and 2000 (Adly, 2012a, 97). While it may be true that the overall weight of manufactured exports did not change much during the two periods, hovering around 40 percent of the total, this took place in a context of expanding energy-based exports, indicating that manufacturing exports were growing at a rate similar to gas and oil, which is unprecedented in Egypt's post-infitāḥ history.

This was also the context of the financial sector reforms between 2004 and 2012 (detailed in the following chapter). These legal and institutional reforms were successfully implemented with the explicit aims of building the Central Bank's monitoring and regulatory capacities, strengthening the banking system's financial position through bank recapitalization, multiplying the number of branches, and improving the overall performance in accordance with Basel I and II international standards.[1] The reform program also included the intensification of competition within the banking system by allowing more foreign banks to operate in Egypt, as well as the partial privatization of state-owned banks and the introduction of administrative restructuring to unprivatized ones. These market-making efforts also involved the expansion of the stock market, which benefited the largest domestic conglomerates and enabled them to raise capital while diversifying away from their traditional reliance on bank financing (Sulṭān, 2015). Indeed, the capital value of the stock market increased from 31.11 percent of GDP (at factor cost) in 2001 (CBE, 2001/2002, 61, 85) to 79.09 percent in 2005 (CBE, 2005/2006, 90, 116) and 82.65 percent in 2007 (CBE, 2006/2007, 88,116).

A much more contentious measure involved the privatization of SOEs, which picked up significantly as of 2004 (Hanieh, 2013, 50–52; Roccu, 2013, 44–45). Despite the success in selling away a significant number of SOEs rather quickly and the subsequent attraction of FDI inflows to acquire these assets, industrial action and labor protest gained momentum. This unrest would continue to expand up to the 2011 revolution and beyond (Beinin and Duboc, 2015; Beinin, 2016). Compared to their counterparts in the private sector, SOE workers were relatively better positioned to move collectively against the degradation in their standards of living due to inflation, downsizing, divestiture or privatization, and austerity. After all, state workers in SOEs or the bureaucracy were the only ones with a formal working relation with their employer, the state, and thus constituted the bulk of those working with permanent or long-term contracts and access to social security and unionization (Gabr, 2018). These were the inheritors of the old Nāṣer-era employment-based social rights, and many of them were concentrated enough to collectively organize in defense of this social contract in a way that could threaten the ability of the state to deliver public services (Posusney, 1997; Makram Ebeid, 2012; Hammad, 2016).

The situation was as complicated within the state bureaucracy, if not more. The Nazīf government's attempts to redefine the size, scope, and structure of the Egyptian bureaucracy failed miserably. For the first time in Egypt's contemporary history, white-collar employees became a source of considerable socioeconomic unrest and protest due to high inflation and the resulting erosion of their real incomes. This further undermined the capacity of the businessmen's cabinet to alter the labor relations that tied employees with the state. Indeed, the law governing these relations (Law No. 47 of 1978) remained intact until 2015 despite much talk of amending it.

Given this sustained weight of the bureaucratic proletariat, the state essentially became in charge of cushioning the sociopolitical impact of liberalization and privatization by acquiring resources, via borrowing, to compensate for the losses of white-collar employees and unionized blue-collar workers in (unprivatized) SOEs. Continuous wage increases were aimed at partly shielding the real income of state employees as they faced a rising inflation tide (Gād, 2017, 8). The increasing inflation would further exacerbate the state's subsidy bill, which the state could not afford to cut because it would add more inflationary pressures to already aggrieved state-dependent workers. This created the circumstances for a sustained use of banking sector resources by the state with great implications for the private sector's access to credit and investment.

The government aimed at decelerating the rate of increase in public job creation. However, this had a limited impact in the short term on the sheer size and relative weight, and hence sociopolitical significance, of the state proletariat. The state payroll kept growing as a percentage of total expenditure. The share of wages increased from 23.4 percent in 1990/1991 to a massive 30.57 percent in 1997/1998 and still hovered around 29 percent in 2006/2007 (CBE, 2017). Throughout the Nazīf period (2006–2011), wages averaged 22 percent of public expenditures.

The increase in inflation was itself partly caused by rising international food and fuel prices after 2006. Egypt became a net fuel importer in 2006 when, for the first time in modern history, its domestic consumption of oil exceeded production (Adly, 2012c). Egypt had already been a net food importer through most of the twentieth century. This structural weakness made the economy vulnerable to external supply shocks in the 2000s that translated into higher inflation and higher budget deficits given that energy and some food items were subsidized.

Protesting Bureaucrats

It was under the Nazīf government that the simmering social unrest exploded, primarily within the ranks of SOE workers and government employees, with both being responsible for nearly two-thirds of the total social protests in 2007 and 2008 (Awlād al-Arḍ, cited in Adly, 2012a, 211) This wave of labor protests in Egypt was considered to be the largest since the 1940s (Beinin, 2016, 10). According to the Awlād al-Arḍ Center and the Egyptian Center for Economic and Social Rights (2011), from the base year of 1998 to 2008, protests quadrupled, rising from 114 in 1998 to 266 in 2004 and 454 in 2008 (Awlād al-Arḍ, cited in Adly, 2012a, 211). These protests took many forms, ranging from strikes and sit-ins to assemblies and demonstrations. This intensification of socioeconomic protest coincided with an increase in political protest against the Mubārak succession project. In this context, the ruling regime was resolved to do whatever necessary to avoid the merger of both channels of protest. This translated into paying higher wages to state workers, even if this meant a higher deficit and larger public debt.

This was the first time state employees within bureaucratic agencies showed a willingness to protest their socioeconomic status. Contrary to SOE workers, employees in the government bureaucracy had no history in unionization or striking; however, according to Nadine ʿAbdalla (2018, 24, 49), due to the falling buying power of their real wages, these white-collar bureaucrats increasingly came to identify with the working class and subscribe to their methods of protest and union formation. Their demands were varied, including the call for wage increases and overtime hours, as well as permanent employment contracts. It is no coincidence that it was among the ranks of such employees that the first independent trade union emerged in 2009, with the real estate tax collectors taking a lead that other civil servants soon followed (Beinin and Duboc, 2015, 2, 9).

Facing mounting fiscal pressures, the businessmen's government went forward with a comprehensive reform of tax policies, laws, and administrative systems. These reforms were explicitly informed by the neoclassical approach to taxation, which was based on reducing the tax rates for all in return for the promise of broadening the tax base and, hence, increasing total revenue(Soliman, 2006, 212). The plan required the simplification of tax laws and administration, an expansion in indirect taxation, and a not-so-progressive income tax scheme. The new legislation removed most of the sector-based tax holidays established throughout the 1970s, 1980s, and 1990s. Moreover, the new tax code set a unified rate for all enterprises regardless of their ownership structure or legal type (partnerships or corporations), establishing a 20 percent rate on commercial, industrial, and capital gains. It gave no tax holidays on the basis of firm size, with the exception of the profits generated by firms receiving micro loans from the Social Fund for Development.

These reforms were primarily targeting large, private enterprises (al-ʿArabī, 2013). It seemed economical to target and reach agreements with a few large taxpayers rather than deal at once with the broad base of the private sector. After all, the reform team had little of the human and administrative capacity required to go after everyone. Ultimately, the political goal of the reforms was to ensure that they generated enough money and that it was done in a way that was accepted by the taxpayer society (i.e., large enterprises), who would be less disposed to tax evasion in the future.

These tax reforms did pay off somewhat. Tax revenues as a percentage of total revenues and of GDP showed some increase, albeit from a very low base. Furthermore, although tax revenues stood for the bulk of total state revenues (averaging 55.2 percent between 2006 and 2011), nontax revenues, made up primarily of rents, still held 40 percent of total state revenues during the same interval (CBE, 2018c).

Moreover, almost half of the tax revenues accrued from indirect taxation (sales taxes and customs), averaging 49.37 percent of tax revenues between 2006 and 2011 and 27 percent of total state revenues. While the collection of indirect taxes was less costly economically, administratively, and politically, it was also less progressive, despite the presence of multiple exemptions on goods consumed by the poorest. It also revealed the state's limited capacity to extract resources directly from big capital and property holders with income taxes, despite the rule simplification and lower rates.

Even within the realm of direct taxation, the final outcome was equally unimpressive. The state-owned authorities and companies, mainly the General

Authority on Petroleum and the Suez Canal Authority, generated about 55 percent of income tax revenues (CBE, 2018c). Originally these were nontax revenues that were directly transferred to state coffers; however, they were simply reorganized and renamed "income taxes" the companies paid, rendering them nontax revenues in disguise. This meant that private sector enterprises of all sizes operating in all sorts of activities and holding around 70 percent of GDP barely contributed a third of total income taxes, or an average of 12 percent of total tax revenue between 2006 and 2011 (CBE, 2018c).

Property taxes had a robust annual increase, averaging 300 percent between 2006 and 2010, though this occurred from an extremely low base. Property taxes, including those on real estate, stood at a negligible 1.56 percent of tax revenue in 2006, jumping to 6.5 percent in 2010 and remaining at an average of 3.9 percent from 2006 to 2011 (CBE, 2018c). The lax and limited application of the real estate tax law demonstrated the reluctance to push for a more elaborate property tax system. This could partly be explained in the light of the contradiction between tax collection and private accumulation. For instance, the construction industry served as a locomotive of growth with employment and capital market expansion in the 2000s, especially during the boom years between 2004 and 2009. It was tied to a great many feeding industries and services, as well as the stock market boom during the same period. Moreover, there was strong representation of these interests in the cabinet, the parliament, and the NDP that enabled them to push back against any application of real estate taxes that could have slowed the sector. Ultimately, allowing private sector accumulation while raising its contribution to state revenues through taxation was a contradiction that could be only partially resolved. Here, the global context is relevant, as increasing capital mobility limited the already restricted capacity of many developing (as well as developed) states to tax capital (Rodrik, 1998). Hence, the tax reforms were far from a game changer and did little to alter how the Egyptian state related to the economy, particularly the private sector.

The modest increase in revenues could not catch up with the increase in expenditures, leading to a widening budget deficit that was reaching levels similar to the pre-SAP era. According to the Central Bank (2018c), the budget deficit as a percentage of GDP increased from 7.7 percent in 2006 to 8.2 in 2009 and 9.8 percent in 2010. The only hope for the businessmen's government was to maintain high GDP growth so as to dwarf the relative increase in the deficit. However, with the start of the global financial crisis in 2008 and the leap in international oil prices, this could no longer be the case. The only way to keep filling the deficit was more borrowing.

The Treasury increasingly began to rely on the banking sector, as the National Investment Bank (NIB) was no longer a viable option. By the early 2000s, the NIB held around 40 percent of the public domestic debt, mainly using deposits of pensions. This de facto mode of financing the public debt was no longer tenable by the mid-2000s as the government had to pay back part of what it had borrowed so as not to undermine the long-term safety of the national pension system. What was being done with these social security contributions became a matter of public debate and some of the demands that protesting retired employees raised ('Abdalla, 2018, 43). By 2010, these pensioners had created an independent union. Under all of these pressures, the state had to diversify away from the NIB for further debt expansion. Indeed, the share of net NIB debt in net domestic debt decreased consistently, from 39.5 percent in 2008 to 29.5 percent in 2011.

The banking sector came to finance 65 percent of the public debt stock between 2001 and 2009, with the NIB financing the rest (CBE, 2005/2006, 104; 2007/2008, 104; 2008/2009, 100). Domestic debt as a percentage of GDP increased significantly from 49 percent in 2006 to 51 in 2007 and 60 percent in 2008. By 2010, domestic debt stood at a massive 76 percent of GDP, increasing at an average annual rate of 15 percent (CBE, 2018a, author's calculations).

No Bringing-In for SSEs

Ultimately, businessmen-turned-politicians occupied the top decision-making posts in the Nazīf government executive, the traditional Egyptian power center. This provided them with the opportunity to address questions of economic policy and capital-regulating organizations. In this light, the ascension of Gamāl Mubārak served as the ultimate end game of this attempted political project. This was a moment when sociopolitical coalitions were being reshuffled and represented an opportunity for fostering further market integration by establishing intermediate institutions and institutional complementarities with the broad base of the private sector.

There is almost no evidence to support that the businessmen-turned-politicians perceived the missing-middle syndrome as a major sociopolitical crisis or an integral part of their agenda for economic transformation. Although the topic appeared in academic and policy circles, it was not tackled as extensively as other items on the reform agenda that were important for large domestic and foreign enterprises, such as business registration and revising land-pricing schemes. In fact, the same dynamics that governed the access of SSEs to capital in the 1990s persisted throughout the 2000s.

International donors, creditors, and sponsors perceived the missing middle as a purely financial and technical problem rather than a political-economic issue. For example, the EU Commission initiated efforts to upgrade SMEs in the manufacturing sector in the wake of the Euro-Egyptian Association Agreement in 2004 (signed in 2001). Established by presidential decree in 2000, the Industrial Modernization Center (IMC) was cofinanced by the EU, the Egyptian government, and the Egyptian private sector (Adly, 2012a, 105). Between 2004 and 2008, the IMC delivered services to 9,726 industrial projects and maintained a membership of 10,319 enterprises, 70.67 percent of which were small businesses (employing ten to forty-nine workers). Nonetheless, despite the amount of funds allocated, the span of its services and overall capacity suggests that market integration was anything but a priority on the agenda. Indeed, according to the IMC (2008, 5, cited in Adly, 2012a, 107), it maintained a budget of 426 million euros for the fiscal year 2007/2008, hardly adequate for such a grand mission as modernizing Egypt's industrial base.

Ultimately, in the 2000s, big business did not rearrange the sociopolitical coalition in a way that fostered bringing in SSEs into the coalition of forces enjoying access to state-regulated capital. The same was true regarding access to finance. While Egypt witnessed the development of a number of institutions and organizations in charge of extending credit to those excluded from dealing with banks due to the high barriers, these new financial providers were largely nonbanking institutions that, similar to the IMC, were part and parcel of international donor strategies where "free enterprise merged with the language of self-employment" (Elyachar, 2005, 81; el-Meehy, 2010).

Crucially, the market making in areas of finance or land disproportionately favored incumbent large businesses with large initial or acquired capital that allowed them to jump the high barriers of interest, collateral, and paperwork. However, it would not be accurate to assume that the exclusion of SSEs was due exclusively, or even primarily, to cronyism (Haddad, 2011, 70).

Cronyism and rent seeking raise concerns about competition between large, politically connected firms and their unconnected competitors, who are often as large but are denied the same access to rents (Chekir and Diwan, 2014). This is hardly the case with regard to enabling masses of SSEs on a sectoral or regional basis to scale up into the ranks of medium-sized enterprises. Here, competition with big business is minimal. SSEs operate in sectors or in market segments that are usually irrelevant to big businesses. Moreover, their scaling up and capitalization may even prove beneficial for large enterprises if they become cheap and efficient suppliers, subcontractors, or outsourced firms. It was within such a context that close ties between big enterprises and the state facilitated the rise of a powerful stratum of SMEs in Japan, South Korea, Taiwan, and, more recently, China.

Besides cronyism, understanding the sociopolitical basis of Egypt's missing-middle syndrome also rebuts many other explanations offered to explain the county's lack of market integration. For instance, some analysts have highlighted ideology and political antagonism as the cause behind the perpetual exclusion of SSEs. Görmüş (2017, 60) claimed, "The way the Egyptian state implemented [the] economic opening—characterized by political corruption and lack of transparency—worked against the integration of micro-, small, and medium-sized Islamic business groups with the market in the peripheral quarters during the Mubārak era." It is true of course that economic actors with Islamist leanings have been largely excluded from state and big business patronage and crony networks since the inception of infitāḥ. The regime even repeatedly targeted some (e.g., Muslim Brotherhood-affiliated enterprises) with sequestration and expropriation ('Abdel-Ḥay et al., 2006; Adly, 2016). However, not all Islamist-leaning businesses were SSEs or SMEs, and definitely not all SSEs or SMEs were Islamist. As already noted, private enterprises in Egypt used nonstate channels for accumulating capital. Brotherhood-related businesses, for instance, could capitalize on the contributions made by a vast, disciplined base of members, while other Islamist businesspeople made use of extensive foreign links in the Gulf countries. Conversely, the sheer number of SSEs and their sectoral and regional diversity have denied them any ideological uniformity to be stamped en masse as Islamist. There is no good reason to suppose that the ruling NDP could not have developed and co-opted a base of competitive and vibrant SMEs within its patronage networks.

In sum, rather than any simple lack of patronage or conscious, politically motivated exclusion, the perpetuation of Egypt's missing-middle syndrome is largely an unintended consequence of complex political processes of competition, co-optation, and cooperation between various bureaucratic actors as well as certain groups within the big private sector. Unlike in other countries in the Global South characterized by more successful capitalist transformations, these sociopolitical processes failed to produce intermediate institutions capable of channeling capital into the broad base of SSEs. No forces with a perceived interest in integrating the broad base of the private sector emerged within the prevailing coalitions, while their lack of capital and political connections rendered SSEs incapable of breaking in themselves.

EPILOGUE TO A FAILED RECONFIGURATION: A BUSINESSMAN'S TRAGEDY

The interests of businessmen-turned-politicians revolved around liberating public assets from state administrative control under the aegis of marketization. They also attempted to redefine the size, scope, and structure of the state bureaucracy in economic matters. Both projects implied deep distributional repercussions for a vast number of state-dependent groups. Some of these groups were closer to being described as a state bourgeoisie, enjoying significant access to public authority that enabled them to accumulate private wealth, whereas others were scraping a living on the bottom of the giant bureaucracy. Either way, many quarters within the state bureaucracy were involved in resisting the businessmen's project in a variety of ways.

Those with a strong share of power struck back. For instance, State Council courts played a vital role in annulling SOE-privatization contracts, as well as ministerial decisions allocating state-owned land to private investors (Adly, 2012b; al-Shawārby, 2015). The military retained its broad mandate and vetoed a number of measures perceived as potential national security threats, such as the privatization of electricity distribution (Shawkat, 2014). For the less powerful agencies and groups within the bureaucracy, resistance was more passive.

The ultimate goals were to allow resources to flow to entrepreneurial (and crony) business groups and away from a variety of bureaucratic beneficiaries. However, this proved to be way beyond the businessmen-turned-politicians' political capacity to fully realize, as it would have required the mobilization of large constituencies from outside the bureaucracy. Alternatively, the strategy of the politicized circles of big business was to strike from the positions they managed to occupy within the regime, which were powerful no doubt, but were ultimately based on the premise of transforming the system from within.

In such an authoritarian institutional setting, opening the political arena was never seriously pursued by the newly configured circles within the NDP or the executive. That sphere remained tightly controlled and manipulated by the security agencies, as was visible in the 2005 presidential and parliamentary elections, the subsequent crackdown on the opposition (2006–2008), and the heavy manning and wide vote rigging of the 2010 parliamentary elections that led directly to the revolution. The clique of big business interests was ultimately serving the interests of limited social strata that gained from the economic liberalization process at the expense of many who lost to inflation and declining real incomes, especially among the bureaucratic proletariat and SOE workers, but also others, such as the state bourgeoisie, who were threatened by further marketization.

The attempt to tie themselves to the extension of the Mubārak regime by grooming the young Mubārak did not help in earning legitimacy in the eyes of many groups within the bureaucracy or in society at large. Many were frustrated by corruption, repression, election rigging, and human rights violation throughout Mubārak's too long reign. After a sharp rise, the influence of powerful private businessmen fell just as suddenly as the 2011 uprising abruptly ended the succession project together with Mubārak's tenure. Gamāl Mubārak's team was the first to be sacrificed. Most were removed from office as an early response to the protests, and many were later prosecuted for corruption charges, including Aḥmed Nazīf and the businessmen-turned-politicians in charge of trade and industry, tourism, agriculture, and housing. The list eventually included the Mubāraks themselves, and the principal leaders of the crony capitalist networks were tried and jailed or fled the country.

The full implications of these political events that aborted the reconfiguration of the sociopolitical coalition governing Egypt's political economy are yet to be fully known; however, they underscore the fact that Egypt was not on a path toward greater market integration and shared prosperity throughout the period of economic liberalization. While a number of crucial sociopolitical hinge points occurred throughout its contemporary history, these moments did not produce intermediate institutional arrangements capable of reorienting the distributional landscape in any meaningful way. This is derived from the fact that the key institutional mechanisms that regulated access to capital remained highly centralized and hierarchical, removing any incentive for those near the top of Egypt's political economic hierarchy—who, by definition, maintained ready access to it—to expand access. In turn, the small size and lack of capital in the broad base of the private sector precluded any break-in from below.

The key institutional mechanisms that held this arrangement in place were those that regulated access to capital: finance and land. The following chapter moves to a detailed discussion of the dynamics of access to finance in Egypt. Despite waves of market-oriented reforms, the overconcentration of credit, mainly extended to the state and a few large private sector firms, has persisted and failed to produce intermediate institutions that could open up channels of credit access for the broad base of SSEs. A familiar story will unfold with regard to land. Taken together, the lack of access to these essential inputs has underlined the inability of Egypt's private sector to integrate, and thus emerge from its cleft state.

Chapter Six

EGYPT'S BANKING SYSTEM

An Exclusive Club

THE BANKING SECTOR IN EGYPT HAS SERVED AS THE MAIN CHANNEL of financial mediation between savings and investments and hence stands as the principal institutional framework through which one must navigate to access financial capital. However, bank-based finance has never been easily accessible for most private small-scale establishments (SSEs) in Egypt. Although this may sound like a generic problem across the world (Acs, Carlsson, and Karlsson, 1999; Ritchie and Brindley, 2000; Decker, Schiefer, and Bulander, 2006; Teoh and Chong, 2008), there is ample evidence that the banking sector in Egypt has been specifically inaccessible for SSEs. The share of total loans that were extended to small and medium establishments (SMEs) in Egypt was firmly below average for MENA's nonoil economies (averaging 13 percent), standing at only 5 percent compared to 24 percent in Morocco and 15 percent in Tunisia.[1] In this regard, Egypt, which also trails Jordan, Lebanon, and even Yemen (before the civil war), is underperforming in an already underperforming region (Rocha et al., 2011, 22).

Indeed, as World Bank surveys show, only 10 percent of SME investment expenditure in the MENA is financed by a bank loan (Rocha et al., 2011, 11), whereas the share of banks as a source of finance for small firms (employing between ten and fifty workers) in other parts of the Global South was significantly higher, such as 20.2 percent in Bangladesh, 14.1 percent in Brazil, 18.2 percent in Croatia, and 24.1 percent in Ecuador (Cull et al., 2006, 3019).

Similarly, el-Kabbani and Kalhoefer (2011, 5) estimated that 95 percent of Egypt's SSEs do not maintain bank accounts at all, relying instead on informal saving mechanisms as their main funding source. This situation strongly aligns with the results of a survey I conducted (Adly and Khatib, 2014) on Egyptian small enterprise owners: 58 percent of the respondents reported access to financing as the principal barrier to growth. The surveyed entrepreneurs in turn cited business profits (73 percent), private savings (66 percent), and credit from family and friends (35 percent) as their three top sources for financing, all of which are informal and based on self- or family financing, which indicates the prevalence of different sources of self-accumulation (Singerman and Hoodfar, 1996, 167).

In contrast, credit and equity from public institutions such as banks, special microfinance- and SME funds, venture capital, and issuing stocks were at the bottom of the list. In fact, a mere 13 percent reported having ever resorted to bank loans, with 6 percent reporting the same for special funds and SME programs. Despite the fact that many SSE owners were able to turn to self-financing or tightly knit social networks to access capital, these informal channels remained imperfect substitutes for formal financing from banks (Mohieldin and Wright, 2000, 667). Self-financing was hence a symptom of SSEs' low adaptation to chronic undercapitalization.

These results illustrate how Egypt's capitalist transformation since infitāḥ has been characterized by the financial exclusion of SSEs. This institutional arrangement was made and remade over time by a coalition of sociopolitical groups that enforced a nonentrepreneurial, risk-averse, and highly concentrated process of credit extension.

Contrary to neoclassical conventional wisdom, this institutional bias was not merely due to the meddling of particularistic interests that stifled capital markets in favor of self-serving incumbents and cronies. In fact, overconcentration and financial exclusion persisted even after the banking sector became more market oriented and aligned with international rules and regulations in the wake of the financial sector reform program that took place between 2004 and 2012.

Ultimately, the banking sector served as a financial intermediary between middle-class depositors, on the one hand, and the state and large private sector enterprises, on the other. Indeed, for the past sixty years, the state Treasury has been the biggest borrower from the banking sector, even without counting state-owned enterprises (SOEs), while large, private enterprises managed to break into the financial system throughout the period of liberalization, raising their share in total banking credit considerably in the 1990s and 2000s. However, these were usually firms that already possessed a large amount of initial or acquired private capital—not only financial and physical but also social and cultural—that allowed them to establish strong business alliances with banking institutions through the creation of mutual trust and private flows of credible information (Stiglitz, 1994, 123).

The root cause of the SSEs' exclusion was institutional rather than policy based. It was certainly possible to increase credit access to SSEs without undermining credit to large businesses, especially in a banking sector like Egypt's that has had notoriously low loan-to-deposit ratios (World Bank, 2009, 23). Indeed, this institutional restraint proved to persist even when state incumbents or bankers showed willingness to increase the share of SSEs in bank credit. Rather, it derived from the long-standing rules, norms, and practices that made it difficult to process credit extension into small-scale establishments that required different financial products and distinct institutional capacities and usually operated in different economic sectors from the large businesses that banks were accustomed to dealing with.

A primary argument of this chapter is that these clients (the state, SOEs, and large enterprises) served as a safe base for the banks in a way that rendered them increasingly risk averse and unwilling to deal with the broad base of SSEs. In other words, access to finance was reserved for the world of dandy and crony capitalisms, while the subsystem of baladi capitalism, and the SSEs comprising it, found themselves cut off.

These SSEs lacked the institutional arrangements that could have facilitated their financial inclusion at lower transaction costs. This system is thus responsible for cleft capitalism as a macroinstitutional condition that emerged and was perpetuated to the detriment of market integration, as well as the broad base of SSEs in particular that found themselves caught in the type of inescapable dilemma represented by the story of the Norse hero Svipdag at the beginning of Chapter 4. Their low levels of capitalization and the little information available about their operations made it quite risky for banks to finance them without demanding significant collateral, which settled back to the chicken-or-egg dilemma of needing capital to raise more capital (Mohieldin and Wright, 2000, 664, 667; Rocha et al., 2011, 9, 27–28; Adly and Khatib, 2014, 34, 75). Thus, a robust and integrated stratum of SMEs failed to materialize as the response to these institutional barriers, self-accumulation, proved to be a suboptimal response to the systemic problem of undercapitalization.

INSTITUTIONAL MECHANISMS OF FINANCIAL EXCLUSION

Chapter 4 introduced the thesis that the financial exclusion of the majority of private establishments in Egypt has been a by-product of a persistently hierarchical and centralized banking system. Its geographic centralization is evident from its exclusive presence in big cities (and even further segregated within well-do-to neighborhoods with a significant problem of a lack of branches), while their administration has had virtually no experience with local communities(Beshāy, 2015). Central offices usually make decisions with a strict hierarchy that manages the rules governing credit extension, be they formal or informal or a mix of both. This process includes formal prudential regulations and monitoring from the Central Bank, as well as top-down power dynamics that are less formally acknowledged, such as the historically intimate relationship between the state Treasury and large state-owned banks in the financing of state consumption and investment or strong alliances between banks and private businesses.

In addition to these formal institutions, informal mechanisms for accessing capital, such as party patronage at the local level, were also marked by a strong degree of centralization. The overly centralized and hierarchical Egyptian banking system allowed only for centralized and concentrated patronage networks that typically included large businesses with enough influence to be present within the inner circles of the ruling elites (el-Meehy, 2010; Soliman, 2011; Menza, 2012). Local patronage networks have played a weak role in extending bank credit to SSEs. This stands in contrast to the example of Turkey in the late 1990s, where the rising SSEs of inner Anatolian cities made use of strong political, social, and religious connections with local politicians who belonged to predominantly Islamist parties (Demir, Acar, and Toprak, 2004, 172).

These characteristics of the Egyptian banking system imply an absence of intermediate institutions through which banks could collect and process credible (and cheap) information about SSEs and individual entrepreneurs, an informational void that raises the risks of opportunism or simple default. This hierarchical and centralized banking system has been structurally inclined to deal with big entities, including the central government, SOEs, and, more recently, large, private businesses that are politically connected, endowed with financial and physical capital, or both.

In such a setting, only a few enterprises in the private sector could afford to access bank credit, leading to a remarkable overconcentration of credit. For those who could not capitalize on their political connections, large initial private financial and physical capital was crucial in providing collateral and other guarantees necessary for accessing bank credit, especially at early stages. Historically, these firms were among the first to occupy strong market positions after infitāḥ by establishing partnerships with either foreign and Arab investors or SOEs in the 1970s and 1980s. Indeed, Zaki (1980, 378) shows that most private firms that secured bank loans between 1975 and 1977 were established according to Investment Law No. 43 of 1974. These were fairly large corporations in the form of joint ventures with Arab and foreign investors and usually functioned as links between Egyptian and international markets (Imām, 1986). Moreover, many had social and cultural capital through prior experiences with banks as depositors or debtors or by belonging to certain personal and family networks within the banking sector. For any of these private enterprises to be able to access bank credit, they had to hit the ground running. As potent and well-established market actors, they were able to overcome the high barriers to dealing with banks in Egypt, be they administrative (high operation costs and private information) or economic (high interest rates and collateral requirements).

The problem did not seem to lie in the overall access of the private sector to credit. Rather, it was in the uneven distribution of access to it, which fell overwhelmingly in favor of larger, more established firms to the exclusion of the broad base of SSEs. As the World Bank observes (2009, 111), "MENA has a deeper banking sector than most other emerging markets, but it has a small client base." In Egypt, domestic credit to the private sector and domestic credit provided by the banking sector, as percentages of GDP, stood around 50 percent and 75 percent, compared to an average of 60 percent and 75 percent, respectively, for other middle-income countries (Stevenson, 2011, 120).

The State as Owner, Regulator, and Chief Borrower

On the eve of actual independence in 1956, Egypt's banking sector was fully privately owned, with a clear majority of banks owned by either foreigners or residents of non-Muslim and non-Arab origins. The one notable exception was Banque Misr, established in 1920 as an expression of Egyptian economic nationalism. After gaining independence, the Egyptian banking sector began to undergo full Egyptianization (*Tamṣīr*) wherein the Nāṣer government sequestered almost all financial and physical assets owned by British and French nationals in the wake of the tripartite aggression toward Egypt in October 1956. This process also targeted the interests of many Jews (some of them Egyptian nationals), who were accused of harboring Zionist sentiments (Tignor, 1984, 135–136; Beinin, 1998, 67, 87). The years 1960 and 1961 witnessed The outright nationalization of all remaining private banks, including Banque Misr, the historical bastion of economic nationalism, changing the landscape of the economy for decades to come.

In addition to the nationalization of some of Egypt's largest private commercial banks beginning in 1957, including Barclays (which later became Alexandria Bank), Banque Misr, and the National Bank of Egypt in 1960, the Central Bank was established in 1961.[2] Thus, this process of bank nationalization took place within the broader context of public sector expansion and state-led industrialization beginning with the first five-year plan of 1960. The state subsequently took over almost all large private enterprises in manufacturing, construction, banking, insurance, and wholesale trade, as well as initiating heavy-industry projects like iron and steel, cement, petrochemicals, and aluminum (Waterbury, 1983, 76; Tignor, 1984, 155–156). Banking decisions were henceforth subjected to a political rationale driven by state development plans that required the extension of bank credit to SOEs in order to realize specific development goals (Waterbury, 1983, 80). This element of the Nasserist political economy endured beyond the ending of state-led development as it began to cater to the consumption needs of state-dependent constituencies after infitāḥ.

The banking system following this period of nationalization was among the first sectors to witness partial liberalization and privatization-cum-internationalization as early as 1975 when foreign banks were allowed to operate in Egypt (Law No. 120 of 1975 and Investment Law No.143 of 1974). This early liberalization aimed at attracting foreign and Arab capital (particularly from oil-rich Gulf countries) to flow into the banking sector (Waterbury, 1983, 131), which presented an effective shortcut to achieving the regime's goals of attracting capital inflows, a significant motive behind infitāḥ all along.

Despite partial liberalization and the internationalization of the banking sector, the state kept a strong grip over the banking system through the continued ownership of large state-owned banks, in addition to its role as regulator through the Central Bank. In addition, the state became the main recipient of bank credit in order to finance SOEs and the budget deficit.

State-owned banks remained predominant. "After five years of the application of Law 43 [of 1974], public sector banks, in terms of the volume of deposits and investments, still held center stage: they held 81 percent . . . and 83 percent of all credits" (Waterbury, 1983, 149). This remained the case throughout the 1980s and 1990s. By the year 2000, state-owned banks held around 70 percent of all bank deposits and 50 percent of loans (Ikram, 2007, 182). Indeed, according to a survey in 1998, state-owned banks held more than two-thirds of all banking assets (Caprio, 1998, 1), and it took almost a decade before private banks began to occupy a relatively dominant position. By 2010, "public banks accounted for 45 percent of total assets and 44 percent of total deposits, with private banks holding for the first time since 1960 the majority of both assets and deposits" (Roccu, 2013, 45, based on Central Bank and World Bank data).

Private banks emerged in the 1970s and 1980s as either subsidiaries of foreign banks (offshore branches) or joint ventures between state-owned banks and foreign ones. State-owned banks such as Banque Misr, National Bank of Egypt, Bank of Alexandria (fully privatized in 2006), and the Industrial Development Bank owned rather large shares of many emerging joint-venture banks throughout the 1970s and 1980s. Despite this state partnership, these banks were nonetheless legally considered private (al-ʿAntarī, 2005, 62).

Although the expanding share of private banks—foreign as well as joint ventures—contributed to a relative increase of competition in credit provision, state-owned banks continued to extend credit primarily on a political basis rather than for profit seeking or risk reduction. Because the central government was the banking sector's biggest borrower between 1970 and 1977, with an overall share of 71.6 percent (compared to 15 percent for SOEs) of total domestic credit (Zaki, 1980, 376), this money was used primarily to finance growing budget deficits. These were often instances where state-owned banks were compelled to extend loans to underperforming SOEs so as to save them from problems of liquidity or insolvency given the inability of the state Treasury to capitalize them fully. Banks were also brought in to finance national megaprojects prioritized by the government (Zaki, 1980, 378).

With the steady rise in the share of private sector enterprises in total output and employment in the general economy, as well as the ventures into new areas under the investment laws issued and amended in 1974, 1977, 1989, and 1997, private sector enterprises began to increase their share of total bank loans from private as well as state-owned banks. According to Zaki (1980, 378), private sector enterprises raised their share of domestic credit from a dismal 6 percent in 1975 to 8 percent in 1977; as of the mid-1980s, private sector enterprises had become the biggest share of borrowers from the banking sector. Their relative share. however, was overtaken by SOEs briefly in the first half of the 1990s as a result of the hard budget constraints that the government adopted following the International Monetary Fund deal of 1991 according to which the Treasury was no longer obliged to cover the deficits generated by underperforming SOEs. This, however, proved short-lived; private sector firms overtook SOEs by the second half of the 1990s. By 2001, private sector enterprises held 58 percent of total bank credit(Figure 6.1).

The decrease of SOEs' shares in total bank credit occurred in parallel to their shrinking role in the economy as a whole: the share of SOEs in total bank loans fell from 11 percent in 2001 to 8 percent in 2005 and 4.7 percent in 2008. This was partly the result of the Central Bank's mitigation of nonperforming loans held by SOEs, combined with the enforcement of new prudential regulations in the context of the financial sector reform program.

Despite this diminishing share of SOEs in total bank credit, the state's direct use of banking sector resources did not wane. It became increasingly reliant on it to finance the ever-widening budget deficit through the issuance of treasury bonds and bills by the second half of the 1990s. The main reason behind the rising deficit was rapidly declining state revenues, which fell sharply from around 45 percent of GDP in 1993 to a bit over 20 percent in 2001 (Soliman, 2006, 229). This revenue contraction resulted primarily from dwindling external rents, such as oil sales, Suez Canal fees, and foreign aid throughout the 1990s and the 2000s, while the state held little institutional capacity to extract taxes from the private sector to which the bulk of output

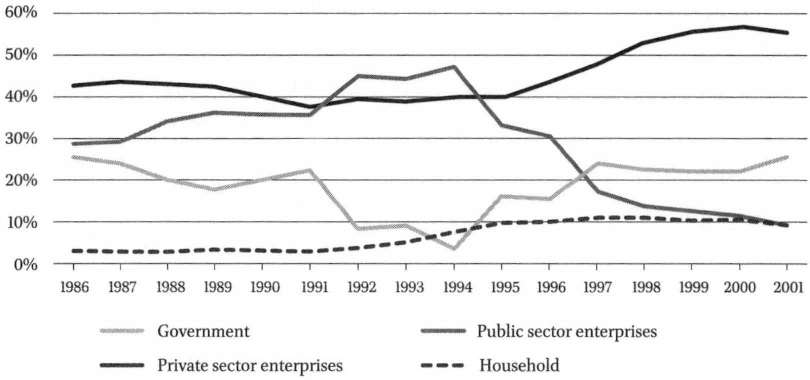

FIGURE 6.1. Sectoral Breakdown of Commercial Bank Credit in Local Currency, 1986–2001 (Percentage Points).

Source: Calculated by the author based on *Central Bank Annual Report* (1996/1997, 132), commercial bank credit and discount by sector, for years 1986 to 1996, and *Central Bank Annual Report* (2000/2001, 113), commercial bank credit and discount by sector.

and investment passed in the 1990s. As expenditures remained constant (around 30 percent of GDP), the budget deficit continued to climb, exceeding 10 percent of GDP in 1996/1997 and hovering around 18 percent by 2000 (Soliman, 2006, 230).

With this rising deficit, the state began to turn to borrowing. For this, the Mubārak regime relied heavily on domestic borrowing. Indeed, "Following the massive debt relief of the early 1990s (through which almost 50 percent of the external debt was cancelled), the external debt stock remained almost constant at around 30 billion dollars, with zero percent growth for the period 1993–2007. . . . Domestic debt soared from 54.49 percent of GDP in 1990/1991 to 85 percent in 2007, with an annual average increase of 13 percent" (Adly, 2012a, 220).

The Treasury first relied on the National Investment Bank (NIB), which came to hold around 40 percent of the domestic public debt stock by the mid-2000s, with the rest held by the banking sector. The NIB was established in 1980 with the aim of controlling all lending to SOEs. In doing so, it was to "absorb the insurance and deposits investment fund that had grouped social security, pensions and postal savings payments" (Waterbury, 1983, 120). However, by the mid-1990s, the NIB's central role had shifted to the financing of public debt, most of which went to recurrent expenditures rather than investment (al-Gebāly, 1999, 11). This marked the shift from state capitalism to catering for state dependents, in addition to expressing the conflicting priorities between accumulation and the distributive claims of politically vital state-dependent constituencies. Herein lies the root cause of Egypt's weak investment performance in the post–Structural Adjustment Program phase (Achcar 2013, 40, discussed in Chapter 2).

The Formation of the Exclusive Club

This extensive public borrowing caused private sector enterprises to contend with the Treasury for financial resources. Although state competition did not crowd out the private sector as a whole—figures provided by the Central Bank reveal that the private sector increased its share rather consistently in total bank credit. The expanded role of the state as debtor had the unintended consequences of contributing to an overconcentration of credit in the private sector in two main ways. The first was through the emergence of private sector cronies in the 1990s who benefited from their political connections and received large sums of credit regardless of their financial positions or the feasibility of their projects—much like SOEs (Adly, 2009). The other way, more indirect, proved to be much more resilient after the financial sector reforms of the 2000s. The state's insatiable appetite for bank credit made state-owned, as well as private, banks risk averse and nonentrepreneurial as the state, together with the SOEs and private cronies it guaranteed, appeared less risky and more lucrative than new clients, especially the broad base of SSEs. These loans to the state covered for the banks' low ratios of loans to deposits (Barth, Caprio, and Levine, 1998; Nasr, 2008, 23–24), allowing them to be pickier when dealing with private sector enterprises.

Indeed, in March 2000, prior to the launch of the financial sector reform program, a mere 343 clients received 42 percent of total private sector credit, 28 of whom (8 percent) obtained 13 percent of total credit. The top 8 debtors (just over 2 percent of the 343) received 6 percent of total credit (al-Ahrām al-ʿArabī, 2002, cited in Adly, 2009, 11).

This overconcentration has usually been explained in terms of rampant cronyism and political favoritism; however, this is far from a comprehensive explanation. Banks established a number of alliances with financially robust business groups that were not strictly crony in the sense of being politically connected to the ruling regime; rather, they were enterprises that already had a large endowment of capital and hence posed little risk. Some examples are Maḥmūd Elaraby's [al-ʿArabī] relation with Banque Misr (Elaraby, 2015, 253–254) and Ḥusein Ṣabbour's joint-venture company with the National Bank of Egypt. These relations began with short-term and small-scale ties with state-owned banks, but their successful upgrading and expansion in product and service markets deepened their alliances with the banks. These relations were largely conducted on a nonmarket basis depending on long-term alliances between banks and business that were economically successful and less risky (Stiglitz, 1994, 123), yet they confirmed the overall feature of overconcentrated credit to the private sector

Financial Sector Reform, 2004–2012

The Egyptian banking system underwent a broad and comprehensive reform program beginning in 2004 with deep implications for credit extension. The result was a more internationalized, privatized, competitive, and profit-oriented sector. This was achieved through the explicit aims of reinforcing the monitoring and regulatory capacities of the Central Bank, strengthening the financial position of the banking system through bank recapitalization, multiplying the number of branches, and improving overall performance in accordance with Basel I and II standards. Indeed, the team of the new Central Bank governor, Fārūq al-ʿOkda (2004–2012), oversaw a series of mergers that served the goal of increasing the size of banks in order to make the system easier to regulate at a lower cost for the newly empowered Central Bank (Beshāy, 2015). The reform program also included the intensification of competition within the banking sector by allowing more foreign banks to operate in Egypt, privatizing some state-owned banks, and introducing administrative reforms in those that were to remain state owned.

The reform process was initiated by a new law governing the Central Bank and the banking sector (Law No. 88 of 2003). The law was meant to provide the legal and institutional framework for the Central Bank's regulatory role regarding commercial banks and went hand in hand with the basic restructuring of the financial elite under the control of the Central Bank. Fārūq Al-ʿOkda, an experienced banker with a long track record in the United States and a doctorate in finance from the University of Pennsylvania, was appointed governor and was joined by a team of individuals with extensive experience in British and American banks. These new bankers represented a strong break with the older state-oriented financial elites who, after the nationalization of the banking sector in 1961, were generally drawn from public sector banks (Roll, 2013). This new elite staffed the Central Bank's leading positions and sat on the boards of state-owned banks that held the prevalent share of the banking sector's assets, deposits, and loans.

Throughout this period, the Central Bank successfully tightened the rules for credit extension and built its capacities to collect and process information and enforce prudential regulations. The Central Bank became significantly more powerful than virtually all other banks compared to the 1980s and 1990s when it lacked the mandate or the human and technological capacity or both (al-ʿAntarī, 2005, 135). Accordingly, the share of nonperforming loans (NPLs) declined from a massive 24.2 percent in 2004 (on the eve of the launch of the reform program) to 14.8 percent in 2008 and 7.2 percent in 2015 (Figure 6.2). This downward trend renders Egypt's position in terms of NPLs more favorable when compared to other middle- and lower-middle-income economies, with such figures as 3.3, 2.98, and 2.4 percent in Brazil, Turkey, and Indonesia, respectively.

In parallel with the consolidation of the financial positions of commercial banks through bank recapitalization and the reduction of NPLs, there was a concerted effort to decrease the number of operating banks: they declined from fifty-seven in 2004 to forty-three by 2006 and forty in 2008 (CBE, 2007/2008, p. c). In addition, the reforms aimed to intensify competition by allowing more foreign banks to operate within Egypt, privatizing publicly owned banks and selling off their shares in joint-venture banks, and restructuring state-owned banks that were not privatized, including the two largest: Banque Misr and the National Bank of Egypt (NBE).

This resulted in the decline of the share of state-owned banks in total banking assets from around two-thirds in 1998 (Caprio and Cull, 2000, 1) to 50 percent in 2012 (total assets held by NBE and Banque Misr). The share of state-owned banks in total deposits and loans also declined from 70 and 50 percent in 2000, respectively (Ikram, 2007, 182), to 34 and 41 percent in 2012 (Roccu, 2013, 46–47). Banque Misr, Egypt's second-largest state-owned bank,

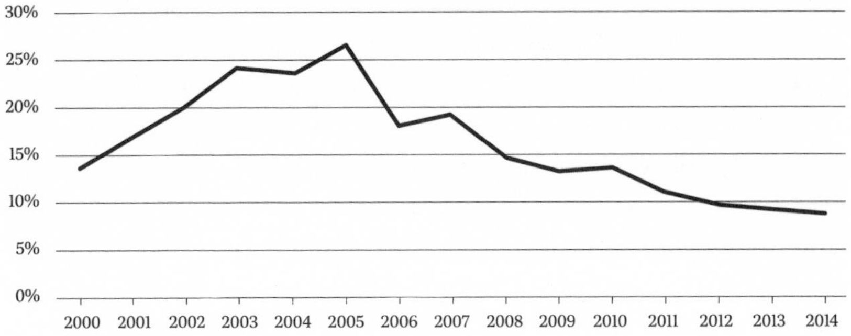

FIGURE 6.2. The Ratio of NPLs to Total Bank Loans, 2000–2014 (Percentage Points). Source: World Bank data, *Egypt: NPLs (2000–2014)*, https://data.worldbank.org/indicator/FB.AST.NPER.ZS?locations=EG.

acquired the third-largest state-owned bank, Banque du Caire, while the former (along with the NBE) was forced to sell off its shares in private banks and joint ventures with foreign capital (Roccu, 2013, 46, 47). These reforms appeared to pay off as the profit rates of both state-owned and private banks increased and finally converged after decades of relative underperformance on the part of the former (Waāīd, 2016).

From a political-economic angle, the financial sector reform program showed that the Mubārak regime had the autonomy and capacity to pursue a seemingly comprehensive process of reform in the 2000s. The state was relatively autonomous from cronies in a way that enabled it to identify the need to save the banking sector from collapse as a security imperative for the regime that went beyond the myopic interests of cronies or even SOEs that were heavily indebted (Adly, 2009).

The roots of the banking sector reforms lay in the interests of sizable social blocks of middle-class depositors and therefore were ultimately sociopolitical. Because the safety and soundness of the banking system in Egypt have long been an organic tie between the state and the middle classes in Egypt, which have usually been the ones with savings deposited in banks, the reforms were part and parcel of the regime's bid to secure state legitimacy and social and economic stability. They represent the largest income group with savings to deposit in banks, where household savings have constituted around 60 percent of total savings in the banking sector since the 1990s (al-ʿAntarī, 2005, 96).

These social groups did not want to undertake the direct risks of investing, especially given the underdeveloped status of Egyptian capital markets (Nasr, 2008; World Bank, 2017g) and thus chose to deposit their money in banks as a safe form for saving, albeit with low returns. In this light, these reforms stand out as a remarkable case of private property protection for a sizable constituency of people, around 10 percent of the adult population (Ḥammād, 2015, citing the head of the Union of Egypt's Banks), in a country characterized by a weak rule of law. This made it imperative for the state to secure their acquiescence by at least preserving the safety of their savings in an environment characterized by the reasonable risks of high inflation and frequent currency devaluations, all the while avoiding catastrophic developments like the loss of principal in the instance of a bank failure

The importance of banks as financial intermediates for the state began to assume even greater importance in the 1970s as workers' remittances began flowing from oil-rich countries, largely through formal channels. Al-ʿAntarī (2005, 95) showed that in 2000, foreign currency deposits in Egyptian banks stood at 23 percent of total deposits, indicating a preference by households with dollar-denominated savings to hold their money in banks. According to Wahba (2010, 173), 61 percent of all remittances in 2006 were sent through formal channels: 22 percent through banks, 32 percent as nominal transfers,[3] and 7 percent through post offices. Conversely, 31 percent were informally sent by family members and friends who were resident in other countries.

In the interests of preserving this sociopolitical relationship, the state has traditionally guaranteed that deposits were not lost in the event of a general collapse of the banking system, especially in state-owned banks that historically held the majority of banking assets, loans, and deposits and continue to have the greatest number of branches and clients. Indeed, it is noteworthy that since the nationalization of the banking sector in the early 1960s, Egypt has witnessed no bank failures in which depositors lost their principal. The sole case of bank collapse was of the Bank of Credit and Commerce International, which ceased operations as a result of its worldwide collapse in 1992. The Egyptian branch's deposits were saved through state intervention after being merged into Banque Misr with a government guarantee that deposits would not be lost (al-ʿAntarī, 2005, 69). Similarly, in the late 1990s, Egypt had a number of ailing small banks that were on the brink of collapse due to imprudent policies and corruption. These included small family-owned banks in addition to a number of tiny public and private banks. The Central Bank targeted these banks in the first round of the financial sector reform by merging them into bigger and more financially sound banks. The result was positive: no bank failed, and deposits were saved.

Since independence in the 1950s, the only case in which depositors lost their money was with the Islamic capital investment companies (CICs; *sharikāt tawẓīf al-amwāl*) in the late 1980s, which could be considered as operating in parallel to the traditional banking sector. As serious competitors to the banking sector (al-Tawīla, 1988, 91–92; Zubaida, 1990, 154), they competed with the Treasury and state-owned banks over the collection and trading of badly needed foreign currency, primarily from Egyptian workers in the Gulf countries (Thābet, 1996, 250, 262). Some argued that the regime perceived them as adversarial toward the end of the 1980s and hence had a political stake in bringing them down (Springborg, 1989; Zubaida, 1990, 160; Henry and Lamm, 2009).

Aside from banks, capital investment companies, which emerged in the late 1970s and numbered 180 by 1985 (al-Tawīla, 1988, 91), were an additional outlet for middle-class savings. In essence, these companies functioned as banks by receiving deposits; however, they were largely unregulated, as they did not fall under the supervision of the Central Bank, a rather glaring indicator of the regulatory weakness of the Central Bank before the adoption of the financial sector reform program in 2003. By the late 1980s, however, many CICs faced serious financial problems, and many were unable to pay back their depositors, leading the state to take advantage of their compromised financial situation and enforce Law No. 146 of 1988, which strictly prohibited nonbanking institutions from collecting deposits (Shuhayb, 1989, 51).

The importance of protecting middle-class savings rose further from the mid-1990s when the state became increasingly dependent on the banking sector to finance its ever-widening fiscal deficit through the issuance of Treasury bonds and bills. Subsequently, the deposits of middle-class households became the main source of the deficit financing that was used to meet the basic state expenses critical for social and political stability. According to the Central Bank, 65.2 percent of the public debt stock between 2001 and 2009 was financed by the banking sector. In the same vein, the share of government indebtedness as a percentage of total banking sector credit increased from around one-quarter in 2001 to more than one-third in 2008 (CBE, 2005/2006, 104; 2007/2008, 104; 2008/2009, 100). Domestic debt as a percentage of GDP also increased at impressive rates, from 49 percent in 2006 to 51 and 60 percent in 2007 and 2008, respectively. By 2010, public indebtedness stood at a massive 76 percent of GDP, increasing at an average annual rate of 15 percent (CBE, 2018a, author's calculations).

MARKET-BASED FINANCIAL EXCLUSION

These reforms indeed had deep implications for credit extension: Egypt achieved a more internationalized, privatized, and competitive banking sector by the end of the 2000s. However, they did not lead to more financial inclusion—a vivid illustration that the unleashing of market mechanisms does not automatically solve the problem of uneven credit allocation if intermediate institutions are lacking.

Politically driven credit to SOEs or cronies did decrease and was subjected to newly enforced prudential regulations. While politics remained central in determining the access to credit, it took place on a more economic basis, representing what can be labeled "safe cronyism." In short, credit extended on a political basis was no longer allowed to undermine the overall health of the banking system as it had threatened to do in the late 1990s. By the end of the first round of reforms in 2008, the Central Bank possessed the institutional capacities to monitor the performance of banks and ensure this would not happen again.

Banks subsequently became more conservative in lending, leading to even tighter credit access for SSEs. The banks cleaned their portfolios and strengthened their established alliances with financially and economically robust private enterprises, which fit well with the profit reorientation of credit relations after the reform.

As credit extension became more profit oriented and risk sensitive, it did not necessarily become more market oriented. The credit market remained constrained by weak flows of public information, a limited client base that included no more than 10 percent of the adult population, and rampant informality in the private sector (Ḥammād, 2015). The beneficiaries of bank credit remained the same—the state Treasury and large, private enterprises displacing SOEs. The reform process thus simply reaffirmed the earlier relationships that characterized the banking sector as a financial intermediary between middle-class depositors and the large private sector enterprises and the state. Credit access for the vast majority of private sector enterprises remained as constrained as ever. Ultimately, these rounds of financial sector reforms would not supply the intermediate institutions that SSEs needed, as they were designed to serve different masters (or coalitions of them).

Figure 6.3 provides comparative indicators for the borrowers from commercial banks per 1,000 adults in selected other countries. This is an indicator of the breadth of the bank-client base in a number of economies in the Global South. It illustrates the extent of Egypt's persistent state of financial exclusion and overconcentration of credit. Between 2004 and 2014, Egypt had a mean of 82.19 adult individuals out of every 1,000 dealing with banks, versus 247.21, 294.00, 272.78, and 786.00 per 1,000 for Brazil, China, Indonesia, and Turkey respectively. This shows not only the particularly limited individual client base of banks in Egypt, where the vast majority of citizens do not use banks either because of underbranching or concentration in cities and relatively well-to-do neighborhoods; it also reflects the limited relation of the financial sector to private sector enterprises.

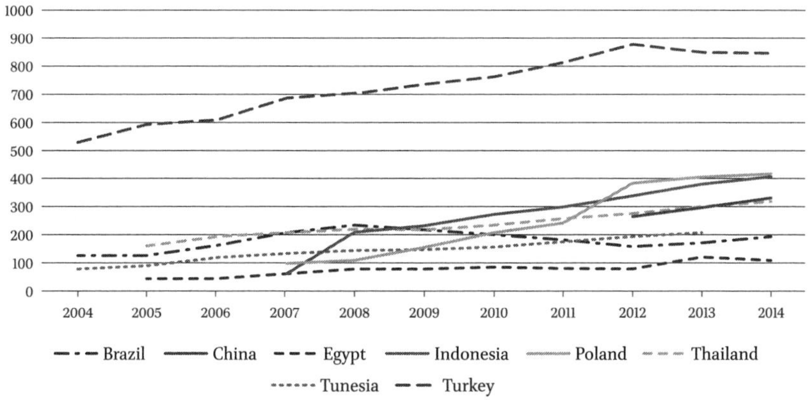

FIGURE 6.3. Borrowers from Commercial Banks (per 1,000 Adults), 2004–2014.
Source: World Bank data, Egypt, Arab Republic, Poland, Brazil, China, Indonesia, Turkey, Tunisia, Thailand, https://data.worldbank.org/indicator/FB.CBK.BRWR.P3?locations=EG-PL-BR-CN-ID-TR-TN-TH.

The problem of weak financial inclusion at both the individual and enterprise levels implied restrained credit for both consumption and investment. According to the annual Central Bank reports covering the period following the launch of the reform program, only a minuscule average of 37.71 per 1,000 acquired bank loans for investment between 2005 and 2009. Overall, the share of the private sector in total bank credit remained high compared to many middle-income countries. Between 2001 and 2014, the share of the private sector averaged 42.21 percent in Egypt compared to 44.81, 42.79, and 38.22 percent in Brazil, Poland, and Turkey, respectively, all high-middle income countries (World Bank 2017i). This could only mean very high concentration within the private sector.

There is ample evidence that the distribution of this private sector bank credit was extended primarily based on informal relations between the banks and their top clients. Such informal relations have often been of a long-term nature and have been known to nurture strong, close, and high-trust relations between banks and their large corporate clients (Beshāy, 2015). This relationship cultivates a level of mutual and long-standing interest between creditors and particular debtors in a way that effectively reduces the costs of monitoring and follow-up on the part of the bank. However, these informal ties often assume a formalized guise in order to at least technically abide by the prudential regulations set and enforced by the Central Bank.

In this way, bank-business alliances have substituted effectively for credit markets by creating tightly knit circles of credit provision at relatively low risk and with abundant flows of private and credible information. One illustration of this feature, and further evidence that private sector credit extension has remained concentrated in a disproportionately low number of large and connected firms, is the low percentage of guaranteed credit, that is, loans extended on the provision of physical collateral. A common practice by commercial banks to reduce the risk of lending in a context of weak information, the insistence on high collateral requirements has been cited by numerous SME surveys as the top barrier to bank credit for private sector actors (Mohieldin and Wright, 2000, 664, 667; Rocha et al., 2011, 9, 27–28). However, it seems that this requirement is relaxed with core clients, where deals are more entrepreneurial and based on higher trust and more information about the borrowers. Between 1999 and 2005, an average of 67.4 percent of short-term credit (due

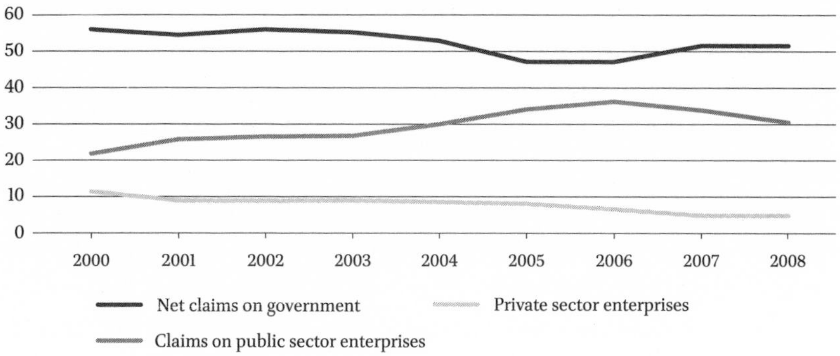

FIGURE 6.4. Sectoral Evolution of Bank Credit in Egypt, 2001–2009.
Source: Calculated by the author based on Central Bank reports (2005/2006, 106; 2006/2007, 102; 2008/2009, 98).

in less than a year, which averaged 58.35 percent of total credit, out of which 54 percent went to the private sector) was granted with no in-kind guarantee versus only 33.5 percent with (CBE, 2004/2005, 122–123, author's calculations).

Some authors attributed these low-collateral requirements to cronyism and political connections in the 1990s (Mohieldin and Nasr, 2003). However, this may not be entirely accurate; the same phenomenon seemed to have persisted even after the launch of the financial sector reforms. Such trustful lending practices curiously went hand in hand with concerted efforts to shed nonperforming loans and engage in generally sounder financial operations, indicating that banks continue to extend credit on a more entrepreneurial basis, even without collateral, within their select alliances with business.

Overall, the reform of the financial sector allowed it to strengthen in a way that did not expand its client base. Indeed, while the system became sounder for middle-class depositors and more sustainable for banks and their major debtors (the Treasury and large businesses), the former governor of the Central Bank, Farūq al-ʿOkda, admitted in a 2013 interview with me that financial inclusion was a big issue that the banking sector continued to face. He stated that the first priority was given to improving the overall health of the sector through consolidating and recapitalizing banks, addressing nonperforming loans, and encouraging the sound and prudential regulations, while few people were thinking about access to finance for the broad base of private sector enterprises.

Once the first round of reforms was successful, a second round followed from 2008 to 2012 that attempted to address the issue of financial inclusion. Among the aims of this second round of reforms was to raise the share of SMEs to total bank loans, while crediting microenterprises was relegated to special programs and business associations. As a first measure, the Central Bank developed a database in cooperation with the Faculty of Economics and Political Science at Cairo University, the Egyptian Banking Institute, and the Central Agency for Public Mobilization and Statistics.

The second measure was the establishment of the first, and hitherto only, credit bureau (I-score) in 2008 in the hopes of providing banks with information about the financial statuses of individuals and enterprises applying for credit. The third measure, which never materialized, was to be the creation of a credit guarantee under the supervision of the Central Bank.

Little progress took place in the area of financial inclusion, however. The second round of reform was interrupted and effectively halted by the political turmoil that followed the January revolution in 2011, while the Egyptian credit bureau, licensed toward mid-2008, did not extend its services to cover microfinance institutions or associations specialized in funding SMEs until 2016. Meanwhile, no credit guarantee has been established thus far.

ATTEMPTED INCLUSION BY NONMAINSTREAMING

Aside from the banking sector, a number of institutions and organizations charged with extending credit to those excluded from the financial sector have been developed in conscious efforts to overcome barriers to credit. These new financial providers were largely nonbanking institutions, ranging from the semiautonomous Social Fund for Development (SFD), established in 1991 and officially integrated into the state bureaucracy in 2002, to networks of nongovernmental organizations (NGOs) and business associations specializing in SME loans or microfinancing.[4] Most of these initiatives emerged from international donors where "free enterprise merged with the language of self-employment" (Elyachar, 2005, 81).

Such strategies, however, did not prove to be a workable solution to the chronic problems of undercapitalization and financial exclusion that the majority of SSEs faced. The market for microcredit and SME lending remained quite small and largely stagnant; any increase in the client base usually came from more people receiving very small loans that served primarily as antipoverty transfers or as selective compensation for subsidy cuts rather than capital for private SSEs with actual entrepreneurial potential. Neither the SFD nor credit-providing NGOs were willing or able to serve as intermediaries between these SSEs and the banking sector, which remained the center of the financial system in Egypt. On the contrary, they were established in order to substitute for the high barriers of dealing with banks as opposed to providing the means to bridge the gap, a reflection of the conservative stance taken by the Central Bank, especially in the wake of the financial sector reform program that limited the potential of banks to engage in microfinancing or SME lending.

Overall, the attempt to "nonmainstream" microfinance and SME funding away from banks only consolidated the well-established triangular relation between middle-class depositors, banks, and the state to the exclusion of the broad base of private sector enterprises. Moreover, microfinance and, to some extent, SME lending (which remained quite limited compared to microfinance focusing on alleviating poverty) increasingly performed the functions of welfare distribution rather than credit provision. This generally occurred through the targeting of economically vulnerable constituencies that the Mubārak regime and its international sponsors thought to be prone to social exclusion, like laid-off workers from privatized or divested SOEs and university graduates among the offspring of civil servants. Thus, microfinance was by no means a solution to financial exclusion, and after more than twenty years of implementation, it has not rectified Egypt's persistent missing-middle syndrome.

The Role of Foreign Donors

The context in which these institutions emerged was the aftermath of the Second Gulf War (1990–1991) and the adoption of Egypt's Structural Adjustment Program in 1991. Both events drew the attention of foreign donors, ranging from the US Agency for International Development (USAID) and a number of European governments to the UN Development Program, to take measures to ease Egypt's transition into a market-oriented economy. In this light, they represented products of the global neoliberal logic that the solution to the increase in socioeconomic marginalization was integrating more groups into the "emerging market." The promotion of entrepreneurship was thus adopted as an antipoverty strategy, as well as a source of relief for the government from the need to provide public employment at a time when SOEs were moving toward privatization. It was also seen as a way to provide alternatives for university graduates and laid-off workers, together with returning workers from the Gulf countries after the war with Iraq (el-Meehy, 2010, 143).

Toward this goal, USAID played a central role in drawing together a group of NGOs to act as microfinance institutions (hereafter referred to as NGO-MFIs). The USAID program began in 1990 as a pilot project involving two NGOs, one in Cairo and the other in Alexandria. The number increased over time, and by 2008, there were around two hundred or so providers in the country. Most began their operations with large donor grants (USAID, 2009, 12). USAID, for example, invested over $150 million in microfinancing between 1989 and 2008, a significant amount considering a total portfolio of $340 million for microfinance in Egypt in 2008. Nevertheless, overconcentration remained a persistent issue even in this sector: five NGO-MFIs held around 40 percent of the total gross loan portfolio and 45 percent of outreach (Sanabel, 2010, 12). While these NGOs are registered under the NGO law and are permitted to deliver services, including credit extension, they are not allowed to operate as companies because the board members cannot receive salaries or commissions in return for what is legally supposed to be "voluntary" work.

In terms of the SFD, its mission was officially reoriented toward improving the standards of living of young market entrants through job creation (el-Meehy, 2010, 146) following the passing of Law No. 141 of 2004 pertaining to microfinance under the Nazīf government (2004–2011). This placed special emphasis on job creation through subsidizing start-ups and microenterprises, and a new financial arm for the SFD was developed in 2005, the Small Enterprises Development Organization (SEDO), with the explicit mandate to provide loans to micro and small enterprises.

The microfinance market expanded considerably throughout this period, and by mid-2008, 360 microfinance programs were serving 1.2 million borrowers (86 percent were served by NGO-MFIs and the rest by banks with special microfinance programs). After nearly two decades of development, the total microfinance portfolio reached $340 million (or 1.9 billion Egyptian pounds in 2008 values). However, the microfinance market extended a negligible 0.0062 percent of domestic credit to the private sector and 0.0027 percent of total domestic credit (CBE report, 2008/2009, 10–11, author's calculation).

Microfinance institutions were not designed to bridge the gap between the banking sector and micro and small enterprises by acting as intermediates. Rather, they merely substituted for banks by assuming the role of credit providers, and hence did not represent a solution to the historic issue of financial exclusion, and the subsequent undercapitalization, that the broad base of the Egyptian private sector faced.

This is derived from inclusion by nonmainstreaming, or the fact that the SFD and donor-dependent NGO-MFIs evolved in parallel to the banking sector. Relying on external donors and, to a lesser extent, government contributions, they had no institutionalized access to the center of the Egyptian financial system: the banking sector to which the bulk of savings flowed and from which almost all credit came. Thus, neither the SFD nor NGO-MFIs could establish strong links with the banking sector in order to mediate between their base of SSE clients and the banks in a way that could have lowered transaction costs and augmented the banks' capacities to monitor the behavior of debtors and enforce repayment.

The SFD never evolved into becoming an intermediary institution between SSEs and banks. "Small business lending under SFD conditions was viewed [by banks] as unprofitable given the small loan amounts as well as the low profit margin of 3–5 percent designated by the fund to the banks versus their regular profit margin of about 20 percent" (el-Meehy, 2010, 211). "As a result, banks often adopted strict collateral requirements, a pattern that has rendered SEDO loans accessible primarily by better-off middle-class civil servants and their offspring" (el-Meehy, 2010, 218–219). Hence, SEDO became a mere mechanism for selective welfare distribution through the disbursement of subsidized start-up loans through the banking sector instead of actually serving as a financial intermediary. Obviously, loans designed to maintain social peace are made by criteria different from those for which one expects profitable returns and repayment. SEDO loans were generally not entrepreneurial, but rather embodied the broader raison d'être of the SFD as an additional financial tool wielded by the Mubārak regime (using donor money) to mitigate the adverse economic conditions faced by the state-dependent middle classes.

The SFD's microcredit program did not fare much better. The SDF attempted to fulfill its original mission to fight poverty through self-employment by disbursing subsidized microloans through an extensive network of community development associations that usually consisted of very small NGOs operating on the village or district level (USAID, 2009, 12). Although these NGOs were primed to function as intermediaries between the local microenterprises and the communities in which they were embedded and the SFD, their capacity to do so remained dubious. According to el-Meehy (2010, 231), many of the NGOs had few grassroots links: "Many SFD implementing agencies could be more appropriately labeled as governmental NGOs and the few NGO partners that work with the SFD are led and managed by members of the political elite or the middle classes, without meaningful links to local communities."

NGOs-MFIs

Despite being donor dependent like the SFD, NGOs-MFIs have been quite different in origin and organization. They have been business-oriented associations from the beginning, targeting operating enterprises rather than offering microcredit to underprivileged or vulnerable constituencies. Their boards have been made up of professional businesspeople, and there is evidence that they have managed to embed themselves into various business communities, usually on regional or sectoral levels.

Hence, they theoretically were qualified to play the role of intermediaries between local and socially embedded micro and small enterprises (as well as some medium-sized ones) and banks, allowing for access to credit on a less personalized basis. However, this has never materialized. The restrictive regulatory framework in which they have operated since their inception in the early 1990s caused them to face many restraints when dealing with banks.

The regulatory framework of NGOs does not encourage banks to provide commercial loans to NGOs unless a guarantee is available. This is due to several reasons: the absence of sufficient knowledge among banks on microfinance as an industry in general and NGO-MFIs operations in particular. Banks have never had access to sufficient information that would help them assess the performance of NGO-MFIs—especially the banks' top and middle management. Moreover, NGO-MFIs are legally declared to be public benefit organizations, which are by definition nonprofit, so their assets cannot be practically pledged as collateral for bank loans.

For instance, under the current regulatory framework, these NGO-MFIs cannot use any of the property the organization owns as collateral, which stands as a significant impediment to their ability to access loans. The usual way in which they engaged with commercial banks was through "depositing the donor grants in banks and borrowing against these deposits from a single consolidated account in their own name (to which borrowers' repayments are also directed) (USAID, 2009, 12).

Microfinance companies (MFCs) could avoid many of the limitations on financial intermediation facing NGO-MFIs, for-profit companies using their own capital to extend loans to microenterprises. However, the regulatory framework governing MFCs remained underdeveloped largely due to the consistent resistance from the Central Bank. As USAID notes in a report, Central Bank regulations do not allow microfinance companies to act as agents for banks (USAID, 2009, 4). The Central Bank, the Ministry of Justice, and the State Council, influential in shaping the regulatory framework governing financial provision, have shown considerable conservatism since the collapse of the CICs in the late 1980s, which impelled the issuance of Law No. 146 in 1988 that explicitly bans the receipt of deposits by any nonbanking financial institution—a law that has been vigorously enforced.

This conservative stance fits well into the triangular relationship of banks, middle-class depositors, and the government, which would restrict competition to banks by excluding MFCs in the name of protecting middle-class savers from potential fraud or risky investments that might entail the loss of their principal. As a result of this restricted credit competition, the average rates charged for microloans in 2009 ranged between 15 and 17 percent, considerably higher than the average annual rate of 12.39 percent charged by banks for one-year loans in the same year (Ministry of Finance, 2009, 51).

Ultimately, the vast majority of commercial banks have not engaged directly or indirectly with microfinance. The four banks that did (out of a total population of around thirty banks in Egypt) held a mere 15 percent of the total (and still tiny) microfinance portfolio as of mid-2008. In turn, the average loan balance in 2008 was a mere $190, or 12 percent of the gross national income per capita, which hardly qualified as any serious capitalization for any enterprise. It is noteworthy that the microfinance law of 2004 set a cap of 50,000 Egyptian pounds in annual turnover, stressing the antipoverty rationale behind microfinance. Indeed, "almost all 14 [NGO-]MFIs would be considered poverty focused" (Sanabel, 2010, 12), with the ultimate result of targeting microloans to categories that were hardly entrepreneurial, unless "vibrant entrepreneurship was equated with simply surviving" (Elyachar, 2005, 30).

In a more ideal case, there would have been mainstreamed intermediate institutions through which the most entrepreneurial among SSEs could have been selected and privileged with cheap credit. However, in this task, business NGOs-MFIs and MFCs struggled under many regulatory and legal restrictions. In essence, this left SSEs to the banking sector, which has historically avoided doing business with them.

Informal Credit: Back to Self-Accumulation

In light of all of the limitations of formal institutions, informal credit markets have often been considered the only remaining resort for SSEs to raise capital. However, the little evidence available about Egypt's informal credit markets indicates they are at best very imperfect substitutes for formal ones (Mohieldin and Wright, 2000, 667).

It is not quite clear whether access to informal credit happens on a market basis that is driven by price signals (i.e., interest rates), regardless of how imperfect they may be. Fieldwork and anecdotal evidence suggest that informal credit in Egypt often takes the form of rotating savings and credit associations (*gamʿiyyāt*), which are generally interest free (Mohieldin and Wright, 2000, 664). Rotating savings and credit associations are informal groups, usually made up of friends and relatives and friends of friends who pitch in agreed-on sums of money, often on a monthly basis. The total amount collected every month goes to one of the contributors according to an agreed-on timetable. (For details about how rotating savings and credit associations function, see Singerman and Hoodfar, 1996, 39, 151.)

These associations depend on high levels of interpersonal trust and myriad self-enforcement mechanisms (Harders, 2003, 207). Hence, they are almost always confined to tight networks of intimately tied individuals who can easily monitor and collectively sanction each other's behavior. In turn, mutual solidarity rather than profit seeking often motivates them, especially in the sense that they are interest free, which is seen as usury from an Islamic religious perspective. This suggests that access to informal credit in Egypt is not subject to the common issue of high interest rates that characterizes the other informal markets underlined in the literature (see, for example, Banerjee et al., 2009,

6). They suffer instead from other problems due to overembeddedness that limit their ability to access capital beyond a small, familiar circle (Uzzi, 1997).

Most informal credit, however, whether obtained on a market or nonmarket basis, is reportedly used to finance consumption rather than production. It is more often than not a means for survival by the urban and rural poor rather than a widely used mechanism for financing small-scale businesses (Harders, 2003, 197). Although Singerman and Hoodfar (1996, 166, 167) mention cases where merchants and artisans resorted to gamʿiyyāt, there is no evidence to support that this is a widespread practice.

However, beyond the specific mechanisms of governing rotating savings and credit associations, access to informal credit in Egypt does not appear to be distinct from the various other forms of self-accumulation that SSEs and emerging entrepreneurs have engaged with for decades. This ultimately involves transforming social capital into access to finance from relatives and friends and is discussed in detail in Chapter 8.

In sum, this chapter has shown how the essential investment tool of debt finance has been made systematically unavailable to the broad base of small establishments through an institutional and organizational framework that has been overly centralized and hierarchical. These institutional traits have ultimately raised the transaction costs for SSEs to an extent that has effectively excluded them from accessing credit, precluding any credible chance of scaling up and thus calcifying the institutional condition of cleft capitalism. In addition to this access to financial capital, centralized and hierarchical institutions similarly characterized access to land that excluded SSEs from accessing the physical capital needed to expand. It is to this story that the following chapter turns. Taken together, the lack of access to these crucial capital inputs has created and perpetuated the institutional condition of cleft capitalism that has robbed the Egyptian private sector of any ability to follow the paths taken by more successful market transformations.

Chapter Seven

EGYPT'S DESERT LAND

Abundant Yet Scarce

IF EGYPT WERE ABUNDANT IN ANY ECONOMIC RESOURCE, IT would certainly be the desert land that constitutes 95 percent of the total surface area of the country. This land is largely uninhabited; around 96 percent of Egyptians live on only 5 percent of the land hugging the banks of the Nile and its delta (World Bank, 2006, 1:11). Thus, this abundant land stands as an open and potentially cheap space for expansion for nearly all socioeconomic sectors. This is particularly true of housing, manufacturing, services, and tourism; the only restrained sector may be agriculture given the limited supply of freshwater. What adds even further to the developmental potential of this land is that "unlike Algeria, Morocco and other countries with large desert tracts, in Egypt the desert begins abruptly and is enticingly near to the core of the country—including the two main metropolises of Cairo and Alexandria.[1] The desert is, in fact, never more than a few kilometers from most densely inhabited areas" (Sims, 2015, 2). Despite this virtual abundance of space, access to this land for productive uses has been quite restrictive for most private sector enterprises. Indeed, entrepreneurs have traditionally underlined access to land, like finance, as a major barrier to growth—a consistent and constant theme since the launch of infitāḥ.

This book pays exclusive attention to the productive uses of land where it serves as a factor—usually the site—of production, with a special focus on nonagricultural activities in urban areas. Here, *land* is broadly defined to include all physical space (e.g., apartments, workshops, storage rooms), while *access to such space* comprises all forms, some of which are legal, including purchase, lease, rent, usufruct, or transfer of property, while others are illegal or extralegal, like squatting.

In one of the most comprehensive studies on land from a business perspective, a World Bank report issued in 2006 showed that Egypt has some of the highest barriers to accessing land for investment in the Global South. The survey I conducted among small-scale establishments (SSEs) in 2013 provided similar results: 38 percent of respondents marked access to land as a significant barrier to growth. This is confirmed in earlier surveys. For instance, an Investment Climate Assessment study conducted in 2006 showed around 27.4 percent of Egyptian firms reporting access to land as a severe constraint on business development, ranking Egypt far below many countries with which it competes to attract investment. Moreover, the World Bank report (2006, 1:1) showed that small and medium enterprises (SMEs) suffered considerably more than large firms in accessing land, indicating a sustained bias toward large firms.

Not dissimilar from access to finance, barriers to land have been predominantly institutional. Accessing land is subject to state regulation, given the fact that desert land is publicly owned and its uses are planned and implemented by a variety of state organizations according to a thick body of laws, decrees, and bylaws. The regulatory framework governing desert land used since infitāḥ has also been marked by the presence of excessively centralized, hierarchical, and authoritarian state institutions. From the outset, the mission of these institutions was to vigilantly enforce the legal, economic, and administrative separation of desert land from the adjacent populated areas, urban as well as rural. Plans for development were thus set and pursued on a national scale in a top-down fashion that lacked any institutional linkage with the socioeconomic dynamics at play in the inhabited areas of the Nile valley and the delta.

As in finance, land-managing public institutions created a bias against the broad base of small-scale establishments by raising the transaction cost of dealing with the state organizations in charge of land management. This resulted in high operation costs due to grappling with complex procedures that consume time, money, and effort, as well as unfriendly pricing mechanisms and major difficulties in securing credible information flows without possessing political leverage, often associated with large business size. Access to information about the availability or pricing of land plots has reportedly been quite difficult for those without connections to the top echelons of the bureaucracy.

Such access is crucial because the state is the primary owner, regulator, and provider of desert land (World Bank, 2006, 1:30). This applies to the direct allocation of desert land for production and investment, in addition to any other noneconomic end, such as defense, national parks, nature preserves, and social housing. The state's role also takes more indirect forms through the impact of the availability and affordability of desert land on prices within the cities where SSEs predominantly operate. Almost all land in urban areas is privately owned, so access to it is largely left to market forces and, theoretically, state regulation of spaces—private as well as public—for economic use. However, due to the explosive population growth and overcrowding of cities and rural areas along the Nile since the 1970s, Egypt's deserts to the east and west of the Nile valley and the delta, in addition to the Sinai Peninsula, have been the only possibilities for economic and housing expansion.

SSEs operating in services or light manufacturing usually require small plots of land that are physically proximate to where they acquire workers, as well as access to their local markets. This is what Elyachar (2005, 63) referred to as an "integrated pattern of residence and work" where "a neighbor open[s] a workshop in the ground floor of the building where they live" (see also Tarbush, 2012, 178). This is a sign of a high degree of embeddedness in the social relations that govern access to inputs and local markets (Stauth, 1991; Hopkins, 1992; World Bank, 2006, 2:61; Schumacher, 2011). It may also explain the concentration of workshops, yards, shops, and storage sites within cities rather than in industrial parks or special zones that have typically been built in the desert. For instance, a 2006 study on Egyptian SSEs found that individual final customers represented 90 percent of the total consumers of SSEs' products of goods and services (al-Mahdi and Rashed, 2010, 110).

Thus, accessing land for SSEs has been dependent on what can be described as the organic expansion of urban centers into adjacent desert land that needs to be available and affordable for multipurposed uses (Shawkat, 2014). Since the 1970s, however, the centralized and hierarchical land-managing state organizations failed to deliver this access to the broad base of SSEs due to their lack of responsiveness and top-down planning and decision making. The outcome was that urban centers became even more crowded, inflicting, likely unintentionally, severe damage on SSEs.

DISCOVERING THE ECONOMIC VALUE OF EGYPT'S DESERTS

Following independence in 1956, Egypt's deserts to the west and east of the Nile valley, and especially the Sinai, served as the national frontiers, as well as battlegrounds, of the newly independent state. Frequent military confrontations with Israel in 1948, 1956, 1967, and 1973 provided the context for decades of military management and control that left a strong imprint on the regulatory and legal framework where military and national security concerns, including border control, put administrative and legal restraints on the economic use of desert land.

During the time of Nāṣer (1954–1970), thoughts did begin to reemerge regarding the use of the desert for urban expansion and industrialization, with the explicit aim of relieving Cairo's massive population pressure. Nonetheless, actual expansion unfolded only at the expense of agricultural land very close to Cairo (el-Kadi, 2009, 38), with the only exception being Madīnat Naṣr, a middle-class neighborhood built in the late 1960s in a desert area east of Cairo.

State institutions in charge of designing and implementing public policies regarding the desert have evolved since the mid-1970s. These developments took place under certain historical conditions, and the initial factors behind them—what may be labeled critical junctures—proved to have long-lasting imprints on later institutions, even when the rationale and functions for which they first appeared had withered away. The overall mission of these centralized and hierarchical bodies nonetheless remained reflective of the concerns and interests of parties who wished to make direct political or economic use of the expansive desert land under their control. Not dissimilar from bank credit, the state, through a great diversity of formal and informal actors with the civilian and military bureaucracies, remained a main beneficiary of a public resource it supposedly regulated and managed for broader socioeconomic goals.

It is nevertheless noteworthy that unlike financial institutions, the institutional and regulatory framework governing the economic uses of desert land was created from scratch in the 1970s and 1980s. This is due to the fact that the economic value and developmental potential of the desert were not discovered (or invented) until that time, and thus had almost no roots in pre-independence times. In fact, ever since the inception of Egypt's modernization efforts in the nineteenth century, "land" meant simply the cultivable space within the Nile valley and its delta (Amer, 1958, 85, 89).

Subsequently, the economic discovery of desert land developed in tandem with the launch of infitāḥ and the realignment of Egypt's economic and foreign policies toward the Western bloc in the Cold War and the peace with Israel (Ḥussein, 1982, 443). Thus, the context of overall economic reorientation created an enduring linkage between planning and using desert land by the state, on the one hand, and attracting investment and generating growth, on the other.

Throughout this period, many of the wartime laws and regulations nonetheless remained in place despite the peace treaty with Israel signed in 1979 and even when the desert, including coastal areas on the Mediterranean and the Red Seas, was discovered to have economic and developmental value. Herein lies the root cause of the extensive involvement of the military and many of its agencies and companies in land management subsequently. The subjection of desert land to military control was one of the driving forces behind the centralized and hierarchical dynamics that dominated land management

The hierarchy was composed of the military at the top, which remained the ultimate regulator of desert land: no property was to be allocated for any economic purpose without prior approval by the minister of defense (Springborg, 1989, 98–99; Dorman, 2013, 5). Legally, the initial allocation of land in the desert also required the prior approval of the Ministries of Petroleum and of Antiquities; however, the ultimate approval lay de facto in the hands of the military given its physical control over most of the land, its strong presence in respective civilian bodies, and its regulatory mandate over the planning process of public land uses. This fact was reaffirmed in a series of laws and presidential decrees from the 1970s when the president, and on some occasions the prime minister, became the supreme coordinator between the military and sectoral ministries and their affiliated organizations and enterprises.

The military has commanded another, though less direct, mechanism of control over land allocation through having a large number of individuals with military backgrounds in senior posts in the civil agencies charged with managing public land use. This has applied to almost all of the specialized public agencies, such as the New Urban Communities Authority (NUCA), which falls under the minister of housing but is significantly staffed by military retirees, as well as the General Authority for Rehabilitation Projects and Agricultural Development (GARPAD), the Tourism Development Agency (TDA), and the General Agency for Industrial Development (GAID) (see Abul-Magd, 2017, 138, 156, 172, 175). Similarly, many retired generals staffing the governorate and municipal levels manage public land within the boundaries of Egypt's governorates. In addition, there is more explicit military involvement at the staffing level, seen in the General Organization for Physical Planning (GOPP), which was established in 1971 and whose head is to be appointed by presidential decree based on the nomination of the defense minister.

Ultimately, the minister of defense determines which desert land is to be used for military or strategic ends, thus rendering a good deal of land unavailable for other public agencies or subsequent private use. In addition to the military's broad mandate over land earmarked for defense and national security purposes, it also retains considerable influence over how the land is subsequently used. The military practices continuous oversight in regulating land use; in many instances, private investors must secure military approval for technical issues such as the heights of buildings or to secure certificates for land mine clearance (Shawkat, 2014).

The military is entitled to compensation from the state Treasury in cases where land previously used for military purposes is allocated for economic ends, a process that requires their prior approval. The military's approval is also required for the allocation of land in coastal areas, defined legally as borders, which typically attract high-value tourism investments, particularly on the North Coast and Red Sea. This reserve of land can thus prove quite lucrative, as Sims (2015, 160) notes: "Military camps remain under control of the Armed forces or security agencies, and they represent a kind of land bank for future urban development that will generate huge profits for developers, whether private or government." According to Presidential Decree No. 531 issued in 1981, the military has the right to auction off any land originally used for military purposes and to collect any proceeds for the construction of alternative military sites or facilities. This arrangement provided a formal channel for the military to convert its regulatory mandate over public lands into direct revenue streams. In 1982, an additional presidential decree (No. 223) established the Armed Forces Land Projects Organization, vesting it with the power to manage these sales of military-owned lands, as well as the returns that would accrue from building alternative military facilities.

The Political Value of Desert Land

Following the October War of 1973, President Anwar al-Sadāt (1970–1981) launched a national program for reconstruction and rehabilitation (*al-taʿmīr*). The original version was primarily concerned with rebuilding three Suez Canal cities, Port Said, Ismaʿīliyya, and Suez, after six years of devastation and population displacement (1967–1973). The Ministry of Housing and Reconstruction was assigned the task of overseeing and implementing the reconstruction plan, which soon developed into building new urban communities and industrial cities in the desert around Cairo (and later in Alexandria and third-tier cities like Asyūt and Damietta in the 1990s and 2000s). The Sixth of October city, the pilot project launched in 1973, heralded the beginning of the establishment of the centralized, hierarchical, and authoritarian institutional framework that still persists. Al-Sadāt and the technocratic and bureaucratic elites made an early decision to bring the direct development of these desert lands into the hands of central state agencies in order to pursue their mission on a national scale (rather than on the governorate level). This pilot project was followed by a host of other cities in the 1980s and 1990s, and by 2015, Egypt had built more than twenty new towns and urban settlements in the previously undeveloped desert land (Sims, 2015, 158).

This desert land was to be managed by several sectoral land-developing organizations under the Ministries of Agriculture, Housing, Tourism, and Industry established in 1975, 1979, 1991, and 2005, respectively. These agencies were assigned the tasks of planning, coordinating, and implementing a modern Egyptian exodus from the narrow Nile valley and increasingly congested delta through the founding of autonomous urban and economic centers in the desert far from the overcrowded cities (Sims, 2015, 117). This exodus was so central to al-Sadāt's economic plans (and for Mubārak after) that it was first underlined in his October paper issued in 1974, which served as a strategic document for the postwar era (ʿOuda, 2004, 116). The mission was to be accomplished through the national management of desert land designated for development: housing, cultivation, tourism, or industry.

In the process, desert land began to be perceived as strategically important for the ruling regime. It became the object on which a certain notion of the public or national good, naturally tightly intertwined to the perpetuation of the ruling regime's control and legitimacy, was to be developed. It was also seen as an indispensable resource to counter security and political threats, actual or perceived.

The beginnings of this development mission to direct urban expansion into the desert was explicitly meant to relieve pressure on Cairo, which "was rapidly becoming a 10 million plus megacity" by the early 1980s (Dorman, 2013, 2). Massive population growth, partly due to rural migration, had strained public services and was thus seen as a sociopolitical threat to public order and social cohesion. For a security-oriented regime, informal settlements around the capital city (*ʿashwāʾiyyāt*) were portrayed as ticking time bombs, especially in the aftermath of the January 1977 riots. It was in this context that government officials began to perceive these self-made housing areas as overpopulated centers of crime, social backwardness, and misery (Tarbush, 2012, 181). In June 1981, in the wake of violent sectarian clashes, President al-Sadāt ordered the removal of a slum area near downtown Cairo known as the al-Turgumān squats (Dawūd, 2014), a practice of physical removal that was not replicated under Mubārak.

The problem of ʿashwāʾiyyāt assumed a more political character by the early 1990s as Islamist militants began taking refuge in a number of informal settlements around Cairo. The Islamic republic of Imbāba, a poor and congested neighborhood overwhelmed with rural migrants from Upper Egypt, became iconic. An Islamist militant group assumed control over significant portions of the neighborhood and claimed to be applying sharia law before being stormed by the central security forces in 1992 (Bayat and Denis, 2000; Bayat, 2007). Thus, being in direct control of the development of desert land was increasingly perceived as critical to mitigating what was seen as an existential threat to the ruling regime and the public order it was meant to sustain.

The development of desert land was closely tied to the careers of political leaders since Nāṣer's time (Waterbury, 1983, 64). It is no coincidence that almost all "national" megaprojects were given names that had explicit reference to Egyptian nationalism, a trend that started under al-Sadāt. Almost all of the new towns created in the desert were given names that were explicitly and directly tied to al-Sadāt's political accomplishments, starting with the first two cities of the Sixth of October and the Tenth of Ramadan, to the west and east of Cairo, respectively. Both names referred to the A.D. and Hijri dates when Egypt launched its military campaign in 1973 against the Israeli occupying forces in the Sinai. Al-Sadāt's al-Sadāt City, was to be built to the southwest of the Nile delta and was intended to become Egypt's new administrative capital. However, the project was abandoned after his assassination. Nevertheless, there remained a continued fascination with "edifice projects"—using Dorman's (2013) expression—tied to the ruler's person throughout the long subsequent rule of Ḥosni Mubārak.

In light of the political significance of the development of desert land for successive rulers of Egypt, the ability to undertake such national projects required direct, centralized, and strictly hierarchical control of the land in a way that may explain the context in which state land-managing agencies emerged and the process through which they kept their administrative structures and mandates. The political, and later economic, significance that top leadership gave to desert land cultivated the seeds of administrative fragmentation and internal competition between different, ironically central, bureaucratic bodies and networks that had some sort of mandate over land management or simply had access to some tract of land. Of course, the first among these was the military, which was among the earliest to invest in retaining the hierarchical and centralized structures first set by al-Sadāt, while land-managing state organizations existed underneath.

Throughout the 1970s and 1980s, the military controlled upstream land supply by possessing ultimate control over the tap from which all desert land came (Shawkat, 2014). Not only was this tied to acquiring economic gains for the institution or to certain groups and individuals within it, but it also soon became tied to the military's search for a political role after the peace treaty with Israel. Indeed, Springborg (1989, 95, 114–116) showed how tight control over desert land served to recast the role of the military in the 1980s as a national vehicle for self-sufficiency, the delivery of development, and the employment of redundant military personnel.

This upstream military control was not the only reason behind the institutional and policy incoherence that marked desert land use. The same logic of viewing the control over this land as the path to greater power and resources dominated interbureaucratic competition more generally. Every governmental agency or body, including some SOEs, was far too jealous to give up control over the land assigned to it, or which it claimed to have been assigned to it, with the final result of extreme bureaucratic and legal complexity and ambiguity, together with a high frequency of interbureaucratic feuds over the ownership and control of public lands.

In 1975, the first piece of legislation governing the economic uses of desert land was issued. Presidential Decree No. 259 established the first sectoral body in charge of land reclamation under the name of the General Authority for Rehabilitation Projects and Agricultural Development (GARPAD), which was put under the Ministry of Agriculture. This was followed by Law No. 59/1979 on NUCA and initiated the long path of using desert land for economic purposes—reclamation, tourism (especially in coastal areas), industry, or, above all, housing and construction (Sims, 2015, 126). NUCA was to be headed by the minister of housing, and it was the body in charge of planning and administering the allocation of desert land for all economic purposes, with the exception of agriculture, throughout Egypt.

In 1981, the NUCA law was followed by Law No. 143/1981, which set the general regulatory framework for the economic use of desert land. Ever since, a heap of laws, presidential decrees, bylaws, and ministerial decrees—not always harmonious or coherent—governed the use of desert land. Next to GARPAD, NUCA remained the most powerful because it retained the largest land bank (World Bank, 2006, 1:30) and was in charge of tourism until a separate sectoral agency, TDA, was put in charge exclusively of the sector in 1991 via Decree No. 7. By 2005, industry was also taken away from NUCA and given to the reformulated GAID.

In 2006, the World Bank estimated that sectoral development authorities and state-owned holding companies "responsible for agriculture and land reclamation, housing and new urban communities, tourism, and industrial development control[ed] over five million *feddans* (the equivalent of 5.189 million acres) of public land in Egypt. This amounts to 2.5 percent of Egypt's territory and is equivalent to about half of the settled land area" (World Bank, 2006, 1:3). As a by-product, the centralized and hierarchical institutions denied any mandate to local authorities on the governorate or municipal levels to plan or allocate the desert land adjacent to them.

In theory, if urban centers were to be allowed to expand organically into the desert in response to population increases, the supply of land would not be a restraint because prices would be relatively low. However, state policies and regulations since infitāḥ and the discovery of the economic value of desert land has either created an artificial scarcity of public land available for investment purposes (as well as for housing) or contributed to raising the prices of private lands inside existing cities. The result has been high barriers to land in general and for small-scale establishments in particular.

Nesting Economic Interests in Existing Institutions

The articulation of Egypt's land management institutions and organizations contributed to the creation of vested interests, which were nested within an established system of rules and structures (Sadowski, 1991, 106). This applied to the state capitalist uses of desert land in the 1980s when state-owned developers dominated the scene, as well as the crony capitalism since the 1990s after a class of large private businesses had emerged. These were results, rather than the causes, of overly centralized and hierarchical structures.

In the late 1970s and 1980s, clear signs of state capitalism were emerging, specifically in the public sector construction companies that were well placed to pursue the national goals of desert development.[2] In the 1980s, these companies fell under the Ministry of Housing and were converted into revenue generators for the ministry under Minister Ḥassaballa al-Kafrāwi (Springborg, 1989, 113–114). These companies enjoyed heavily subsidized desert land plots, together with a host of incentives and exemptions. In turn, they progressively shifted from supplying low-income housing to targeting higher-income groups, especially with the influx of workers' remittances from the Gulf (Amin, 2001).

Other manifestations of state capitalism in this period were less explicitly tied to public sector developers; rather, they were linked to the private accumulation of high-ranking bureaucrats in the civilian as well as military branches of the government (Springborg, 1989, 105). Civilian bureaucrats and professionals working for state institutions began establishing cooperatives in the 1970s and 1980s with the goal of building housing units for their members. These cooperatives were given a number of privileges in the new urban communities' law of 1979, among which was heavily subsidized land. Unlike developers, the cooperatives were legally required to deliver units to their members, not generate profits. Nevertheless, this was indeed a vehicle for exploiting subsidized desert land for private accumulation by military and police officers, judges, university professors, bankers at state-owned banks, and journalists for national newspapers, among many others.

These particularistic economic interests emerged as intended or unintended consequences of the centralized and hierarchical land management system installed in the 1970s. Despite modest outcomes in policy terms, the beneficiaries became the sociopolitical force that maintained the resilience of such an institutional setting.

These trends of state capitalism in the land sector, however, did not translate into the central government's direct and conscious use of desert land to generate revenue for the Treasury. Thus, it is imperative to understand the strategy of desert land use in the light of its political rather than pecuniary economic value. While sectoral agencies like NUCA, GARPAD, and TDA continued to subsidize land in the hope of luring investors and final consumers, they did not become centers of accumulation of public wealth until very recently, particularly in the 2000s, when attempts were made to capture part of the speculative value of desert land designated for housing through new pricing mechanisms like bidding (Sims, 2015, 81).

Explicit private interests emerged relatively late, as late as the second half of the 1990s and 2000s, when private construction tycoons broke into the previous process of desert land allocation dominated by the public sector and the military. These private interests made use of the centralized and hierarchical structures that they had little role in creating but that served their goal of asserting direct control on desert lands via the political leadership. Within this institutional framework, a few socioeconomic actors—groups of investors as well as upper- and upper-middle-class consumers—were able to skim off the economic value of the land.

In terms of investors, there was a sustained bias for large capital, be it state owned in the 1960s or private domestic and foreign capital from the 1970s (Shawkat, 2012, 208). Priority was given to megaprojects in the form of land reclamation and the establishment of new urban centers and industrial zones in the desert. At the time, large capital was best positioned to generate economic returns from these projects given its access to finance, technology, and markets. Moreover, the overly centralized structures, as well as the enforced artificial severance of desert land development from rural and urban populated areas, made it more feasible to deal with large economic actors. Thus, the institutional operation costs, as well as the locational costs of initiating production and distribution from desert spaces, excluded small-scale establishments by design (Elyachar, 2005; Sims, 2015).

Desert land development went to serve various strata of middle-class consumers who were either state dependent and corporately organized, or otherwise to higher-income groups that had savings to invest in real estate (often the same depositors in the banking sector).

Contrary to the World Bank's (2006) rather technical assessment, the problem did not simply lie in red tape, administrative fragmentation, weak monitoring and assessment capacities, and information asymmetry. Rather, the centralized, hierarchical, and authoritarian land-management organizations served the interests of certain sociopolitical coalitions. These coalitions were fairly broad, including hundreds of thousands of middle-class consumers, as well as entire economic sectors, ranging from the construction industries, such as steel, cement, glass, and related services like real estate, that were all tied to banking and stock markets. Hence, this was not a simple story of rent seeking where private interests took possession of state power, distorting markets and generating rents at the expense of social welfare. On the contrary, the notion of the public good that was expressed in the exodus from the narrow valley had social constituencies that fed into the regime's legitimation and social control.

EGYPT'S REGULATORY APARTHEID

The institutional and regulatory framework governing public land in Egypt has been based firmly on the administrative, legal, and economic separation of uninhabited desert land from the vibrant rural and urban areas, where almost all Egyptians live. As early as 1979 and 1981, when key pieces of legislation were passed, public land in Egypt was divided into two main administrative categories: lands inside the *zimām* and those outside it. *Zimām* is defined as "boundaries of cultivated and uncultivated agricultural lands that have been historically surveyed by the Egyptian Survey Authority and included in the Real Estate Tax Department's land and property tax registry and which are subject to the agricultural land or property tax" (World Bank, 2006, 1:12).

Respective local authorities, namely governorates, have administered the inside-zimām lands, nearly 96 percent of them privately owned as agricultural plots or property in urban areas (el-Kadi, 2009, 283). Conversely, outside-zimām land was publicly owned by definition.

In addition to the zimām dividing line, cities and villages are subject to artificial cordons that limit their potential expansion into unoccupied desert land. The cordons were originally demarcated based on the boundaries of already established cities and villages with the aim of protecting agricultural land from urban expansion in the central delta region. However, this model was generalized to include cities in governorates with adjacent desert extensions, creating an artificial administrative boundary and curbing the natural expansion of these urban agglomerations into the desert (Shawkat, 2012, 210–211). The aim of this regulatory regime was to provide state land-managing agencies with a clean slate from which to plan and coordinate the relocation of the population from the valley to the new cities and towns in the desert without having to deal with existing socioeconomic activities.

The logical result was that high administrative and legal barriers suffocated urban areas by creating an artificial scarcity of land inside the cities that were adjacent to vast, uninhabited desert, causing prices of inside-zimām lands to skyrocket. This meant that SSE owners were squeezed out of the market because they were unable to afford the very high prices demanded. They therefore stood as collateral damage to a process of centralized, authoritarian, and top-down desert land management. It is remarkable that the relative diligence with which the state maintained separation between desert development and the actual population's social and economic activity was contrasted with their almost complete laxity in regard to urban expansion into adjacent privately owned agricultural lands. As a result, the latter absorbed almost all of the urban population growth, namely, in Cairo, since the 1960s. By 2006, 65 percent of Cairo's population, for instance, lived in informal areas (Tarbush, 2012, 177).

The organic expansion of urban centers did occur; however, it occurred largely informally, and technically illegally, on private agricultural land adjacent to large cities, especially Greater Cairo. As access to public desert land has been generally restrained for productive as well as housing purposes, there has been a secular increase in informal land use through the building of illegal housing units. This has been most apparent in the sheer expansion of squatter settlements and shantytowns in Egypt's big cities since the 1960s and 1970s (el-Kadi, 2009, 84). Most of this expansion occurred on private agricultural land adjacent to major cities, with Cairo again absorbing up to 70 percent of rural migrants from 1960 to 1996 (el-Kadi, 2009, 38).

Agricultural land in Egypt has been historically subject to a well-developed and elaborated system of private property registration since the late eighteenth century and was enforced further by the 1840s. By the 1850s, private property was formalized in a series of official decrees (Cuno, 1980, 247), a system that survived, or perhaps was even reinforced by, Naṣer's land reform rounds from 1952 to 1961 (Hansen, 1991, 127). In these reforms, private property in rural areas was widely extended to new social strata: small and middle peasants who formed up to 10 percent of the rural population (Amer, 1958, 148). Nevertheless, the private property system remained unscathed, explaining the very limited share of state ownership of land inside the zimām, where 96 percent remains privately owned. By the 1970s, the share of the state in agricultural land was almost negligible.

Despite the fact that such building on agricultural land remained illegal, the state was systematically lax on enforcement. Indeed, the state has not intervened in a single case to remove any of settlements that have expanded onto private agricultural property (el-Kadi, 2009, 167). Semiformality allowed a market of informal housing units to emerge and expand with a de facto set of stable legal relations that were predictable and often permanent. All of this occurred in the absence of a comprehensive and functional property registration system, as land tenure effectively substituted for building without a permit. This created customary and semiformal property rights that were nonetheless respected and functional, demonstrating little need for the formal registration of housing units that was stressed by De Soto and other neoclassical institutionalists who emphasized formal property registration as the only path away from dead capital. In Egypt, more than 95 percent of urban land and property is not formally registered, including housing units built with permits and in line with building regulations (World Bank, 2006, 1:19).

In terms of informal housing settlements that emerged on the desert, publicly owned by definition, these have been the exception rather than the rule throughout the past few decades. The legal status of desert land, in contrast to privately owned agricultural land, was a salient issue in creating stable relations between urban developers and dwellers. Only two out of the informal fifteen settlements in Cairo were built on desert land: Manshāt Nāṣer and 'Ezbet al-Haggana (el-Kadi, 2009, 104; Sims, 2015, 174). Indeed, according to el-Kadi (2009, 60–61), by 1996, informal settlements on desert land in Greater Cairo constituted less than 10 percent of the total surface area of informal settlements, demonstrating the overwhelming expansion that had taken place on agricultural land and the absence of organic expansion to adjacent desert land.

Throughout the decades, this informal urban boom has caused a number of small and medium-sized construction enterprises to thrive. They have supplied over two-thirds of Egypt's total housing units and filled the niche of supplying relatively cheap apartments that was left when the larger public and private developers preferred to address the demands of higher-income brackets. However, this is quite different from the general question of accessing land for productive uses; the predominant, if not exclusive, use of urbanized agricultural land was for housing purposes rather than as production sites for manufacturing or services.[3] For those producers, access to land remains highly restrained and far too costly.

In a few cases, informal land was used for productive purposes; however, this has usually been on a very small scale and often for household enterprises that operated on the fringes of informal housing. For instance, I have come across several workshops in the Zabālīn slum area in Cairo where garbage recycling takes place in small workshops and warehouses annexed to informal houses (Fahmi, 2005, 158). The workshops were established in total breach of industrial and environmental safety rules and thus would never be granted permits by respective authorities; nevertheless, they were not closed or removed, as the law requires, despite the health and safety hazards they posed. Workshop owners (and residents of the slum area) reported that local authorities periodically collected fines for operating such workshops without permits, but they never closed them down. While these fines were official, they were often collected alongside other informal payments, such as bribes and gifts to policemen and local officials.

However, this case aside, organic expansion on adjacent agricultural land did not present a solution to the inaccessibility of land for SSEs (or for housing purposes for the general population). There was only so much agricultural land to build on. According to el-Kadi (2009, p60–61), by 1996, the total surface area of informal settlements (again, predominantly built on agricultural land with desert spots constituting less than 10 percent of the total) was 30,625 feddans in Greater Cairo (around 31,784 acres). This area hosted a staggering 6.9 million inhabitants in 1996, growing into 8.9 million by 2006. Overcrowding is quite evident, and the high cost of acquiring land within the city has been a logical consequence. Such developments may stand to explain the difficulties that SSE owners have reported regarding access to land as a major barrier to growth.

Small-Scale Establishments as Collateral Damage

The high artificial administrative and legal barriers that were set to separate desert plots from populated urban and rural areas stifled access to land for SSEs within and outside the zimām. This paradoxical outcome occurred despite the generous incentives provided by the state in the form of heavily subsidized property to investors, final consumers, and even SSEs as a means to encourage the resettlement of economic activities from the overcrowded Nile valley and delta (World Bank, 2006, 1:23).

On the supply side, NUCA and other sectoral land managers had a wide array of pricing mechanisms at their disposal through which they could pursue their mission. These ranged from administrative pricing by technical committees and extended periods of usufruct to allocation by decree based on preferential agreement and market-based sale in auction. Despite all this, prices of developed desert land around major cities, particularly Cairo, continued to increase, even igniting competition with the much more limited supply of land inside the zimām. The final outcome was a general increase in prices, causing even more crowding in the already overpopulated urban centers. However, this was more than a mere policy bias; it had been ingrained in the governing institutional and regulatory framework with its centralized, supply-driven, and strictly hierarchical structures.

Since their inception in the 1970s, land-managing organizations had missions that bore evident conflicts of interest. The Ministry of Housing and Reconstruction, and NUCA as of 1979, were assigned the developmental mission of planning and managing the economic uses of desert land for a better distribution of the population. But they were also expected to maximize the direct economic returns from such desert land for the state or other groups or agencies formally or informally tied to it, ranging from public sector developers to cooperatives representing corporatist groups of state employees, such as the police, judiciary, journalists, engineers, and military officers.

Thus, NUCA ended up as a planner and regulator on the one hand, and a developer and investor on the other. Whereas the first pair of tasks required supplying adequate infrastructure to desert land at the cheapest price possible in order to encourage socioeconomic activities, the second pair entailed raising the prices of the lands they owned and developed. By the time of infitāḥ, desert land was hoped to attract foreign, especially Arab, investment from the General Cooperation Council (GCC) countries in real estate. This proved a critical juncture, as it set incentives for major market actors to raise the prices of desert land in order to maximize direct returns as opposed to keeping these prices as low as possible to realize the original mission of conquering the desert.

This regulatory framework set the incentives for all market actors in subsequent decades—primarily the state as the landowner and occasional developer, as well as the developers themselves (foreign and Egyptian, including public and private sector) and final consumers. The path was inaugurated under al-Sadāt with the decision to build luxury summer resorts on the northwestern coast of Egypt (el-Kadi, 2009, 49), with NUCA directly building its first resort, Marāqya, on the northern Mediterranean coast in 1980 (el-Kadi, 2009, 44). That example was followed by a number of other NUCA-owned resorts in the 1980s and 1990s, "catering to both Egypt's rising middle classes and its various elites" (Sims, 2015, 192).

The model of planner-regulator-developer that NUCA laid out was generalized to the new expanding urban communities in the late 1970s and throughout the 1980s and 1990s around Egypt's large cities, especially Cairo. In the late 1990s, NUCA started partnering with large, private sector developers in the establishment of gated communities and luxury compounds. In these deals, NUCA allocated desert land plots to developers at very low prices in return for a commitment from the developer to provide the required infrastructure and utilities. NUCA would hold a percentage of the housing units to sell later when the value would have risen considerably (World Bank, 2006, 2:60; Adly, 2011, 8–9).

As early as the mid-1990s, Land Law No. 96 of 1995 allowed state agencies to sell the plots they owned as private land. This allowed many public agencies to become de facto urban investors and developers that could use their originally publicly allocated land for commercial purposes with the aim of attaining the highest price possible in the land market (Shawkat, 2012, 211). This began with the appointment of Moḥamed Ibrāhīm Soleimān as minister of housing in 1993 (through 2005). As Sims (2015, 128) asserts, under Soleimān, "Large private real-estate developers became the main agents of progress, enhanced by an extremely friendly relationship with NUCA." Soleiman's tenure has since been tied to the emergence of New Cairo (al-Qāhira al-jadīda) in the mid-1990s, which has developed into a gigantic urban settlement, equal roughly to the total surface area of all the new cities that preceded it (World Bank, 2006, 2:60; Sims, 2015, 130).

Like other new cities, New Cairo had been planned to offer low-cost housing for the urban poor in Egypt's overcrowded capital city. However, this changed as of the mid-1990s when the state began to target the establishment of high-income and luxury compounds and gated communities. State policies started to favor large, private businesses in land allocation, often through opaque and highly corrupt dealings (Mitchell, 1999; Sfakianakis, 2004; Adly, 2012b; Mitchell, 1999), along with a heightened appetite by big Egyptian investors to grab land for speculation.

The maximization of the value of desert land also led to the creation of intermediaries who used privileged political and social ties, as well as insider information in the state bureaucracy, to appropriate portions of the rent resulting from higher speculative prices. The arbitrary inclusion of desert plots into New Cairo manipulated land prices and granted higher values for some plots over others based on insider information regarding urban plans for future development (Shawkat, 2014). Furthermore, there is anecdotal evidence that such practices were not confined to cronies and rent seekers but also emanated from bureaucratic bodies as a whole (Barayez, 2016).

With desert land to the east and west of Cairo catering explicitly to high-income groups, the value of land began to rise considerably. Although NUCA continued to offer desert land at subsidized rates through the 1990s in the hope of attracting investments and residents, the premiums were often captured by intermediaries. A change in pricing mechanisms was looming as the government became eager to catch these rents, or a portion of them, through the adoption of more market-oriented (and sometimes openly speculative) pricing mechanisms. By the early 2000s, NUCA had sold a number of land plots at auction. The most famous of these, held in 2004, tripled the final land price from the original allocation price (World Bank, 2006, vol. 1). Here, the aim was to increase state revenues and cut out the middle people and speculators.

These sharp increases in land prices did not make things much better for SSEs that now faced high prices in addition to bureaucratic hurdles. Indeed, according to the World Bank report on land in Egypt (2006, 1:iv), "Access to land and the price of land represent the only constraints that firms perceive to have worsened in a climate of reform."

ONCE AGAIN, MARKET-BASED EXCLUSION

With the advent of the Nazīf cabinet (2004–2011), desert land management took a clear market-oriented turn in terms of pricing policies. In 2007, Nazīf issued Decree No. 350 that allowed investment companies to buy land through public auction. These measures reportedly led to a 130 percent increase in land prices in new urban centers like New Cairo, as well as the new industrial cities like the Sixth of October (Shawkat, 2012, 214). In turn, the new cabinet had an unmistakable bias toward large, private developers, Egyptian as well as Arab, mainly from the GCC countries. The cabinet also suffered from a considerable conflict of interest as one of the largest private developers, Aḥmed al-Maghrabi, sat as the chair of the Ministry of Housing and NUCA head between 2007 and 2011. Rent networks were reconfigured accordingly. Ironically, there was a move toward relatively more transparent and market-based pricing mechanisms with the declared intention of cutting out intermediaries in favor of larger revenues accruing directly to NUCA or the state Treasury.

Making pricing more market based did not change the inherent bias against SSEs; the institutional and regulatory framework remained strongly skewed in favor of market actors with large initial and acquired capital. Ultimately, what the auctions did was raise prices to new heights, leading to even more speculation and thus indirectly exacerbating the problem of access to land inside the zimām. Similar to the case of bank finance after the two reform rounds of 2004 to 2012, this meant that increasing market orientation could be just as exclusionary to the majority of economic actors. Ultimately, the institutional biases and antidevelopmental incentives remained as they always were, with the only possible positive aspect of this market reorientation deriving from the fact that noncrony large capital was now provided a level playing field, especially to foreign investors. This was of little consequence to those excluded from the system altogether like SSEs.

While there is ample evidence that the business elites of the late Mubārak era were self-serving (Mitchell, 1999; Adly, 2012b; Roccu, 2013; el-Tarouty, 2016), particularly in the case of large plots of desert land in prime locations to the east and west of Cairo being reserved for a handful of politically connected developers, how this land access was distributed is but a detail in a much larger and more complex story. There was indeed a larger institutional and policy bias toward large businesses at the expense of SSEs and, more generally, against local communities in populated areas.

The big private developers of Mubārak's later years were market actors, and not mere intermediaries who confined their activities to speculation (i.e., rent seekers and middle people). They supplied large numbers of housing units, while the construction and real estate sectors acted as the locomotive of growth for many feeding industries in the 2000s like cement, iron and steel, aluminum, and glass. In turn, they operated within an institutional framework that was geared toward high-income groups and required heavy capital investment. This supply, or even oversupply, of luxury units built on desert land hardly contributed to solving Egypt's housing problem.

Thus, the institutional framework that created and perpetuated this bias did not serve a narrow coalition of rent seekers or state captors; rather, it tied land uses to a broad socioeconomic constituency that had vested interests in maintaining the centralized and hierarchical institutional order. These included domestic, foreign, and Arab private capital, as well as large segments of middle-class households and high-income savers and investors. Hence, it cannot simply be reduced to a story about bad management, rent seeking, corruption, and cronyism; policies have also included some notion of the public good (the exodus from the narrow valley and delta; the building of new communities; reclaiming desert land for cultivation, industrial cities, and touristic centers) with a view toward growth and development. State and private sector interactions indeed happened within this context, and thus the true tragedy lies in the fact that the notion of the public good and the coalition of interests aligned with the institutions governing land use was conducive to the development of cleft capitalism.

In this regulatory framework, private (and, earlier, public sector) developers, as well as foreign companies (and military-affiliated developers after 2013), stood in the middle between the state and final consumers/investors. Developers received desert land designated for real estate development by NUCA. From there, the developers built compounds, apartments, and villas and sold them to upper- and upper-middle-class consumers looking not only for housing units but also seeking safe investments in the face of chronically high inflation. The rising land prices served a relatively broad social constituency that depended on investments for their families. For example, they have been able to secure housing for their adult children or indirectly benefit by investing their savings in real estate property.

In sum, the regulatory framework governing desert land use throughout the past four decades has become the site for the socioeconomic reproduction of a sizable stratum of the middle classes in Egypt. Herein lies its resilience in the face of its now well-corroborated social and economic dysfunction.

Industrial Parks: Unrealistically Affordable

The chapter thus far has linked the institutional arrangements that governed desert land use with the artificial land scarcity that faces SSEs. However, there remains a more specific issue in this regard. The plans for new communities and cities included the establishment of large industrial cities and special zones and parks in developed desert areas, usually with below-market land prices and subsidized infrastructure. The original idea was to move polluting industries from overpopulated cities, with major implications for Cairo given the big concentration of industries in it, to the desert while establishing new, integrated communities where people could live and work away from the Nile valley and delta. The law empowered the Council of Ministers to issue a decree banning all new industrial activities in the existing cities. In 1983, Cairo was declared closed to new industries, and plans were set to move them to the new urban communities surrounding the city (World Bank, 2006, 2:2). The state plans failed to materialize, however. The fact that these small enterprises needed to be close to their local markets, labor pools, social networks, and both forward and backward linkages (i.e., baladi capitalism) was simply ignored. "Supply-side thinking again trumped all else" (Sims, 2015, 228).

SSEs continued to operate within the city even in the face of higher informal costs, primarily in the form of paying bribes and fines to local officials. As Elyachar (2005, 42) found in her fieldwork, "Working without a license was a small expense, in comparison to moving out to the desolate reaches of the desert, far from any customers." Again, this stands as an additional illustration that SSEs' access to desert land could occur only in a broader context of the organic urban expansion of neighborhoods into geographically proximate desert areas. However, this could not be so because small-scale establishments had no intermediate institutional channels that could have linked them to state land-managing agencies.

Not only was there a lack of formal intermediate institutions; they were also missing informally because patronage networks were just as centralized and hierarchical. Patron-client relationships have served as intermediate channels and mechanisms for the capitalization of SSEs in certain contexts, particularly in Asia. This often took place through local governments, often mediated by party networks. However, for localized patronage to work, and hence grant SSEs access to state-owned land, the ownership and management of such assets must be in the hands of local governments rather than be overly centralized and hierarchical. In Egypt, local governments, in the form of governorates, were denied almost all access to owning or managing the desert land plots adjacent to them and to which their populations could have organically expanded. Undoubtedly governorates in Egypt have notoriously lacked administrative competence and integrity in the management of their assets; however, even by corrupt and cronyistic practices, they may have served partly as intermediaries for local entrepreneurial communities in a similar manner to the regional and municipal governments in China that enjoyed access to physical and financial resources under Deng Xiao Ping's fiscal federalism.

In contrast, Egyptian desert land was made inaccessible to local governorates and local residents alike as it was subjected to NUCA's mandate (Sims, 2015, 231). As the World Bank noted, "All industrial zones established in areas beyond 2km from the cordon of a city require that NUCA transferred the land to the governorate in whose jurisdiction the site is found" (World Bank, 2006, 2:2). As expected, NUCA lacked the intermediate institutional capacities or the social and political local connectedness to develop plans in accordance with existing SSEs. Most of the desert land that seemed to have developed any semblance of economic value was systematically taken from local governorates and handed over to the centralized sectoral agencies—GARPAD, NUCA, TDA and, later, GAID. In turn, governorates in Egypt have been generally denied any credible chance of developing their own local financial resources and have relied heavily on the central government to cover their recurrent expenditure (Soliman, 2006, 111).

Moreover, the overly centralized nature of NUCA made it quite costly, if not impossible, to get access to reliable information regarding the availability of land and the quality and exact locations of the developed plots. As with housing and construction, this translated practically into an institutional bias to large capital that retained the political connections or sheer economic weight to tweak the rigid supply-driven plans of NUCA, and then GAID, to which the mandate over industrial land management was passed in 2005. These asymmetries of information and the discrepancies in the land management system have led to the creation of middle people who often control, or de facto own, the parcels of land allocated to small and microenterprises in new industrial zones and sublet them to end users at higher costs (Wahba, 2013; Shawkat, 2014).

Due to the high locational costs, subsidized desert land has not seemed desirable for SSE owners (Elyachar, 2005; Sims, 2015). According to Article 10 of Law No. 141 of 2004 on small enterprises, it was decided that 10 percent of all public land available for investment would be allocated to small enterprises at subsidized rates. Article 11 stipulated that land prices were to be decided on an administrative basis and set at a below-market rate within the limits of the cost of extending public utilities to the plot of land. There is little evidence that these articles have been observed by the respective state agencies, especially given that the law left the terms of land allocation, price collection, and ownership transfer to the discretion of the allocating agency. Indeed, it is odd that the law provided no incentives to small enterprises in terms of accessing land within cities that were suitable to their markets and their mode of operation.

Nevertheless, the institutional bias against the majority of SSEs and low-income dwellers, urban and rural, persisted as the incentives of all major actors were geared toward overvaluing land prices. The losers were the ones never included in the coalition at any phase and were trapped in the cities and villages that were denied any organic expansion into the adjacent, uninhabited, and virtually subsidized desert land. Ultimately, they were left to figure out their livelihoods through the informal settlement of private agricultural land; however, land for productive purposes was neither available nor affordable.

This situation has derived from the fact that the broad base of private sector enterprises was never party to the political process that created market actors. This applied to both financial and physical capital and resulted in the undercapitalization that has underscored the institutional condition of cleft capitalism, which denotes the development of parallel and polymorphic subsystems with uneven access to capital. The following two chapters explore two of these subsystems in detail: baladi and dandy capitalism. Largely invisible to existing accounts of Egypt's economic sphere, particular diagnoses of its ills (which generally focus on of crony capitalism), these two subsystems exhibit the underlying vibrancy, and entrepreneurial potential, that has been stifled by the institutional factors we have explored. By painting a vivid picture of how these constraints act on Egyptian enterprises, as well as the limited ways in which they are overcome, we gain a clearer picture of Egypt's actual economy and the institutional filters that maintain its cleft state.

Chapter Eight

BALADI CAPITALISM

AFFECTIVE CAPITAL

Egypt's path toward market making generated a cleft order where the subsystems of baladi, dandy, and crony capitalisms coevolved. This chapter focuses on baladi capitalism, providing a detailed anatomy of its structures and operations in light of extensive fieldwork, surveys of small-scale establishments (SSEs), and numerous interviews conducted in Egypt in mid-2013.

The defining feature of baladi capitalism is the low degree of differentiation between the social and the economic. A low degree implies that the social life of an individual or group—family, friends, neighbors, community, and so on—is deeply intertwined with that person's economic activity. Low differentiation makes most transactions rooted in private knowledge and interpersonal trust; hence, it is directly contingent on the concrete social identity of the respective SSE owners and managers.

Generally, SSEs are socially embedded and less economically differentiated, a trait that has been observed throughout the world (Beckhard and Dyer, 1983; Zimmer and Aldrich, 1987). Indeed, SSEs typically rely on trust, group solidarity, and emotional commitment in order to accumulate financial and human capital, conduct economic transactions, minimize the risk of opportunism, access information, and explore markets (Granovetter, 1985; Shapiro, 1987; Grayson, 2007, 65). This trust mitigates risk and uncertainty (Moorman,

Zaltman, and Deshpande, 1992; Halpern, 1994; Mayer, Davis, and Schoorman, 1995; Das and Teng, 1998; Soule, 1998; Wicks, Berman, and Jones, 1999).

Social networks, usually consisting of family and friends, serve to reduce the asymmetries of information between parties. Such networks are quite prevalent in the Global South due to the weakness of formal contract enforcement and the high risks associated with impersonal transactions. From an analytical view, networks of family and friends are labeled "affective capital": interpersonal affection and the intrinsic and mutual concern over well-being are used to create, exchange, and distribute economic value (Dasgupta, 2000, 78). This concept draws heavily from Pierre Bourdieu's definition of *social capital* as "the sum of resources, actual or virtual, that accrue to an individual or group by virtue of possessing a durable network of more or less institutionalized relationships of mutual acquaintance and recognition" (Bourdieu and Nice, 1980, 2; see also Nahapiet and Ghoshal, 1998; Lin, 1999).

Affective capital accrues from two main sources: consanguinity, which includes the nuclear family next to other forms of kinship (e.g., an urban extended family), and nonconsanguine relations, which can be grouped under the many forms and degrees of friendship. The two are based on intense interpersonal knowledge that extends over long periods of time in ways that engender mutual trust and belief in goodwill (Halpern, 1994; Montgomery, 1998).

Family

The sociological and anthropological literature has extensively addressed the family in the Middle East (Joseph, 1999; Fargues, 2001; Haney and Pollard, 2003; Pollard, 2005)—for example: "The family serves as an economic and political institution, as much as a social or affective one, and individuals maintain very close ties with their relatives throughout their lives. Individuals both compete for family resources and/or cooperate to use the family to further collective interests. Family has a pervasive role in allocating and distributing resources, in regulating morality and arbitrating conflict" (Singerman and Hoodfar, 1996, 146). Indeed, the reemergence of the Egyptian private sector after infitāḥ relied heavily on preexisting family structures and networks. Hansen (1991, 31) noted about the formative period that "family connection and wealth made a strong comeback."

The central role of family in mediating economic and political relations between entrepreneurs and both markets and the state has been the result of the continuous stabilization of nuclear family relations in Egypt through the twentieth century (Fargues, 2001, 247; Pagès-El Karoui, 2012, 6). "Throughout the [Arab] region, marriages are much more stable than in Europe; for example, the divorce rate per 100 marriages decreased in Egypt from 26 to 18 from 1940 to 1995" (Conte and Walentowitz, 2009, 226). Hence, the prevalent structure has increasingly become the nuclear family, with a consistent and constant decline in women's fertility rate since the 1960s (al-Ḥūty, 2015).[1] This made nuclear families more efficient and tightly knit than before, and thus potentially stronger centers for private accumulation and small-scale business operation, organization, and exchange. Nuclear families could also capitalize on patrilineal or matrilineal ties with other related nuclear families, creating a dense web of paternal and maternal uncles, aunts, cousins, and second cousins (Conte and Walentowitz, 2009, 228).

The form of primarily urban social relations— exemplified not only in family but also in gender, state-society relations, the market, religious communities, and neighborhoods, among others—have by and large been the product of top-down modernization since the nineteenth century. Top-down reforms and the progressive integration of Egypt's economy into the European division of labor through debt, military conquest, foreign capital relations, and trade all contributed to the destruction, or at least displacement, of the prevailing social relations and structures that could be labeled traditional according to modernization theory (Pagès-El Karoui, 2012, 2).

Earlier forms of tribes or clans, sects, guilds, Sufi orders, neighborhood associations (*ḥāra*) and other institutionalized forms of nonstate collectivized actors have either withered away or become too ceremonial to perform any significant economic role.[2] This was especially the result of urbanization in the twentieth century, favored a direct relationship between the state and its subjects and citizens (Hourani, 1981, 40; Ayubi, 1995, 100; Menza, 2012, 35). According to Issawi (1947, 95), "The medieval guilds may be said to have been completely dissolved at the beginning of the British occupation. For some ten years, no organization rose to take their place, but after 1890 unions began to be formed, mainly on the lines of friendly societies among the better-paid workers." Thus, no intermediary institutions have existed between the state as a centralized bureaucratic authority and the individual since independence, with the exception of the nuclear family and informal networks of relatives, friends, and neighbors (Joseph, 2000; Haney and Pollard, 2003; Pollard, 2005).

Friendship

In contrast to family, friendship ties are typically less recognized in any formal or legal sense and are thus held to be more flexible and voluntary (Silver, 1990). Nonetheless, the survey I conducted in 2013 on Egyptian SSEs suggests that friendship plays a relatively significant role as a socioeconomic institution, creating the space for trust-based economic exchange and joint activity. These friendship ties usually develop through common experience in schooling or university education, professional experience, past military service, and neighborhood ties. Furthermore, tight friendships often lead to the fraternization of friends who become increasingly considered as blood brothers despite not being born of the same mother. Indeed, the Arab proverb holds: *rubba akhin lakka lam talidhu ommuk* (*Best friends are the siblings that one's mother did not give birth to*).

These social networks on which SSEs rely go beyond the functionalism of transaction cost theory (Ouchi, 1980; Doney and Cannon, 1997); they are not purposefully formed in order to lower transaction costs or provide information or inputs at below-market rates. Rather, they are formed prior to and, on many occasions, independent of their potential economic uses. They thus primarily serve the social, personal, and affective ends of their members, as one does not make friends or have relatives in order to start a business. These latter economic uses can be taken as the latent functions of interpersonal relations and affective capital (Merton, 1968, 117). Economic transactions and access to human, financial, and physical resources through interpersonal relations are manifestations of common interests and instances through which mutual trust and concern with mutual well-being are reproduced among many other social transactions.

Moreover, as economically functional as affective capital could be, it certainly carries some of the many tensions inherent in economic exchange (Elyachar, 2005, 130). Because both family and friendship relations are socially constructed, they can become strained and dissolve if conflicts over the distribution and allocation of resources overwhelm the mechanisms of cooperation or undermine feelings of mutual trust and loyalty (Frenzen and Davis, 1990; Beatty et al., 1996;Heide and Wathne, 2006).

A much-cited example is the succession process of family-owned enterprises, which is not always smooth despite presumed strong family ties and collective solidarity (de Vries, 1993; Handler, 1994; Harveston et al., 1997; Davis and Harveston, 1998; Miller, Steier, and Le Breton-Miller, 2003; Sharma, Chrisman, and Chua, 2003). There are ample anecdotes regarding siblings and friends who dissolve partnerships or otherwise refrain from entering them so as to avoid endangering their social relationship. In addition, there exist a number of cases of succession fights between relatives and siblings that end up in court as they overwhelm the dispute resolution mechanisms of family structures. For instance, a study by the Egyptian Ministry of Justice in 2010 (cited in Naṣr, 2017) revealed an increase in succession-related disputes before the courts, from 119,000 in 2006 to 121,000 in 2007 and 144,000 in 2009. These figures are by no means insignificant, especially if they are calculated as a percentage of the rather limited number of wealth-holding families in which succession is worth fighting over in a country that is generally poor. In a nutshell, trust may and does fail (Granovetter, 1985; Shapiro, 1987; Kramer, Brewer, and Hanna, 1996).

Social relations can make access to economic opportunities possible, however imperfectly, but they make it impossible for those who are socially excluded. The economic sphere is thus an extension of the social—tensions, conflicts, and all. Hence, there is little reason to romanticize baladi capitalism as something "natural," "authentic," or as an arrangement spared from tension over the allocation of resources. It is socially constructed and historically constituted and is rife with power asymmetries.

This chapter explores the creative ways in which small-scale establishments overcome the trust barriers endemic to all economic transactions, formal and informal. It outlines the many ways social relations are put to work for economic transactions, from the accumulation and exchange of financial and human capital, the sharing and exchange of information, to the social mechanisms of trust and enforcement. Ultimately this vibrant intersection of the social and economic in Egypt's private sector reveals no genetic predisposition against capitalist activities; rather, the broad base of Egyptian SSEs has suffered from systemic undercapitalization that has precluded their growth and expansion.

ENTERPRISE AS A SOCIAL UNIT: "KNOWING PEOPLE IS A TREASURE"

Love, Money, and Self-Accumulation

Networks of family and friends provide the opportunity to convert affective capital into financial and human capital.[3] Because both forms of capital are considered essential for the growth of SSEs in Egypt as well as elsewhere in the world (Stiglitz, 1994, 207), these social relations serve as channels for mobilizing private savings or securing interest-free credit directly from family and friends (Singerman and Hoodfar, 1996, 39; Harders, 2003, 207) or by acquiring the necessary guarantees and collateral to access bank loans (Mohieldin and Wright, 2000). In addition, they enable the acquisition of essential human capital such as managerial and technical skills

To look at this in terms of the life span of an enterprise, in the start-up phase, affective capital essentially substitutes for financial markets, including formal banking, as money provision becomes related to one's access to social networks. A massive 94 percent of surveyed enterprises reported relying on private savings to raise their start-up capital, followed by 50 and 30 percent who depended on funds from family and friends, respectively.[4] Table 8.1 shows that private savings stood at an average of 63 percent of the reported start-up capital composition.

It is worth noting that sole proprietorships were largely cut off from channels of financing by family and friends' financing in this initial start-up phase. This was reflected by their complete dependence on private—or individual—savings and business profits at all phases (Figure 8.1). This highlights the fact that private social capital is unequally distributed in society, which generally contributes to social and economic inequality (Endress, 2004, 71).

Networks of friends and family prove important not only through shares in enterprise capital. They also rank first with regard to accessing credit for micro and small enterprises. Indeed, family- and nonfamily-owned enterprises reported securing sizable percentages of their start-up capital through borrowing from family and friends.

Beyond the start-up phase and into the later stages of business operations, finance from family and friends was reported to also be of utmost importance. In the survey, one-third of respondents (35 percent) noted that credit from family and friends was a source of financing. If credit from family and friends was added to the sale of private and family assets as a means for financing, the total number of reporting respondents would approach 53 percent.

Source of Finance	*Average Percentage of Start-Up Capital Reported by Respondents*	*Percentage of Respondents Using Each Source of Finance*
Private savings	63	94
Funds from family	17	50
Funds from friends	10	30
Credit from banks or associations	5	17
Other	5	7

TABLE 8.1. Sources of Finance at the Start-Up Phase as Reported by Entrepreneurs (Percentage of Respondents) .
Source: Adly and Khatib (2014, 81). Reprinted with permission.

Entrepreneurial Skill Acquisition

The importance of private social capital in providing access to financial capital is supplemented by its role in acquiring human capital—the basic managerial and technical skills required to run a business. Indeed, survey results indicate that networks of family and friends have largely been the main source of skill acquisition in SSEs. While respondents overwhelmingly expressed the need for accounting, marketing, managerial, and financial skills, 60 percent noted that the main source of such skill acquisition was family relations, followed by apprenticeship and informal ties. In contrast, formal institutions such as governmental agencies, including training and education facilities, were reported to have been accessed by only 7 percent of the respondents. Business and developmental associations were mentioned by 21 percent. This picture is similar to Elyachar's (2005, 130–132) study of workshops in two Cairene popular neighborhoods where mastery, skills, and knowledge were passed through social channels of kin and as-if-kin apprenticeships.

In Egypt, these socialized channels of entrepreneurial skill transfer and acquisition seem to play a significant role across sectors, firm size, and ownership categories. Within family-owned businesses, family ties were the most important (82 percent). Sole proprietorships and nonfamily partnerships depended

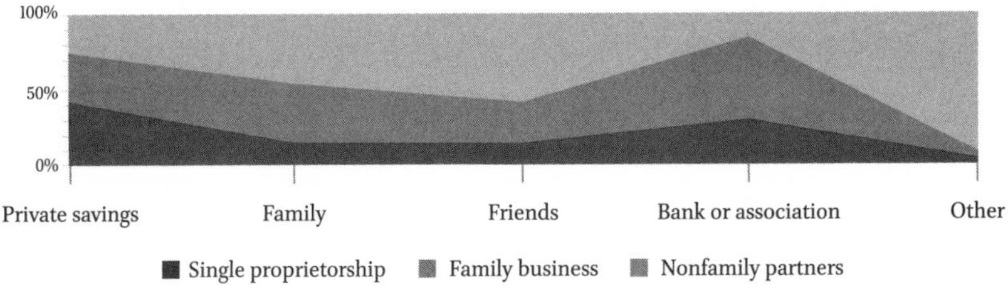

FIGURE 8.1. Start-Up Capital Sources by Ownership Structure as Reported by Entrepreneurs (Percentage of Respondents).
Source: Adly and Khatib (2014, 91). Reprinted with permission.

more on apprenticeships and mentorship channels. Nonetheless, family ties remained important for these nonfamily-owned enterprises: almost one-third of such entrepreneurs held them to be the main source of skill acquisition.

Overall, private social capital is the most significant factor in enabling small-scale establishments to enter and survive in the market, and it therefore represents a clear instance of the low degree of differentiation between the private social and economic. However, it is worth mentioning that larger and older enterprises show a tendency toward more differentiation between their social and economic identities, functions, and finances.

INTERBUSINESS TRANSACTIONS

Socialized Market Transactions

As much as social networks and interpersonal trust may lower transaction costs, mainstream neoclassical institutionalism regards them as at best suboptimal substitutes for functioning property rights and the rule of law. Beyond a certain point, they even become a strain on potential growth and expansion as the modern market is, after all, based on the possibility of anonymous or impersonal exchange (Greif, 2006), while transactions dependent on social ties and personalized knowledge run the risk of being overembedded (Uzzi, 1997) or falling captive to overly "strong ties" (Granovetter, 1973). This bars enterprises from accessing resources or information about markets and may limit them to suboptimal conditions of exchange wherein their horizon of potential customers and suppliers is constrained by their immediate social circle (François, 2004, 4).

Despite the logical validity of this transaction costs argument, it is not as strong sociologically. Practically, as a mode of governance that comprises socially embedded and family and friends' network-enabled transactions, community does not completely replace market mechanisms all the time. The two modes of governance often coexist, interact, and co-constitute each other. The different mixtures or modes of articulation between the two may explain the variety of socialized transactions in developing and developed economies wherein social ties continue to play a significant role in the production and distribution processes.

In fact, network capitalism and socially embedded practices in many Asian countries have led to vibrant private sectors capable of growing and competing nationally and internationally despite the absence of strong formal institutions (Boisot and Child, 1996; Park and Luo, 2001; Luo, 2003; Demir, Acar, and Toprak, 2004; Wu and Leung, 2005). In addition, they paved the way for the rise of more impersonal market transactions at following stages, growing out of their initial social embeddedness, in the absence of reliable formal rule of law and property rights all the same.

Building economic exchange on social relations is a mode of governance that is different from market and hierarchy (Adler, 2001). In the tradition of Karl Polanyi, Adler defined *community* as extended social networks of firms, entrepreneurs, and managers. Whereas markets depend on price signals and hierarchies on authority, community works through trust as a central mechanism. This is how transaction cost is kept low, opportunism is limited, and information flows are secured. In addition to trust as a central mechanism of self-enforcement, other social mechanisms of enforcement that involve nonstate organized sanctioning that deters actors from defecting (Walker, Kogut, and Shan, 1997).

In light of these successful and more competitive Asian cases, it is safe to state that the prevalence of socialized transactions does not in and of itself denote exceptionally negative, precapitalist, or premodern traits in regard to Egypt's baladi capitalism. Neither does it fully explain the weak capacity of small-scale establishments to grow and expand—and thus the subsequent structural features of the missing-middle syndrome. The real question is not how socialized transactions have been inherently anemic to market making but rather why, in the case of Egypt, they have not paved the way for further capitalist development as in East and Southeast Asia.

Familiarized Markets

Survey results suggest that socialized and personalized transactions could contribute to the rise and constitution of a market since infitāḥ, defined as the space where price-driven exchange occurs. However, they could not substitute perfectly for the missing ingredient of access to capital that could propel Egypt's baladi capitalist subsystem into a robust and integrated private sector. This articulation between community and market as two modes of economic governance creates what I call a familiarized market. In such a market, price signals are indeed considered in any decision for exchange, while community networks are used to navigate markets, serving as a social interface to deal with parties lying beyond immediate high-trust circles (Stiglitz, 1994, 85).

This derives from the fact that membership in social networks of extended family, friendship, and community (e.g., religious denominations, common geographical origin, or ethnic affinity) helps in accessing information, finance, land, and skilled labor through exchange on the market. Thus, networks of family and friends work in tandem with market forces. For instance, social networks may provide access to cheap credit, skilled and semiskilled labor, and even informal or below-market-rate access to land (e.g., shops, offices, and storage houses). They also perform the tasks of information collection, verification, and circulation in a way that may, and often does, provide privileged access to private tacit information that is confined to members of the social network (Doney and Cannon, 1997, 610; Grayson, 2007, 65).

This is demonstrated in product markets, which are more often than not competitive given the low-capital and low-skill requirements for entry in many of the sectors where SSEs usually operate (Zimmer and Aldrich, 1987). Small-scale establishments often combine both social and economic transaction modes of governance at once; for instance, narrow socialized relations often substitute for financial markets in providing for credit while coexisting with less personalized and more price-oriented arrangements with suppliers and clients. Similarly, interpersonal networks can be used to ease access to skilled and semiskilled labor for enterprises that deal with other actors on a market basis. Hence, price signals are important and cannot be dismissed, even in such a socially embedded setting.

The survey indicates that the movement toward familiarized market transactions is associated with the size of doing business, defined here in terms of working capital and turnover.[5] Intuitively, this often implies a wider circle of suppliers and customers as enterprises grow, usually in accordance with more sensitivity to price signals. However, the causation here is not very clear. Whether more impersonalized transactions are the source or the result of larger business size must be separately examined, though there is likely some interplay or coevolution at play when enterprises enter a virtuous cycle conducive to growth. This dynamic harmonizes with the earlier observation from the survey that a higher degree of relative differentiation between the social and economic functions of SSEs gradually emerges as firms grow older and develop larger turnover and capital.

Ultimately social relations may either substitute for the market completely or otherwise serve as an interface for market actors to gather and verify information, as well as limit transaction costs and the risks of opportunism. As the survey results suggest, the degree of the former versus the latter depends on the enterprise turnover. Figure 8.2 demonstrates the various combinations between the two modes of governance. It suggests that the size of the enterprises, expressed in terms of their capital, employment, and turnover, is the decisive factor that determines a more market-oriented mode of articulation between community and market (see Figure 3.1). This underlines the essential argument of the book that undercapitalization, the main cause as well as effect, of cleft capitalism, has been and remains the principal problem plaguing the broad base of private enterprises in Egypt.

Based on Figure 8.2, community systematically replaces market mechanisms. Here, social networks constitute the space for exchange, while price matters little—if at all. Exchange takes place on the basis of trust, mutual care for the well-being of the different parties in the transaction, solidarity with other group members, and even a sense of group belonging that overrides the pecuniary interest of the individual (Halpern, 1994, 661). Anecdotally, there are indeed instances where business decisions appear based on social considerations—*yenaffa'ḥad*, meaning to conduct business with someone with the sole aim of benefiting that person, usually out of social solidarity or altruism along family or communal lines.

Whereas one extreme indicates oversocialization, the other shows disembeddedness or undersocialization of market actors. While this latter mode may not be possible in many economies in the Global South due to weak contract

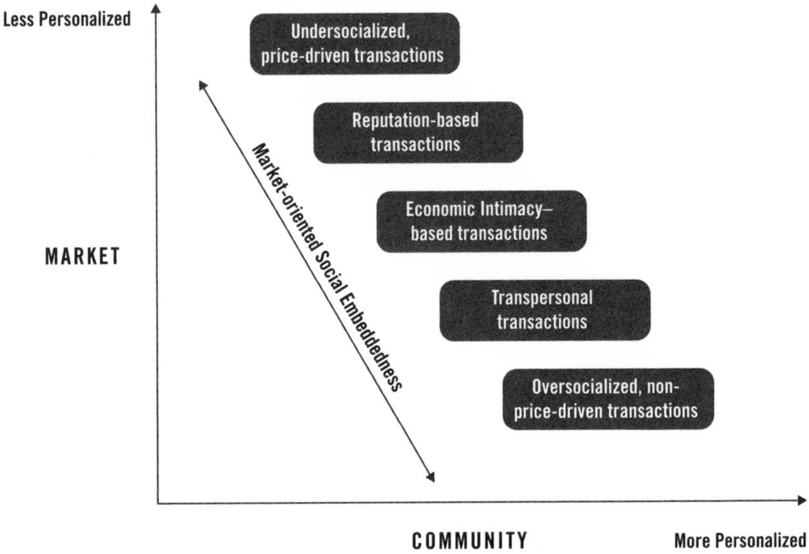

FIGURE 8.2. Modes of Articulation Between Market and Community.

enforcement and the absence of reliable public information, there do appear to be cases where "pure" impersonal market transactions take place, especially in transactions that involve spot deals with little anticipation of future or repeated interaction. This typically occurs in the context of low-cost and often low-quality final goods and services, such as street vendors or kiosks and food peddlers who sell cheap or perishable products. These transactions occur in a literal marketplace (*sūq*) suggesting the possibility for anonymous price-driven exchange.

Unskilled labor is another instance of anonymous price-driven exchange in the absence of functioning formal market institutions. In fact, low-skilled labor in Global South economies is often part of an informal and unregulated market where the forces of supply and demand determine wages (usually daily or weekly) and little long-term commitment exists between employees and employers. In these settings, labor turnover is normally quite high and skill requirements (as well as acquisition) are low, causing little distinction between laborers on the market (World Bank, 2014, 35).

However, once higher-quality requirements or longer-term commitments enter the picture, anonymous exchange becomes riskier and entails a potentially higher transaction cost. Thus, with the exception of large enterprises that manage to develop brands and trade names, many SSEs tend to combine the two modes of governance, community and market, in conducting business. These social ties do not completely or continuously replace market signals in these instances, but they serve as an interface between entrepreneurs and the markets (Stiglitz, 1994, 85), effectively rendering them market-making and market-mitigating mechanisms.

Transpersonal Transactions

Whereas personalized transactions are by definition built on the concrete social identity of their parties and hinge on preexisting ties, there are other social mechanisms through which mutual trust and personal experience may be transferred beyond the immediate parties by reference or recommendation (*tawṣiyya*) or intermediation (*wasṭa*). These are instances where affective capital can become transferable from one individual or group to another, stretching the possibility of conducting personally rooted transactions to people who may not know each other in person.

Sharabi (1988), in his well-acknowledged study, described wasṭa as a nepotistic dynamic with many negative social and economic repercussions. This is undoubtedly true in many instances, such as when personalized transactions constitute moments when the market mechanisms of price differentials and other competitive edges are sidelined in favor of nonmarket ones based on social networks and community ties. This can surely stand as a source of inefficiency; however, for small-scale establishments, such mechanisms serve as nonmarket alternatives in highly informalized economies with prohibitively high risk, high transaction costs, and little access to effective and cost-efficient legal enforcement. Transactions remain conditioned by some interpersonal relations at the core. However, they allow third (and more) parties to capitalize on such intimate personal relations without being direct parties to them.

Indeed, production inputs and skilled labor are often accessed through such transpersonal mechanisms as tawṣiyya and wasṭa. For instance, informal credit can be made available by the recommendation of a creditor, or employers may rely on references from trusted friends to acquire employees, especially in posts that require some special skill.

Accessing such semiskilled and skilled labor is also a salient example of the functions of familiarized markets. Although it requires reaching beyond the direct circles of friends and relatives, the labor market is often navigated using these informal and highly socialized networks. Employers as well as employees depend heavily on socialized information, assessment standards, and mechanisms of enforcement in accessing laborers, which again harmonizes with Hansen's (1991, 185) remark that "the labor market surrounding a particular small enterprise is very small (family, personal acquaintances, relatives of employees and so forth)."

Moreover, according to an International Labor Organization report (Barsoum et al., 2014, 33) regarding youth employment in Egypt, a massive 63.9 percent of young workers interviewed reported that "consulting informal networks of family and friends" was the primary factor in finding their current jobs, versus a mere 2.5 percent who mentioned labor offices and 3.7 percent who had formal interviews. A World Bank study (2014, 35) revealed similar figures, with 45 percent of surveyed workers reporting that they acquired their work through friends or relatives in the formal private sector and 46.4 percent of informal private sector workers stating the same.

These dynamics "may also imply structural problems in the labor market that go beyond simple favoritism. Reliance on preexisting connections between workers and employers can also be a response to information or contract based market failures" (Sahnoun et al., 2014, 36). Indeed, some evidence suggests that this is the case, especially with semiskilled and skilled labor, as the great mismatch between the supply and demand of skills renders formal certification an unreliable reference for recruiting the right people (Barsoum et al., 2014, 3).

Skills are often enterprise or sector specific and are informally obtained on the job rather than through formal education or training (Elyachar, 2005, 39). Furthermore, there is no formal referral system for sector- or enterprise-specific skills in Egypt and no reason to believe that most formal certifications issued by schools, institutes, and training centers can convey accurate information. This is true even with the traditional formal route of education attainment, as research reveals that dependence on personal connections hardly varies between different education levels—something one would expect if these formal avenues were indicating skill level correctly. According to the World Bank (2014, 36), dependence on personal connections to secure a job was reported by 42.3 percent of people who are illiterate compared to 48.3 percent for those with a below-secondary education, 48.1 percent of people with a secondary education, and 43.1 percent for those with a postsecondary education. Nor did these figures vary much with regard to age, with 48.3 percent of youth and 46.4 percent for young adults ranging from their early twenties to thirties reporting reliance on such networks. This suggests that although experience tends to increase with age, it is not indicated through any formal recommendation, reference, or certification but rather through social connections.

Economic Intimacy and Reputation

The second in-between mode of articulation between market and community is that of economic intimacy—solid, intimate, and concrete knowledge shared between business parties to transactions. Economic intimacy is similar to the concept of economic networks that tie the managers and owners of firms together (Uzzi, 1996) or between customers and sellers (Browne and Blank, 1997) or banks and certain firms or business groups. For instance, interfirm networks may maintain nonmarket relations (i.e., nonprice driven) with different managers or even different owners so long as they meet each other's expectations and share the belief in longer-term exchange (Uzzi, 1997). Such networks may even serve as drivers of less personalized market exchange and contribute to market making in countries that lack formal contract enforcement and suffer from high transaction costs and information asymmetry.

These ties need not be social in the sense of knowing personal details about business owners or managers (e.g., to whom they are married or their personal conduct in nonbusiness settings unless relevant to the transaction). Rather, the information generally pertains to the behavior of the entrepreneurs, particularly in terms of whether they meet their obligations and honor their word or about the performance of their businesses (e.g., creditworthiness, competitiveness, sales).

These ties are thus different from the transactions based on mutual affection that can be found among household members or close friends (Dasgupta, 2000). For instance, as François (2004, 30) underlines the case of the Sinos valley in Brazil, "By the 1990s, cooperation had come to have an entirely different basis, and, though not legalistic, the trust had come to be more *process* than *individual* based [emphasis added]. That is, it grew to depend on the reputational considerations that are central to neoclassical accounts of clusters." Gaining close and up-to-date knowledge about customers, suppliers, and competitors was also presented as the most plausible explanation for the expansion of credit extension to growing Vietnamese enterprises since the 1990s (Steerb and Senc, 2008).

The final mode of articulation between the economic and the social is reputation. Because the reputation of an entrepreneur, an enterprise, or a product is relatively impersonal and generally belongs to the realm where certain enterprises occupy a niche and manage to establish an edge over their competitors, the development and nourishment of a reputation is one familiar way out of the dependence on socialized transactions and into market-based and price-driven exchanges (Stiglitz, 1994, 88). A reputation, and the efforts associated with maintaining it, lowers transaction costs and limits the risks of opportunism in transactions that require long-term commitments such as deals with suppliers and credit extension to customers. This is something that entrepreneurs refer to as *aʿmel ism fī al-sūq-*, which means literally "making a name in the market." (For a detailed case of workshop masters in Cairo who could develop a reputation of honesty, competence, and efficiency over time, see Elyachar, 2005, 113–114.)

Taking these concepts regarding interbusiness transactions together—familiarized markets, economic intimacy, and reputation—this chapter has thus far emphasized the dialectical relation between capitalization, and hence business size, on the one hand, and the movement beyond dependence on preexisting social relations, on the other. Thus, economic intimacy and reputational mechanisms have been less common in the Egyptian context due to the chronic problems of undercapitalization; they have merely served as intermittent signals, especially among the relatively better-capitalized SSEs with some potential to grow beyond merely socialized transactions if sufficiently capitalized. They appear more frequently under dandy capitalism, where enterprises typically have higher levels of capitalization.

THE VAST GRAY AREA OF SEMIFORMALITY

In addition to the socially embedded elements of interbusiness transactions, there is a third analytical component of baladi capitalism that revolves around state-business relations and the vast realm of semiformality in Egypt's private sector.

In conformity with much of the literature on entrepreneurship in the Global South, survey results clearly show that dealing with state agencies or invoking formal rules that are set and enforced by the state is problematic for private enterprises. This is especially the case with small-scale establishments that largely lack the resources and political connections to limit the costs and risks of dealing with such state bodies. Hence, SSEs generally limit their invocation of formal rules and regulations in order to avoid the high cost, high risk, low return, and low trust associated with their relationship with formal institutions.

Formal market entry through registration (e.g., permits, licenses, tax registration) is an expensive, arduous, and wasteful process in terms of time and money, and the returns following such registration are limited and far from guaranteed. Contrary to neoclassical conventional wisdom, there is little evidence to suggest that formally registered SSEs have better access to finance or land or even protection against extortion and predation by state officials. These high costs and low returns also infect interactions involving the state as a third party in interbusiness transactions, primarily through contract registration and enforcement. Indeed, surveyed owners and managers of SSEs have expressed limited trust in the functionality and predictability of formal institutions, and hence the ability of these institutions to provide a predictable business environment.

In light of this problematic relation with formal institutions, outright informality, where SSEs operate without invoking any state-set and enforced rule at all, seems to be the natural institutional alternative. However, survey results surprisingly show that outright informality prevails only for the tiniest and usually subsistence-driven SSEs, whereas the relatively larger, more capitalized, and more market-oriented SSEs conduct their business on the broad spectrum between formality and informality. These practices are characterized by familiarized market transactions that take them beyond the comfort zones of perfectly socialized information, high interpersonal trust, and functioning social mechanisms of enforcement. This primarily derives from the fact that their relatively larger size makes them more visible by the state, and their expanded turnover requires the occasional invoking of formal rules. Indeed, the survey results confirm the correlation between increasing business size, expressed in reported capital and annual turnover, and resorting to formal rules. This is especially the case in the absence of systemic and universal nonstate organized mechanisms of enforcement, such as a mafia or autonomous clans.

This partial invocation of formal rules, however, occurs through their articulation into broader social, and hence informal, rules and mechanisms. Survey results suggest a variety of combinations of formal and informal rules that market-oriented SSEs turn to in a way that limits the cost and risk of doing business formally yet enables them to protect their property rights to the largest extent possible against opportunism and defection by other market actors.

I label this tendency to invoke formal rules despite the inherently high costs and low returns "organic formality." It means that greater capital and turnover, as well as the absence of universal nonstate enforcement organizations, leads to a higher frequency of invoking formal rules without necessarily rendering these formal institutions less costly or more lucrative.

Ultimately these findings contradict many of the tenets of neoclassical institutionalism. First, they show the limitations of the supposed dichotomy of formality and informality because market-oriented SSEs often combine both, making it imperative to understand the sociological and political-economic underpinnings of semiformality rather than focusing on two separate and hermetically sealed sectors of the economy.

Second, they suggest that formality is not merely a legalistic and formalistic status. Formality is much more complex than the mere business registration or the acquisition of permits and licenses. From an economic sociology perspective, looking at transactions that are formally recorded and registered by the state regardless of the legal status of the enterprise is much more relevant in understanding how the broad base of private sector enterprises actually operate in the Global South.

In many instances, formally registered enterprises conduct most of their business informally— for example, employing labor without contracts or social insurance and underreporting revenues to evade taxes—and unregistered enterprises and entrepreneurs also may conduct some aspect of their business formally. Examples include the use of checks, trust receipts, and bills with customers, suppliers, or creditors, making it possible to bring in the state as an enforcer in the case of any dispute and thus limit the risk of defection. They therefore turn to the state as a last resort if all trust and social sanctioning mechanisms fail. What neoclassical scholarship misses (or dismisses) are the mixes of formal and informal mechanisms of enforcement while favoring a more legalistic approach to formality that focuses almost exclusively on business registration.

The following sections highlight in more detail the survey results, which reveal the specific modes of combining formal and informal rules by Egyptian SSEs. I demonstrate how these enterprises have strategically, though partially, interacted with formal state institutions and how organic formality, or a more formalized micro and small private sector, could have been possible had SSEs had adequate access to financial and physical capital. I then present a number of theoretical implications for the conventional wisdom that neoclassical institutionalism poses and ultimately suggest a more sociological approach to the question of state-SSE interaction.

Formal Market Entry: High Cost and Dubious Returns

Survey results confirm the findings of earlier World Bank Governance Indicators and Doing Business reports: that state-business regulatory transactions (e.g., those governing business registration, permits and licenses, bankruptcy, and asset recovery, among others) are quite costly and denote limited or uncertain returns for the majority of SSEs in Egypt. More than half of the surveyed registered enterprises (56 percent) reported that the process of registration was either difficult or very difficult; 69 percent of them blamed this difficulty on laws and 84 percent on the ways in which the laws were implemented or how the government bureaucracy functioned.

In addition to the high cost of registration, the results suggest that economic returns on business registration were indeed uncertain, if not altogether negative. Registered enterprises reported they had suffered more than unregistered ones from administrative incompetence and inefficiency, political instability, and exposure to extortion and corruption by state officials. In fact, surveyed owners and managers of unregistered SSEs said that one of the reasons behind not registering was to avoid such problems. Obviously, unregistered enterprises are generally spared administrative incompetence or inefficiency.

Furthermore, and contrary to neoclassical institutionalism, survey results revealed that registering did not appear to have contributed to better access to capital for SSEs in the form of credit or land, nor did it shield them from the costs of extortion and bribery. In fact, owners and managers of registered enterprises reported the inaccessibility of land at a much higher rate than unregistered ones. The likely explanation is that unregistered, and hence informal, activities are generally based in service and commercial sectors that require few physical assets (al-Mahdi and Rashed, 2010, 102).

Registration also showed a limited impact on accessing bank credit. Figure 8.3 demonstrates the different sources of finance that surveyed entrepreneurs reported. Here, surveyed SSEs were broken into three subcategories by size and legal status: micro, small, and unregistered microenterprises. The distinction by size was based on the number of employees reported in the survey, with small enterprises hiring more than five workers and microbusinesses hiring fewer.

Ultimately, registration displayed little effect in accessing bank finance: all three categories reported strikingly similar dependence on self-accumulation (i.e., business profits and private savings) as the most significant source for funding. In contrast, bank loans and special funds and programs (including microfinance and SME programs and schemes) were the least used for both registered and unregistered enterprises. Although the percentage of enterprises using bank loans is greater for registered ones compared to their unregistered counterparts (17 versus 6 percent), this figure is hardly impressive and does not indicate any dramatic gains from being registered. Overall, the financial profiles of the two enterprise groups are roughly similar and display major restraints on accessing institutional finance for micro and small enterprises regardless of their legal status. Indeed, such systemic discrimination against SSEs is both a main manifestation and cause of undercapitalization.

Another intriguing piece of evidence of the paradoxically disadvantageous position of registered SSEs compared to unregistered ones comes from the views expressed regarding corruption and extortion as barriers to growth. Whereas 53 percent of entrepreneurs running registered enterprises said that corruption was a barrier to growth, only 33 percent of unregistered ones stated the same. This finding almost entirely contradicts what Schneider, Buehn, and Montenegro (2010) frequently held—that informal enterprises were more exposed to corruption than those formally registered—and refutes the logic that formal legal status grants better property rights protection and business security to enterprises. Moreover, whereas 57 percent of registered

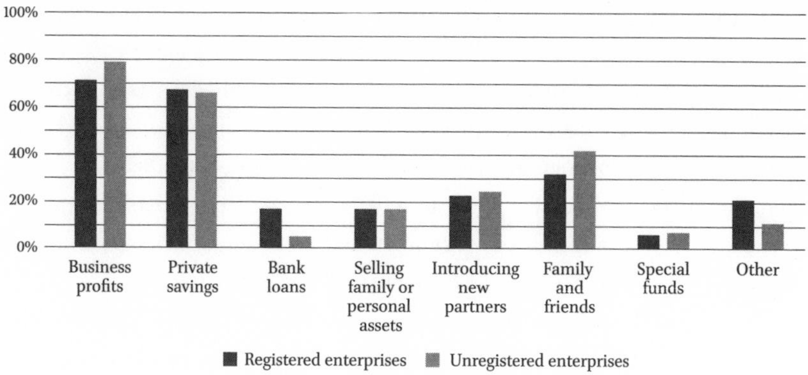

FIGURE 8.3. Sources of Finance as Reported by Registered and Unregistered Enterprise Owners/Managers (Percentage of Respondents).
Source: Adly and Khatib (2014, 79). Reprinted with permission.

SSEs indicated that they had to pay bribes in order to do business, only 44 percent of their unregistered counterparts reported so. Despite the fact that both percentages are quite sizable and show a high level of exposure to corruption and extortion for almost all SSEs, the percentage is again counterintuitively higher for formally registered enterprises.

In addition, state-mediated transactions, where the state stands as a third party to interbusiness dealings, are reportedly costly in terms of the fees, time, and effort consumed in navigating the process, as well as exposure to informal payments and extortion. Moreover, less than half of the surveyed entrepreneurs (48 percent) expressed the belief that formal contracts and procedures were enforceable and defendable, a clear sign of the poor status of the rule of law in which contracts do not provide sufficient protection. This led ultimately to conducting business transactions informally, thereby counting on a set of mechanisms of self-enforcement or socially enforced norms.

Organic Formality

The business reaction to these institutional constraints is quite complex, nuanced, and by no means uniform. Outright informality, which refers to doing business with no reference to formal rules or any interaction with state agencies, is affordable for only the tiniest SSEs. These fully informal establishments typically involve one or two people, are often subsistence driven, have an extremely small turnover with no wage workers, and are confined to local markets and closely knit social circles (al-Mahdi and Rashed, 2010, 110).

Resorting to formal contractual tools and procedures increases with both registration and size, indicating the process of organic formality (Figure 8.4). These two trends are complementary: registered microenterprises tended to be larger than unregistered microenterprises as 73 percent of registered small enterprises reported some use of formal papers and procedures, compared to 53 percent of registered microenterprises and 34 percent of unregistered microenterprises.[6]

The fact that an overwhelming majority of the biggest SSEs noted that formal contractual tools were not substitutable with informal agreements supports the hypothesis that organic formality correlates with size. In contrast, a much larger percentage of owners and managers of microenterprises, registered as well as unregistered, held that both had equal enforceability. Furthermore, small, registered enterprises provided the most favorable views of formal procedures and contracts, with only 11 percent believing that formal and informal agreements were equally enforceable. Conversely, 50 percent of microenterprises, registered as well as unregistered, held informal and formal agreements to be equally enforceable, reinforcing the assumption that larger turnover generally implies doing business beyond the heavily socialized circles of high trust and mutual solidarity.

A significantly lower percentage of small, registered enterprises held formal procedures to be costlier, more complicated, inflexible, and exposed to extortion than informal agreements in comparison to microenterprises.

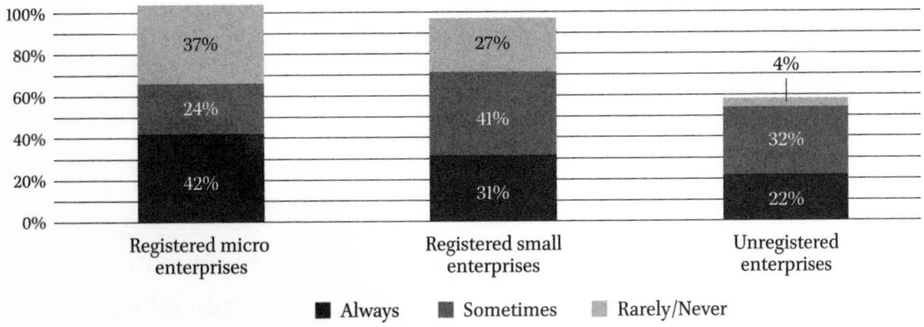

FIGURE 8.4. Frequency of Using Formal Contractual Tools by Enterprise Size and Legal Status (Percentage of Respondents).
Source: Survey conducted by Adly and Khatib (2014).

Figures 8.5 and 8.6 indicate that formal procedures are almost indispensable for business transactions beyond a certain turnover size. Informal agreements were considered riskier and clearly less enforceable.

This larger turnover both requires and results from wider, market-oriented circles that go beyond the comfort zones of high interpersonal trust and intimate knowledge, while informal agreements here are risky because access to nonstate enforcement is not easily available in urban areas. The only option remaining is to weave formal rules into largely informally conducted transactions.

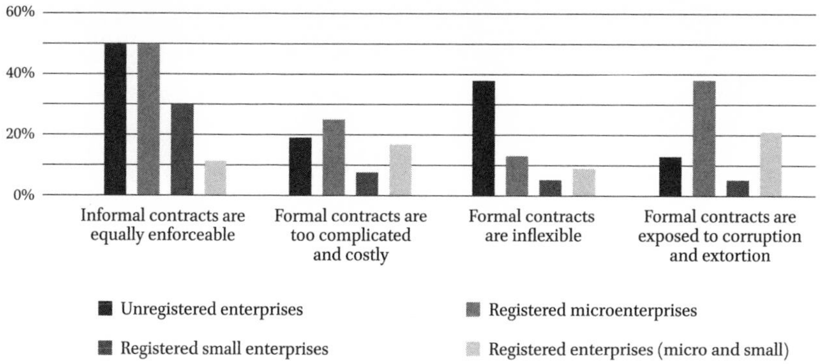

FIGURE 8.5. Reasons for Not Using Formal Contractual Tools as Reported by Entrepreneurs (Percentage of Respondents).
Source: Adly and Khatib (2014).

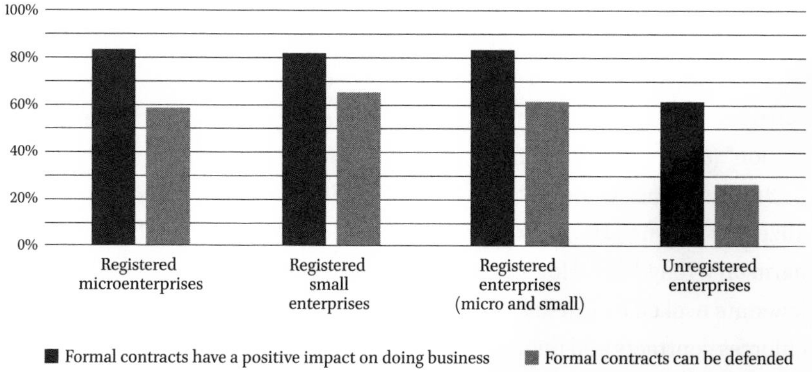

FIGURE 8.6. Views Expressed by Entrepreneurs on Formal Contract Enforceability (Percentage of Respondents).
Source: Adly and Khatib (2014). Reprinted with permission.

STATE-MEDIATED TRANSACTIONS: HOBBES RATHER THAN VON HAYEK

Survey results suggest that the larger, and hence more market-oriented, SSEs resort to formal rules at higher frequencies, despite the well-corroborated inefficiencies of formal institutions. Here, market-oriented transactions increase the need for a third-party enforcer, and while state institutions are not completely reliable, there have been no nonstate organizations capable of assuming the role of enforcer, at least systematically and in a more reliable manner than the state.

The solution to such a suboptimal institutional choice on the part of market-oriented SSEs was to bring in the state as a potential punisher for defection rather than an actual enforcer of agreements, a key function of the Hayekian state. As the process of organic formality dictates, interbusiness transactions acquire formal status as they grow and take on a long-term nature, especially when they involve socially unfamiliar parties. Still, the state is not ultimately brought in unless all social mechanisms of enforcement and trust fail. At this point, state involvement through police action or lawsuits is not expected to enforce the agreement, retrieve assets, or protect the private property rights of the wronged party; rather, it is a form of retaliation that parties initially, and often implicitly, agree on as a deterrent to defection. Indeed, this is suggested by the general preference for invoking the criminal law, as in the case with using checks or promissory receipts: the state is brought in to inflict harm on the miscreant regardless of its limited capacity to bring back what was lost. Again, such threats often serve a deterrent role for potential wrongdoers, reflected in a number of colloquial sayings: "dragging someone through the courts" (*yegargar fī al-maḥākem*) or "inflicting harm and insult on someone through taking them to the police station" (*bahdala fī al-aqsām-*).

In this capacity, the state is closer to the idea of the sovereign conceptualized by Thomas Hobbes that solely possesses the right to inflict physical harm on wrongdoers. However, it is much further from the neoliberal rule-of-law state evoked by Friedrich von Hayek and Wilhelm Röpke, which actively enforces contracts and upholds the private property rights of individuals and entities. Moreover, it also departs from Avner Greif's (2006a, 2006b) stress on the role of private-order institutions at the dawn of capitalism in Europe as the state did not initially perform any enforcement acts. Economies in the

Global South today are not exactly there, as their market constitution has largely followed the creation (or the inheritance) of centralizing bureaucratized state apparatuses. In other words, SSEs and other private sector actors in the Global South are not stuck in the sixteenth or seventeenth centuries; they simply have modern state structures that do not perform what neoclassicals expect them to.

This observation has considerable sociological and political implications for the broad base of private sector enterprises. It indicates that nonstate organized violence in Egypt is not costless or fully reliable as a substitute to the state, especially in urban areas where the survey was conducted. Nonstate systematic, and hence institutionalized, enforcement of contracts requires strong intermediate social organizations that can perform functions of enforcement stemming from physical coercion that the state cannot perform. This has been the case only with clan-like organizations such as the mafia (Paoli 2002, 79–81), which retain features of premodern hierarchical authority over their members in a manner that goes against the essential claims of modern states regarding their monopoly of the use of force (Paoli, 2002, 74). Skaperdas (2001) attributed the prevalence of such nonstate organized violence to power vacuums created by the absence of state enforcement, which usually results from geographic remoteness, the presence of ethnic enclaves, or the collapse of state institutions (Volkov, 2016)—none of which apply to the main Egyptian cities where the survey was conducted.

Indeed, Egypt has scored relatively well on the Word Bank index for political stability and the absence of violence prior to the 2011 revolution when compared to other nations in the Global South. Political stability and the absence of violence and terrorism measures perceptions of the likelihood of political instability or politically motivated violence, including terrorism. In 2004, Egypt's score was 22 (out of 100; larger scores denote more stability) compared to 13 for India, 4 for Indonesia, 8 for Russia, and 2 for Colombia. The score improved by 2009: Egypt scored 26 compared to 11, 21, 18, and 5 for India, Indonesia, Russia, and Colombia, respectively. While this score serves as a very rough proxy of the absence of business-related violence because it includes many other factors, such as civil conflict, riots, and military insurgency, it nonetheless can indicate the extent of any power vacuum left by dysfunctional state coercive institutions.

In the urban environs of Cairo, market-oriented SSEs have adapted to any functional vacuum left by the state's limited enforcement capacities through different mixes of formality and informality. Baladi capitalism usually operates in a gray area of semiformality constituted by two essential institutional modes: selective formality and twisted formality.

TWO MODES OF SEMIFORMALITY: SELECTIVE AND TWISTED FORMALITY

Selective formality refers to a strategy SSEs use when they unevenly invoke formal rules while doing business; in other words, they conduct some transactions formally and others informally. *Twisted formality* implies invoking of formal rules in a manner that serves ends other than the ones they were originally set for. This change in function corresponds to the integration into broader social, and hence informal, mechanisms of trust and enforcement. Thus, rule twisting usually takes place through a systematic and often institutionalized use of loopholes in the law or in the way it is implemented, while selective formality is characterized by entrepreneurs' choosing which transactions to conduct through formal rules.

The choice of SSEs to employ one or more of these strategies seems to depend on three factors. The foremost is enterprise size. Indeed, there is a general correlation between firm size and the frequency of using formal rules in doing business. The second factor is the nature of the parties to the transaction. There is anecdotal evidence that SSEs resort to formal rules more often when dealing with other enterprises than with customers or workers. The final factor is the time range of the transaction. Fairly intuitively, the longer term the transaction is (e.g., credit, installments, future consignment delivery), the more likely it is done using formal rules and vice versa. According to an Egyptian business lawyer, size and time range are correlated and mutually reinforcing via the mechanism of the credit term (*al-taʿāmol bi-l- ājil*): "Once you hit a certain size, you deal in credit. Unless you do this with suppliers, you can't grow. Once you start involving credit, you grow. This then becomes mutually reinforcing" (Gabr, 2017).

As for more selective modes of formality, surveyed SSEs reported different frequencies of resorting to formal contractual tools in a manner that correlated with business size. A small minority of surveyed enterprises reported the regular use of formal rules in conducting business (14 percent), and only 11 percent said that they never invoked formal rules. The rest reported different frequencies of using formal contractual tools. Conversely, 34 percent reported that they "sometimes" use formal contractual tools. Five percent said that they "often" use them. Figure 8.7 depicts the ratios.

Twisted formality is expressed through a number of practices. One is the incomplete or partial use of formal procedures in a way that largely guarantees the security of the transaction against opportunism by other parties, while also lowering the cost of relying on state-mediated rules. This is reflected, for instance, in the use of preliminary sales contracts (*'uqūd ibtidā'iyya*), which denotes the partial registration of relatively large business transactions, particularly the transfer of valuable physical assets such as land or expensive movables like cars or machines. Preliminary sales contracts, which business parties often use without following up with the full registration of property transfer, create obligations on the part of the buyers and sellers; however, they are not valid for third parties, especially good-faith buyers (those unaware of the previous sale). Despite these limitations, preliminary contracts often serve the end of creating a chain of ownership that is accepted by the courts in a dispute, which indicates the overall semiformal character of the rules governing transactions (Gabr, 2017).

Such incomplete invocation of formal rules helps in evading the cost of property registration and the risk of providing information to the state, while acquiring partial or minimal property protection at the same time. Indeed, formal

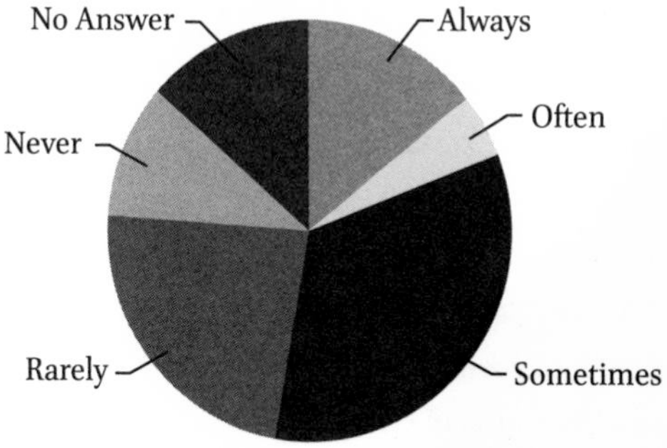

FIGURE 8.7. The Frequency of Resorting to Formal Contractual Tools (Percentage of Respondents).
Source: Adly and Khatib (2014, 67). Reprinted with permission.

land and property registration barely captures 5 to 10 percent of urban land and property in Egypt (World Bank, 2006, 1:4) implying that the cost, both formal fees and informal payments, of conducting land-related transactions according to formal rules and institutions is quite expensive and thus largely avoided.

Registration is hence effectively replaced by alternative formal measures such as *ṣaḥat tawqīʿ* or *ṣaḥa wa-nafāz*. *Ṣaḥat tawqīʾ*, which can be defined as a "procedure undertaken in court to authenticate land/property transfer deeds, often used to confer some form of legality on informal transactions of land and property and perceived by some as a proxy to registration" (World Bank, 2006, 1:111). *Ṣaḥa wa-nafāz* describes a "low-cost procedure undertaken in court as a proxy to registration, in which the claimant upon purchasing land/property uses the transfer deed to dispute the right of the seller to the property in question, and which leads the court to examine the chain of ownership (lasts several years)."

Power of attorney (PoA); *Tawkīlāt*) constitutes yet another popular legal tool that exemplifies twisted formality. It is widely used in transactions of valuable movables and occasionally in real estate. In these instances, sellers write out irrevocable PoAs to buyers, with the power to buy, sell, and delegate to third parties. Although these PoAs are not sales contracts, they effectively act as such because sellers generally receive payments and renounce property rights, enabling the buyer to sell the property or delegate this power to third parties (usually subsequent buyers) to do the same (Gabr, 2017). This legal tool enables some official documentation of transactions, as the registry certifies a PoA without incurring the cost of registering property transfers, especially if they are of a short-term nature (which is typical of brokers and merchants).

However, a PoA is technically just that: the object of transaction legally remains the property of the principal (the first seller), and all delegates are treated as agents (the de facto buyers). As long as the PoA is irrevocable however, the risks of opportunism remain limited. A number of cases have witnessed challenges to PoAs on the death of the principal in which those inheriting would seek to reclaim the property from the agents (the de facto buyers). Amazingly, the Court of Cassation (2003) issued a ruling upholding a PoA as an implicit sales contract (Case No. 2595, May 28, 2003), a ruling that was taken as a precedent that formalized the rather twisted use of a PoA to serve as a sales contract. This has further confirmed the semiformal nature of the Egyptian property rights system that has been widely acclaimed by both market actors and state agencies in charge of settling disputes.

Indeed, twisted formality appears to be a good adaptation to a property registration process that despite the reforms introduced between 2004 and 2010 designed to reduce the cost and simplify procedures, remains cumbersome and costly. According to the 2015 World Bank *Doing Business Report*, Egypt ranked eighty-fourth worldwide with regard to property registration, requiring 8 separate registration procedures, compared to an average of 6.1 for the MENA region and 4.7 for Organization for Economic Cooperation and Development countries. Furthermore, the real operational cost of registering property appears in the number of days required to complete the process: 63.0 days in Egypt compared to an average of 31.3 days for the MENA region and only 24.0 days in the OECD countries.

The second example of formal rule twisting is the use of commercial papers like checks and trust receipts (*iṣalāt amana*) as security documents (*adawāt i'timān*) rather than payment instruments (*adawāt wafā'*) and are, as such, used as guarantees against wrongdoing without ever having the intention of collecting the check at any stage (al-Sharqawi, 1990). A trust receipt, though not legally considered commercial paper, is a document signed by a party stating receipt of a deposit, which can be any movable valuable, including cash, on the basis of trust from another party. The document includes a date on which the deposit is to be returned, is kept by the original owner as proof, and may be submitted before the court in case the deposit is not returned on the designated date. In some instances, a trust receipt is a bipartite agreement of a depositor and a trustee. However, it is more commonly used in Egypt as a tripartite agreement, wherein a depositor deposits a movable to a trustee who must deliver it on a certain date to a third party, known as the beneficent (Ḥamdi, 2014, 149).

From a strictly legal angle, checks are not designed as security instruments. Egyptian commercial law (article 503/1) states that "checks shall be payable upon sighting. All statements otherwise added shall be null and non-existent. If the check is presented for honoring before the date mentioned in the issue date, it shall be honored on the day it is presented," with the exception of crossed checks. The full amount pledged in a bearer check must be available the moment the check is written (Court of Cassation, 1952; el-Kalioubi, 2002; Mokhtār, 2010, 6). Nonetheless, such guarantees against wrongdoing or as a means for the delivery of future financial commitments remain the most prevalent uses of checks in Egypt. Moreover, businesspeople and merchants tend to prefer checks over other security instruments like promissory notes because an unpaid check is overseen by a criminal court, whereas failing to pay a promissory note is dealt with as a civil case (Khairī and al-Amīn, 2011). Such commercial paper allows the potential invoking of state agencies, like courts or public prosecution, in the face of wrongdoing or dispute that signify moments in which the social mechanisms of interpersonal trust and enforcement fail.

The use of checks and trust receipts specifically opens the way for invoking the state in a dispute, with serious repercussions for the wrongdoer. The prevailing logic is not the enforcement of the agreement or the recovery of money or assets due because the procedures are too cumbersome, costly, and lengthy. The aim instead is retaliation against wrongdoers by inflicting as much damage as possible on their financial position, reputation, and even personal freedom in the case of imprisonment. According to Egyptian commercial law (No. 17/1999), the merchant faces one of three situations on failure to pay a check: instant payment of the amount with a fine, trial, and potential sentence of up to two years in prison, or both. The law adds more penalties for repetition of the same offense, including depriving retractors from attaining future checkbooks from banks or their denunciation in the commercial bulletin issued by the Federation of the Chambers of Commerce, or both (Mokhtār, 2010, 45).

The case of trust receipts (*iṣalāt amana*) is even more dramatic. Failure to return the complete deposit on time (and unspoiled in case of a noncash movable) is a violation of the penal code (Article No.341) and can lead to a prison sentence or a fine, or both. Such mechanisms are commonly used among microenterprises and small merchants who lack bank accounts and thus cannot issue checks and are used widely for financial noncommercial purposes among poorer Egyptians(Gabr, 2014).

In addition, the translation of long-term transactions, especially transactions with credit terms, into commercial paper adds a formal mechanism of enforcement to informal mechanisms such as familial ties or interpersonal trust and friendship. For example, it is often used to hedge against the risk of the loss of direct personal relations on the occasion of the death of one of the parties to the transaction. Here, the presence of formal contractual tools in the form of a promissory note, check, or trust receipt provides a po documented enforcement tool against the beneficiaries of the deceased. Su formal rules are nonetheless well integrated into broader social mechanisms of trust and enforcement. For instance, despite high interpersonal trust, parties to a business transaction may agree to write down their obligations, invoking such proverbs as "*maḥadesh ḍāmen ʿomroh*" (No one guarantees living until tomorrow), indicating that the death of one of the parties, between whom high levels of trust exist, may endanger the transaction; or "*ḥarraṣ wa-la tekhawen*" (Be cautious without necessarily mistrusting others). Writing down obligations is often used when parties to the transaction have some mutual social knowledge and trust, yet at least one of the two wishes to write the agreement down.

Egypt's baladi capitalism is a socially embedded business subsystem of relations, structures, norms, and networks that can perform multiple economic functions: initial capital accumulation, skill acquisition and transfer, information circulation and verification, and social mechanisms of trust and enforcement. Crucially, this social embeddedness of Egyptian baladi capitalism has no exceptionally negative precapitalist or premodern traits in comparison to more competitive economies in the Global South, mainly in East and Southeast Asia. Thus, it does not in and of itself explain the weak growth and expansion capacities of the broad base of Egyptian small-scale private establishments, as well as the missing-middle syndrome.

The survey evidence discussed in this chapter has highlighted the evidence that Egyptian SSEs have a tendency to move toward more formal and less personalized transactions as they grow and acquire capital. Thus, undercapitalization stands as the primary difficulty of the Egyptian private sector: undercapitalization derives from the lack of complementarity between the private-order institutions of baladi capitalism and the state-controlled and -regulated institutions governing access to physical and financial capital. Such complementarity, and thus better access to capital, could have translated into higher turnover and larger working capital in a way that could have led to virtuous circle of growth, increasing (organic) formality and more market-oriented transactions.

DANDY CAPITALISM

DANDY CAPITALISM REPRESENTS THE THIRD BUSINESS SUBSYSTEM of Egypt's cleft capitalist order. Defined by the higher degree of relative differentiation between the economic on the one hand and the social and the political on the other, it has granted a few private enterprises the ability to conduct impersonal transactions less contingent on their social relations. This higher differentiation has had observable effects on growth potential, ushering a minority of enterprises into the ranks of Egypt's thin layer of medium-sized and large private enterprises.[1] The concept of dandy capitalism captures private enterprises that have realized some ability to grow rather than merely survive, like the majority of private sector entities in Egypt.

The ability to grow and scale up was largely a function of their initial or acquired capital endowments that enabled them to overcome institutional barriers to operating and accessing financial and physical capital and made some of them attractive partners for international capital. By the 1990s, these dynamics gave birth to a layer of large and medium-sized enterprises (Waṣfi, Waṣfi, and Shawqi, 2013). The traits of dandy capitalism could also be found in a limited number of small enterprises that operated in nontraditional sectors like high-tech and Internet-based services ('Olama, 2015), constituting an enclave of skill- and technology-intensive entities in an economy dominated by labor-intensive and generally low-technology economic activities.

The chapter discusses the rebirth of the Egyptian private enterprise as a relatively autonomous entity, legally, financially, and organizationally. It then examines all three aspects of dandy capitalism as a business subsystem covering intra- and interfirm dynamics and then relations with the state.

THE REBIRTH OF THE EGYPTIAN PRIVATE *SHARIKA*

Article 505 of the Egyptian Civil Code defines a company (*sharika*) as "a contract according to which two people or more are committed to contribute to a financial project with a money share or a work share with the purpose of sharing the possible return of profit or loss" (el-Kalioubi, 2002, 65). Legally, all kinds of commercial companies enjoy a juristic personality once their contracts are made (Shamsān, 1994, 142, 299). However, the common use of the term *sharika* is much narrower than the legal one: it refers almost exclusively to market actors that are largely differentiated—financially, organizationally, and operationally—from the social identities of their owners and thus generally exhibit a high degree of administrative complexity. This chapter stresses this economic-sociological connotation rather than the legal one.

The birth of the Egyptian sharika can be traced to the 1920s. It was in that context of nationalist exultation and the limited autonomy the British had granted to the Egyptian state that an industrial national bourgeoisie began to develop. Until this period, foreigners, foreign residents, and members of ethnic and religious minorities almost exclusively owned the *sharikāt* (the plural of a *sharika*) that could qualify as differentiated market entities in industrial and service sectors (Abdulhaq, 2016). It was mainly with the advent of Banque Misr in 1920, an economic joint-stock organization that enjoyed a market identity and was operationally and financially differentiated from its shareholders, that an Egyptian sharika finally emerged (Issawi, 1947, 125; Tignor, 1984, 188).

Following the end of World War II, many foreign- and minority-owned sharikāt were subject to Egyptianization, which refers to a series of laws and regulations that aimed at increasing the share of Egyptian nationals on management boards and as owners and workers in big foreign-owned enterprises and were further sequestered and nationalized in the aftermath of the 1956 Suez crisis (Tignor, 1984, 188). Simultaneously, successive waves of land reform targeted the Egyptian landowning class from 1952 to 1961. In 1961, the nationalization of large domestic commercial and industrial enterprises led to the effective extinction of the first generation of private Egyptian sharikāt. A look at the three decree laws concerning nationalization—Nos. 117, 118, and 119—in 1961 reveals that Egypt by that time had witnessed the growth of an indigenous class of large enterprises that had the corporate identities and legal statuses of genuine market organizations. The first two laws listed 250 companies to be nationalized, with the valuation of the companies indicated in the value of their stocks, demonstrating that they were corporations rather than simple partnerships. The third law set limits on the maximum value of stocks to be held by any legal or natural person, with the excess flowing to the state. It affected 159 companies, virtually all corporations with stock, publicly or privately traded (ʿAbdel-Faḍīl, 1980, 252–258, 261–263). Hence, from the early 1960s through the mid-1970s, state-owned enterprises became the only *sharikāt* in Egypt.

The launch of infitāḥ in 1974 marked the rebirth of the Egyptian private sharika. Market opening allowed for the progressive differentiation of the social and economic identities and functions of a few private enterprises—those with large initial capital. These enterprises came to constitute Egypt's thin layer of middle and large businesses by the 1990s. This rebirth of the private sharika was not an intentional consequence of infitāḥ, nor was it a premeditated plan by private sector entrepreneurs. Indeed, social relations remained crucial for the formation, control, and operation of private sharikāt (Hansen, 1991, 31), though this developed in a very different way from the broad base of private small-scale establishments (SSEs) caught in the realm of baladi capitalism.

The higher degree of relative differentiation among dandy enterprises resulted from three principal sociohistorical factors that marked their evolution. The first is the large initial private capital that allowed early opportunities to conduct larger transactions, access final markets, and ultimately grow and develop organizational sophistication. Many of these traditional capitalists with private wealth date to the pre-1952 period as they were able to retain their financial capital informally in the form of cash or otherwise in the trade sector, allowing them to continue accumulating capital on the margin (Sadowski, 1991, 101). In addition to those who took shelter in domestic trade and small-scale construction, largely left untouched by nationalization schemes (Zaki, 1999, 74), others moved their businesses abroad following the nationalizations of 1961; among them were Onsi Sawiris and Ḥusein Ṣabbour, who moved their construction businesses to Libya in the 1960s (al-Wafd, 2016; ʿAbdel-Naṣer, 2015). Such was also the case with Loṭfi Mansour [Manṣūr], the founder of Mansour Group, who relocated to Geneva in 1966, where he was able to resume his private cotton trade after shifting from Egyptian to Sudanese cotton (Mansour Group, 2017).

In these moves, the corporate form was apparently the means through which joint ventures with Arab, and to a lesser extent Western, capital were formally struck. Indeed, Samia Imām's (1986, 61–72, 74–77) remarkable depiction of early private big and middle capital in Egypt shows that they were registered as *sharikāt Amwāl* (corporations) since the 1970s. Moreover, most of the companies that were later registered under investment laws were corporations rather than partnerships.

The second factor behind higher differentiation was a by-product of the first: the ability of some enterprises to play the role of intermediary in Egypt's early import liberalization in the 1970s (Sadowski, 1991, 104). This enabled them to capture sizable shares of the burgeoning Egyptian consumer markets and associated them with brands and trademarks of international companies in a way that allowed them to separate their concrete social backgrounds from what they supplied to the domestic market. Here again the Mansours provide a good example of a foreign-local intermediation. Capitalizing on the ties they cultivated in Europe in the 1950s and 1960s, they were able to establish partnerships with foreign capital and play the role of intermediaries amid the consumerist expansion of the 1970s and 1980s. They positioned themselves as brokers for multinationals looking for entry into the local Egyptian market, including American Chevrolet, Caterpillar, and Philip Morris. By the late 1980s and 1990s, their agency ties had developed into more complex schemes of assembly industries and technology transfer programs under the guise of state-sponsored strategies for local-market industrialization adopted by the Mubārak regime (Mansour Group, 2017).

The third factor was the strategies pursued by these early traders and merchants to move away from acting merely as intermediaries and brokers and into higher value-added and capital-intensive sectors. The fact that some of the agency offices (*Makāteb tawkīlāt*) and showrooms of the 1970s developed into diversified business groups certainly indicates an entrepreneurial spirit that early capital accumulation both encouraged and enabled (on the earlier forms of tawkīlāt, see Zaalouk, 1989, 279).

THE INNER WORKINGS OF DANDY ENTERPRISES: FORMALLY COATED INFORMALITY

In terms of control, these reborn Egyptian private sharikāt remain generally entrepreneurial rather than managerial, meaning that their individual founders or their offspring, not professional managers, play a central role in both owning and running them. These enterprises are relatively young, dating back to the mid-1970s or later. Thus, many founders are still managing their enterprises and making strategic decisions, if not handling daily operations. Capital markets have been persistently shallow, narrow, and underdeveloped in a way that raises the returns on control (Nenova, 1999; Khanna and Palepu, 2000; Morck, Nakamura, and Shivdasani 2000; Claessens and Fan, 2002).

In the Egyptian context, higher differentiation meant that formal rules and structures underlay social ties and personalized networks. However, unlike baladi capitalism, the concrete social identity of the owners becomes less central to capital accumulation and access to economic opportunities, and the social components of entrepreneurship, like family and friendship, retreated into the functions of ownership control and top management.

Unlike advanced capitalism, the development of the corporate identities of these enterprises did not take place on the capital market, which remained underdeveloped. Rather, it occurred on the final product markets where trade names in service sectors and (initially international) brands in manufacturing were the critical factors in developing corporate identities (Dawar and Chattopadhay, 2002, 14). Once these were associated with these corporate abstractions, consumers would become less interested in the identity of those who owned and managed these enterprises. Indeed, some of the businesspeople deemed most successful in Egypt have kept a low profile and are barely known to the public, including most of their suppliers and final customers. For example, Nāṣif Sawiris, the CEO of Orascom for construction, Egypt's biggest nonfinancial enterprise, has consciously avoided the media (Evans, 2018). Similarly, no member of Elsewedy family, which owns the largest producer of electrical cables in Egypt and the Middle East (Elsewedy, 2015), has ever been politically active or a public figure.[2]

In turn, the Talaat Moustafa [Ṭalʿat Muṣṭafa] Group presents a revealing incident of how some Egyptian enterprises have outgrown the social identity of their owners and managers. Hishām Ṭalʿat, the CEO and second-generation founder of the construction giant, was implicated in the murder of his divorced wife in 2009 and was sentenced to fifteen years in prison in 2012 (France 24, 2012). His conviction did not bring down the company with him even though the growth of the group in the 1990s had been closely tied to his career after succeeding his father. Following some initial shockwaves in the weeks that followed the sentencing, shareholders, contractors, and customers renewed their trust in the publicly traded group. Management stressed the strength of the company, with its large land bank and sound financial position (ʿAskar, 2010).

Granted, social and personal ties, mainly family and friendship, assume an important role in the ownership and management of enterprises due to the high returns on control given the absence of strong, regulated financial markets and the general weakness of the rule of law (Almeida and Wolfenzon, 2006). However, unlike baladi capitalism, they do not mediate business transactions as frequently, and hence do not strictly condition access to inputs and market outlets. For those who operate under dandy capitalism, social and informal relations are internalized within the formal and legal structures of the enterprise, a phenomenon described as "formally coated social informality" (in contrast to mere legal formality).

By the turn of the century, the evolution of the corporate identities of large Egyptian enterprises was ensured with free-floating shares in the Cairo and Alexandria stock market. This stock market, a remnant of Egypt's pre-independence era, was effectively defunct after the nationalizations of the 1960s, but was reactivated in the 1990s with the passing of Law No. 95 of 1992. However, it did not gain steam until the mid-2000s when some of Egypt's large private and state-owned companies issued shares. Orascom telecom and Orascom construction were among the first to issue shares again, as early as 1998 and 1999. Others followed suit in the 2000s, such as Elsewedy electric in 2006, Talaat Mostafa [Muṣṭafa] and Ghabbour Auto in 2007, and Palm Hills in 2009 (al-ʿAntarī, 2005, 298). These proved to be critical junctures for the evolution of corporate market identities of large business groups in contemporary Egypt.

INTERBUSINESS TRANSACTIONS: INTERNALIZATION OF MARKET OPERATIONS

This section explores the various modes of coordination that rendered impersonal access to inputs and markets possible for a few enterprises and hence granted them the opportunity to grow from big to bigger. First, their higher degrees of differentiation contributed to the ability of enterprises to access inputs and market outlets on national and sometimes international levels by conducting impersonal transactions. This was not necessarily based on an exceptional ability to conduct anonymous, price-driven and arm's-length transactions. With an institutional context characterized by a weak rule of law and contract enforcement, as well as high levels of information asymmetry, many could not afford impersonal transactions. Conducting anonymous exchange has rather been derived from the ability of these enterprises to externalize some market transactions while internalizing others.

Dandy enterprises succeeded in externalizing sales of their final products on a market basis. This process has been related to the evolution of the corporate identities of a number of enterprises, as anonymous transactions on final markets were made possible by trademarks, brand names, and the reputations of certain enterprises or their affiliation with international brands or countries of origin (Dawar and Chattopadhay, 2000, 14). These factors reduced risk and conveyed trustworthy information to consumers about the quality and content of final products without any direct allusion to the concrete social identity of the owner(s). Indeed, businesses in Egypt, and the Global South generally, that sustained ties with multinational corporations (MNCs) were those that could dominate and even establish national markets beginning in the mid-1970s.

However, what worked in final market outlets was not as readily applicable to input and intermediate markets due to the weak rule of law and rampant information asymmetry and the risks of opportunism. This became increasingly important by the 1980s and 1990s as large, private enterprises started moving into capital-intensive and higher-value-added sectors in industry and services. With the exception of short-term transactions conducted on the spot for raw materials or unskilled labor, market-based and arm's-length transactions have never been a reliable option due to the fact that the cost of private enforcement through monitoring and testing could be prohibitively high. In the face of such limitations, alternative modes of governance and coordination emerged, allowing the internalization of many market transactions. This gave dandy capitalism its distinctness as a business subsystem.

The internalization of market transactions was sought through two modes of governance. The first was the erection of private hierarchies (i.e., bureaucratization and conglomeration) through which inputs could be processed and final markets accessed through related and unrelated diversification, in addition to the creation of internal capital markets. The other mode was to establish combinations of formal, semiformal, and informal institutional rules that governed long-term cooperation and exchange among suppliers, customers, banks, and others. The best of these combinations are found in business alliances, which allow long-standing cooperation between enterprises (including banks), usually based on past relationships and mutual trust. These alliances are not sensitive to immediate changes in price signals; rather, they are geared toward securing longer-term competitiveness in final markets (Helāl, 2016).

Business Groups: Private Hierarchies

With the externalization of markets for final products, business groups simultaneously developed a mode of governance based on internalizing the production of some inputs within a single organizational structure, with the aim of cutting the costs of acquiring them on the market (Schneider, 2009, 557). Because business groups are a collection of enterprises with the same ownership and control (Khanna and Yafeh, 2007), decisions on the allocation of resources and investments happen in accordance with a well-defined, centralized, and often formal command structure (Leff, 1978, 662). Furthermore, they can be composed of sectorally diversified and unrelated enterprises that do not share the same production chains or require similar inputs or markets, as is the case with the Mansour group, which runs enterprises in the food, tobacco, and car industries and in retail and financial services. Conversely, they may be sectorally concentrated with full vertical integration, whereby the group enterprises correspond to different components of the supply chain of a single product or products that require similar inputs, skills, and markets.

Business groups can assume myriad legal forms. For instance, there are holding companies with strict pyramidal structures (Almeida and Wolfenzon, 2006). At the top, a holding company owns subsidiaries that may themselves own, partially or totally, other companies. Other times, business groups assume a looser form with a single entrepreneur or a business family holding the ownership of affiliated companies. For instance, the Sawiris family uses cross-shareholding of diversified holding companies, each roughly specialized in one of three sectors: telecommunications, construction, and industry and tourism. The Mansours' business group is similarly organized, with the family jointly owning and managing six holding companies that operate in unrelated sectors (Mansour Group, 2017).

The size of these groups is also a factor; only the largest in terms of number of firms, capital, turnover, assets, employment, and market shares end up with sophisticated legal and administrative structures. They also reflect patterns of capital accumulation and embody certain strategies for growth and risk mitigation, especially in contexts like Egypt with high macroeconomic and political uncertainties.

As a hierarchical mode of coordination, business groups should not be confused with sectoral or national hierarchical modes of governance that exist in coordinated-market capitalisms (Soskice and Hall, 2001). In Egypt, there is a general lack of nation- or sector-wide business associations through which some institutionalized interest aggregation and representation might take place in relation to the state or organized labor (Schneider, 2004). Chambers of commerce and industry federations have been extensions of the state bureaucracy since the time of Nāṣer (al-Sayyed, 1983; Bianchi, 1989; Sulaymān, 1998; ʿEzz al-din, 2003), and because of their large compulsory membership, they often suffer from major collective action problems.

There are no semipublic business organizations or associations in Egypt that play any role in a broader corporatist setting (Streeck and Schmitter, 1985). While business associations do exist, they are largely closed clubs more interested in politics than policy (Schneider, 2009, 557). Business groups have often used their size and weight in critical sectors to cultivate individual and informal connections with bureaucrats and politicians. This hardly functions as a robust mechanism for economic coordination on macroeconomic issues in negotiating with labor. This situation resonates with Rettberg's (2005) claims in her study of Colombia that large "business groups have strong incentives to act outside of business associations to advance their particular interests."

Hence, the heavy presence of generally large and diversified family-controlled and -managed conglomerates creates a mode of governance within each business group (i.e., private hierarchy) that has an impact on the overall functioning of the private sector and the economy without much formally institutionalized interbusiness or state-business coordination. This is similar to what Schneider (2009) described in Latin America and labeled as hierarchical capitalism. In turn, these business groups, as expressions of strategies of conglomeration, fed into either vertical integration or sectoral diversification.

Vertical Integration: Replacing Supplier and Distributor Markets

Vertical integration implies the internalization of the supply or distribution chain under the same business group control and management structure. Such vertical integration could be seen in terms of Ronald Coase's (1990) concept of cutting transaction costs, which may apply to any firm in any economic context. However, in the Global South, including Egypt, vertical integration is more often linked with market failure in terms of accessing intermediate goods and services. Indeed, supplier and distributor markets suffer from the lack of free, reliable, and public information, as well as rampant informality, and hence high costs of transaction and risks of opportunism (Williamson, 1971; Klein, Crawford, and Alchian, 1978). It thus makes sense that growth strategies in agriculture, manufacturing, construction, and services include expanding the business group to contain firms or divisions that perform the tasks of backward and forward linkages.

Examples of such vertical integration include PICO Agriculture, owned by the Diāb family, that has internalized its entire value chain, from cultivation of crops to the production and distribution of final products in national and export markets. In addition, La Poire, one of the biggest pastry producers, has two distinct business lines: production and distribution, and thus has "complete control over its supply chain" (PICO, 2017).

Elsewedy Cables offers yet another case of vertical integration. In 2010, the business group was made up of sixty subsidiaries and sister companies. Within the group, many companies are specialized in the production of inputs necessary for cable production, ranging from plastics and plastic molds to wires and metals (Elsewedy Electric, 2010). Similarly, Elaraby [al-ʿArabī] group, which produces a wide range of electronics and durable goods, produces some of the inputs necessary for its product lines (mainly intermediate goods) like plastics and foams (field visit by author in 2016). The group also has its own outlets and a marketing company specializing in durable goods and home appliances.

Vertical integration can be partial or whole, practiced on a grand scale by big business groups and on smaller scales by medium-sized enterprises that establish backward and forward linkages. In all of these, vertical integration replaces intermediate markets that are either nonexistent because middle and small enterprises capable of producing reliable inputs may be lacking or are imported.

Related and Unrelated Diversification

Diversification is another key feature of business groups in Egypt. Like vertical integration, it is an investment strategy, an organizational structure, and a mode of coordination. As a strategy, it refers to investment in different sectors, often unrelated, where activities do not intersect in any of the backward or forward linkages. As an organizational form, it can be defined as "a multi-company firm which transacts in different markets but which does so under common entrepreneurial and financial control" (Leff, 1978, 662). Institutionally, diversification within large business groups is a mode of governance and coordination where a wide array of business and investment operations are brought within the same private bureaucracy and control structures. This latter institutional element is the most relevant for this discussion.

Leff (1978, 666) provided a functionalist explanation for diversification: "The group pattern of industrial organization is readily understood as a microeconomic response to well-known conditions of market failure in the less developed countries.... Some of the inputs are inherently difficult to market efficiently for example: honesty and trustworthy competences on the part of high-level managers." In these instances, owners and managers of a firm decide to capitalize on their human, financial, and social resources to move from one sector to another under the same private bureaucratic structure.

Diversification not only constitutes a microeconomic solution to the failure of intermediate markets, especially whenever high-quality inputs are required, in addition to trustworthiness and strict timing, it also substitutes for underdeveloped capital markets (Dyck and Zingales, 2004; La Porta, 2001). Such a substitution can occur in two principal ways. The first is the creation of internal capital markets, where business groups become so large and diversified that they allocate, on a bureaucratic basis, their capital among their subsidiaries by moving resources from one sector to another. This also assists in capitalizing on brands, trade names, and trademarks by using them in different product markets.

The second is making use of high returns of control by diversifying into new sectors under the same ownership structure. This marks economies with underdeveloped capital markets where it may be too risky for owning families to freely float their ownership structure (Nenova, 1999; Khanna and Palepu, 2000; Morck, Nakamura and Shivdasani, 2000; Claessens and Fan, 2002). Such diversification has one main benefit in terms of mitigating macroeconomic instability in the form of countercyclical current accounts, consumption volatility, and sudden stops in capital inflows (Gopinath and Aguiar, 2007). Diversification offers more maneuverability for enterprises. Some of the literature also suggests that it can serve as a means to counter the political risks of state predation and erratic shifts in public policy (Oh and Varcin, 2002).

By the 1990s, the Egyptian private sector witnessed diversification in some of the largest business groups, such as the Mansour, Sawiris, and Diāb family holdings. The Mansours began their automotive business after infitāḥ in 1975 in partnership with General Motors. In 1977, they branched out to become Caterpillar's distributor in Egypt and the Middle East, and in 1992 the al-Mansour for financial investments was established. This company itself owned companies engaged in a large variety of activities, most important of which was the production and distribution of cigarettes in partnership with Philip Morris, which occurred alongside owning and managing two supermarket chains in Egypt toward the late 1990s and early 2000s: Metro and Kheir-Zamān. In 1994, a fourth company was established, MANSFOODS, which solely owns and operates McDonald's in Egypt. Further diversification took place in 2005 as the enterprise branched out into construction and real estate by establishing Palm Hills, a partially publicly traded holding company in the Egyptian stock market since 2007. Finally, in 2010, the Mansours stepped into equity investment by establishing MANSCAPITAL L.L. (Mansour Group, 2017).

Another example is the Sawiris family, which Forbes considered to be the wealthiest in Egypt in 2012. The family has retained their position since then. The family business began in the late 1950s when its founder, Onsi Sawiris, owned a construction company in Upper Egypt. He relocated to neighboring Libya in the 1960s to escape Nasserist nationalization policies. Following infitāḥ, he established ORASCOM in 1976, which began as a construction company that soon expanded into other areas from the 1980s, including tourism, hotels, real estate, telecommunications, and cement and fertilizers.

There are smaller-scale cases of related diversification, where family-owned businesses have preferred expanding into related activities that share common inputs, technology, and distribution, such as the Elaraby [al-'Arabī] group, which began as a store selling a variety of goods, including home appliances, and then moved into assembling and later manufacturing

Japanese-originating durable goods (Elaraby, 2015). The history of the group is marked by a general diversification into different lines of production of durable goods. Currently, the holding firm owns companies operating in trade and industry, engineering industries, air-conditioning and refrigeration, electric bulbs, home alliances, musical instruments, and home appliance marketing (Elaraby Group, 2017).

Other cases of related diversification include the Talaat Mosfata [Ṭalʿat Muṣṭafa] Group, a construction and real estate giant that began in the mid-1970s after Ṭalʿat Muṣṭafa capitalized on crony ties with the local government in Alexandria to access land and contracts using his NDP membership (Thābet, 1996, 259). In the early 1990s, with the second generation in charge, the company departed from its early dependence on political patronage and morphed into a genuine market actor that introduced integrated urban centers on the outskirts of Cairo for the first time, developing a strong reputation for the on-time delivery of housing units and high quality after-sales services. By the 2000s, the company had moved into hotel construction and management (Talaat Moustafa Group, 2018).

Business Alliances as a Mode of Governance

Despite their overall functionality, private hierarchies, as a mode of business coordination, could not deliver everything. When inputs could not be internalized within business groups through vertical integration or diversification or acquired on a pure market basis, an in-between mode of governance developed: interbusiness alliances. These alliances were institutionalized networks of economic organizations that encompassed formal and informal rules for establishing long-term and predictable patterns of interbusiness exchange. Unlike baladi capitalism, such alliances transcend immediate personal relations and social ties (Dasgupta, 2000). They are more process oriented and centered around the economic performance of enterprises (François, 2004, 30) and usually pass from one manager to another in allied organizations (Uzzi, 1997).

Similar to vertical integration and diversification, interbusiness alliances are investment strategies and modes of coordination. The rationale behind them is mutual utility maximization and cost reduction through the setting and observance of rules securing long-term transactions between economic actors. Such business alliances are generally horizontal, wherein parties do not come under the same hierarchy and have, at least formally, equal power. For instance, this is how banks create informal long-standing partnerships with debtor firms, something close to what Stiglitz (1994) called market interfaces.

Business alliances operate according to several mechanisms. The first is the continuous flow of highly credible and reliable private information that is either shared among alliance members formally (e.g., financial reports submitted to banks) or informally (as may be the case with recommended suppliers or distributors). In all cases, these flows of private information limit risk, enhance the capacity to make decisions, generate opportunities, and lower the cost of information gathering and processing. The second mechanism is the presence of a long-term prospect for decision making that is generally insensitive to short-term price fluctuations (Uzzi, 1996, 683), and the third is a familiarity with the behavior and performance of alliance members in a way that makes opportunism unlikely and lowers the cost of dispute settlement and contract enforcement (McMillan and Woodruff, 1999).

These business alliances in Egypt can be traced back to the seeds of private sector expansion after infitāḥ. In this period, close and long-range relations began between certain private enterprises (or the entrepreneurs or families owning and managing them) and other enterprises, including suppliers, distributors, and banks (al-ʿAntarī, 2005, 109, 111). These alliances even found their way into state-owned enterprises (SOEs) and their private counterparts in partnerships established in the 1970s and 1980s (Sadowski, 1991, 100).

Some entrepreneurs could build on earlier, short-term and initially small-scale exchange with state-owned banks to establish long-term, process-oriented, and institutionalized alliances. Prime examples include Maḥmūd Elaraby's relationship with Banque Misr (Elaraby, 2015, 253–254) and Ḥusein Sabbour's [Ṣabbūr] partnership with the National Bank of Egypt (discussed below). There is also evidence that such bank-business alliances were not confined to big business groups or politically connected persons. As alliances served as governance and coordination mechanisms that regulated credit extension at relatively low transaction costs (see Stiglitz, 1994, 90, 123), the enterprises that made it by the 2000s could be seen as cases that grew with banks rather than simply dealing with banks after growing.

According to a survey conducted in 2006 by the Egyptian Banking Institute in cooperation with the Central Agency for Public Mobilization and Statistics

(CAPMAS), 47 percent of the surveyed SMEs indicated interacting with banks (el-Said, al-Said, and Zaki, 2013, 10), only 16 percent of which reported experiencing any trouble in such dealings. The fact that a majority reported none of the problems that SMEs traditionally experience, such as high collateral requirements, indicates that engaging in some sort of bank-business alliance (long-range close relationships with banks) provides them with privileged access to bank credit—bearing in mind that the total share of small and medium enterprises (SMEs) in bank credit in Egypt does not exceed 5 percent (Rocha et al., 2011, 22).

In the 1970s and 1980s, such bank-business alliances may have stemmed from social networks based on familial and shared educational or professional backgrounds. While this is hardly distinguishable from practices under baladi capitalism, with the notable exception of being linked to formal credit-providing institutions like banks, the twist that occurred later was the rise of economic networking that went beyond the immediate solid social identity of the owners and managers of private enterprises and banks. From here, these relations developed into sustained patterns of economic exchange based on past records, shared experience, and accumulated firm- and industry-level information. All of these factors contributed to the creation of a long-term time horizon and mutually recognized interfirm interest, or what has been called relationship banking (Beshāy, 2015).

Overall, alliances such as these exist between private bureaucracies and organizations (Uzzi, 1996) in a way that adds a more impersonal, differentiated, and institutionalized element that effectively substitutes for markets and hierarchies as modes of economic governance.

Bank-Business Alliances: Separate But Close

The banking sector in Egypt historically has been characterized by a persistent and firmly institutionalized separation between nonfinancial and financial enterprises. Throughout the past four decades, no domestic businesspeople, business families, or groups have ever acquired a controlling share in a commercial bank that would have enabled them to direct or substantially influence credit provision decisions.

This separation of financial businesses from nonfinancial ones was reinforced by the financial sector reform program launched in 2003/2004 that set and enforced legal and prudential regulations to secure the highest degree of separation possible. The law has also set limits on the methods used for calculating the shares held by natural or legal persons. Similarly, article 50 of the banking sector law requires that the Central Bank be notified of any natural or legal person holding 5 to 10 percent of the issued capital of any bank.

In practice, the Central Bank has maintained a firm stance throughout the 2000s in not allowing the overlap of ownership or control between nonfinancial business groups, especially those run by families, and banks. For instance, this has affected the Sawiris family in its failed attempts to secure a license from the CBE to establish a commercial bank (Ḥassan, 2017; Qotb and Ghāleb, 2016). Hence, the shares of businesspeople in commercial bank–issued capital have remained below 10 percent, as has been the case with the Mansours and Crédit Agricole–Egypt. The Central Bank has also counted on the presence of the French Group Crédit Agricole as a buffer against any attempt by the Mansours to gain control of investment and credit decisions (Beshāy, 2015). The same applied to Oriental Weavers in its shares of Piraeus Bank (5 percent), as well as Saudi, Emirati, and Indian individual investors who held shares below 5 percent in the Commercial International Bank, Egypt's largest private bank.

Such regulatory restrictions in Egypt impeded the emergence of the Turkish or Russian models wherein commercial banks are owned and controlled by nonfinancial business groups (Perotti and Gelfer, 2001, 2002; Demirag and Serter, 2003). It also precluded a Japanese-style banking sector where banks own and generally finance nonfinancial business groups (Morck and Nakamura, 1999; Hoshi, 2001; Caballero, Hoshi, and Kahyap, 2008).

The Central Bank has also set restrictions on the ownership of commercial banks in shares of nonfinancial businesses and their ability to extend credit to businesses where banks are shareholders. The CBE's annual report of 2002/2003 (p. 51) demonstrates that the largest share of the banking system's investment portfolio in Egypt has been made up of loans and discounts (49.3 percent in 2003 on the eve of the financial sector reform program), while investments in other securities, including private company stocks and bonds, were merely 4.2 percent of the total. This situation has not changed significantly since implementation of the financial sector reform program in 2003/2004, as the Central Bank has used its broad regulatory mandate to liquidate assets held by commercial banks, primarily publicly owned ones, that were once acquired as collateral for unpaid loans (Beshāy, 2015). According to Law No. 88 of 2003, all assets and movables acquired by commercial banks as collateral for unpaid debt must be sold within a year.

Bank-business alliances nevertheless formed a nonhierarchical yet coordinated mode of governance that dominated the provision of financial capital to the private sector in Egypt. These patterns of exchange have been characterized by long-term horizons and relative immunity to short-term price (and other market) fluctuations. Within these alliances, there are streams of private information that are shared between allied managers in a way that limits information asymmetry (the lack of public information), reduces risk, and contributes to the creation of business opportunities for both parties (Beshāy, 2015; Waḥīd, 2016).

Such bank-business relations developed in the 1980s and 1990s based on two main mechanisms. The first was politically driven: extending bank credit, primarily from publicly owned banks, to cronies with strong ties to the Mubārak regime (Adly, 2009, 11). The other has been more economically driven; it included private enterprises that were not necessarily politically connected. These were the early roots of bank-business alliances that came to dominate access to credit in the 2000s following the implementation of the financial sector reform program.

Through the first mechanism, "Privileged private sector borrowers were . . . allowed to borrow despite their poor financial condition and insufficient collateral" (Dean and Modeildin, 2001, 29). These alliances were forged on political bases, usually neglecting prudential regulations. For example, Aḥmed Bahgat, a leading businessman and industrialist in the 1990s, held loans in excess of 1 billion Egyptian pounds in the late 1990s and has been reported to be personally close to Mubārak's elder son 'Alā' (Mitchell, 1999, 463; el-Tarouty, 2015, 121–130). Another striking example from the 1990s was *Nuwāb al-Qurūḍ* (Loan MPs), a case known in which twenty-eight bankers, businesspeople, and former politicians, together with four members of parliament from the ruling party, were indicted for embezzlement (Adly, 2009, 12–13).

Despite the rampancy of politically based alliances, the 1980s and 1990s also witnessed the emergence of economic bank-business alliances between commercial banks, private as well as public, and businesspeople who were not necessarily politically connected. For instance, the Elaraby Group has been party to a strong and durable alliance with Banque Misr since the 1970s. According to the memoirs of the founder and chairman of the group, Maḥmūd Elaraby, the enterprise secured a 100 million pound loan for factory expansions in the early 1990s (Elaraby, 2015, 253–254), and, in a personal interview with me (2016), Elaraby claimed to be the biggest client of the bank. The former chairman of the bank, whom I met during my field trip to the Elaraby complex in 2016, was also appointed at Elaraby Group following his retirement. He mentioned that the group was an excellent client for Banque Misr, given its successful expansion into the Egyptian durable goods market and its sound finances. He highlighted the experience that he had inherited from former chairmen as a model between a bank and a business. According to the former chairman of the bank, the relationship has been so fluid and close to the extent that the bank used to call on the group to expand into new areas and offer to extend specially designed loans to the business's needs.

Another enduring example of a bank-business alliance that dates back to the early 1990s is that between the Ṣabbour group and the National Bank of Egypt (NBE). In 1994, the NBE formed a joint-venture company, Al Ahly for Real Estate Development, with Ḥusein Ṣabbour, the owner of a prominent and pioneering consultancy firm. According to the company's website in 2018, the NBE owned 40 percent of the shares, while the Ṣabbour family retains the remaining 60 percent, an exceptionally enduring partnership between an individual entrepreneur and his family that the CBE has tolerated thus far. The joint venture seemed to have begun thanks to the strong personal ties between Ṣabbour and the then chair of the NBE, Maḥmūd ʿAbdel-ʿAzīz. The partnership assumed an institutional character as it has outlived ʿAbdel-ʿAzīz's tenure as chairman of NBE, which ended in 2000. Moreover, this particular bank-business alliance could not have been derived from political connections because Ṣabbour did not join the former ruling NDP under al-Sadāt or Mubārak (Saʿīd, 2017), nor did he play any direct political role throughout his career.

STATE-BUSINESS TRANSACTIONS

The third component of dandy capitalism is state-enterprise interaction, which presents in two principal forms. First, it involves transactions that private businesses conduct directly with state agencies, be they regulatory (e.g., business registration, permits, licenses) or economic (e.g., tender, subsidies and incentives and taxes, public land allocation). Second, it captures interbusiness transactions to which the state is a third party, generally through acting as an actual or potential enforcer of agreements between market actors.

As a by-product of their relatively large amount of capital and turnover, dandy enterprises are generally more visible to the state. Hence, none of them can afford outright informality with their transactions conducted away from any state record or registration. Rather, they must adhere to formal rules and regulations, or at least make it appear as though they were (e.g., tax avoidance or evasion, temporary contracts for workers). However, this certainly does not preclude invoking informal rules in dealing with officials by pulling strings or paying bribes in order to grease the wheels and lower costs of transaction or cut through red tape (Hoogvelt, 1978, 137). Such practices are enabled by their superior access to social, political, and economic resources. In short, dandy enterprises are too big to hide and have a better chance to show high adaptation to formal rules, even if they were not of their own making.

An additional by-product of their relatively large size is that these enterprises are better disposed to access to state-created rents such as desert land sold at below-market rates, fuel subsidies, tax rebates and exemptions, and tariff and nontariff protections among others (Sadowski, 1991, 104). By possessing large initial or acquired capital, they are important to policymakers (Adly, 2017, 22). On the one hand, they can deploy their resources so as to align with state policies and projects, such as developing new towns in the desert, populating industrial parks, and reclaiming land plots (Sadowski, 1991, 106). On the other, they have often possessed social and cultural capital in addition to their financial and physical capital, providing them with information and leverage to influence or reduce the operation costs of interacting with state agencies (Imām, 1986, 56).

Influencers Rather Than Captors

Because dandy capitalism is characterized by a relative differentiation between the economic and the political, dandy enterprises, unlike captor firms (see Chapter 3), have had to operate under formal rules that were largely not of their making. With some notable exceptions, many private businesses that managed to grow under Mubārak have never wielded enough political weight to influence the parliament, bureaucracy, or executive to amend formal rules or issue new ones (Zaki, 1999, 121, 123).

In contrast, captor firms in Egypt often belonged to state organizations—namely, the military or the intelligence and security agencies—either formally or informally, and they have thus been powerful enough to carve out their own fiefdoms and dictate formal laws and regulations designed to protect their claims on state resources and furnish them with economic opportunities (Adly, 2012b, 2; Adly and Palluelo, 2013, 22–26).

While most Egyptian captors have originated in these state security and military circles, Mubārak's rule witnessed significantly fewer cases of private sector captors. Aḥmed ʿEzz, the notorious steel tycoon who wielded considerable power in the NDP and its majority in parliament between 2005 and 2010, stood as a notable exception when it came to private business's capacity to set formal rules in their favor. In 2008, ʿEzz successfully amended the antimonopoly law by reducing the fines placed on enterprises found guilty of monopoly, which effectively protected his firm's position in the steel market (Selim, 2006).

However, Aḥmed ʿEzz's case remained exceptional in terms of private sector actors in Egypt. Bureaucratic actors have dominated economic policy and regulation making throughout most of Egypt's capitalist transformation. Even under Aḥmed Nazīf's businessmen's cabinet, seen as exceptionally business friendly, the power to formulate and pass economy-governing laws remained largely in the hands of the state bureaucracy, namely the Ministry of Justice and the State Council courts. Both entities could outweigh the influence of business-friendly ministers in key positions like tourism, agriculture, and industry and trade as they continued to express a certain legal culture and practice inherited from the statist legal tradition of the 1960s (al-Shawārby, 2015).

In this case, most private enterprises, including some of the largest, had a limited capacity to dictate formal rules to serve their direct and narrow interests. This does not mean, however, that they did not benefit from state-created rents; it merely notes how they had little sway over the formal rules governing the creation and distribution of these rents. Nonetheless, they were relatively capable of using their political contacts or economic weight in order to influence the implementation of formal regulations through twisting or evading them via their financial, cultural, and social capital (Hellman, Jones, and Kaufmann, 2000, 9–10). This would render them influencers rather than pure captors.

However, being influencers rather than captors came with the risk of being prosecuted (or persecuted) by the political leadership, judiciary, or bureaucracy. This leads to the idea of buying protection rather than seeking rent, such as the telling example, illustrated by Kassem (2004, 33–35), of Rāmi Lakaḥ, a businessman who ran successfully as an independent candidate in the parliamentary elections of 2000. Lakaḥ used his vast financial resources to secure himself a seat, despite being a Christian Catholic in a Muslim-majority district and facing a heavyweight NDP candidate (Soliman, 2006, 248). However, his subsequent decision to remain independent and his refusal to join the NDP cost him his hard-won seat. Arrears owed to state-owned banks were made subject to prosecution, and he was eventually expelled from the parliament and fled to France.

A majority of Egyptian private enterprises thus had to live with a number of regulations, laws, and verdicts that were neither of their choosing nor always in their immediate interest. For instance, Tender Law No. 89 of 1998 posed a number of risks for big business investments, including those with robust political connections, regarding public land that was allocated for real estate, tourism, industry, and land reclamation purposes. The law set formal restrictions on land that could be directly allocated by ministerial decree. This created a large gray area wherein large urban developers had to cooperate with the Ministry of Housing (ʿAbdel-ʿAẓīm and Fawzy, 2015), including the Talaat Moustafa Group with strong political links within Egypt and with Gulf Cooperation Council–based investors and medium-sized ones like al-Ahly/Sabbour.

Similarly, several ministerial decrees concerning the allocation of land plots, as well as SOE privatization contracts, were subject to challenge before the State Council courts. Being designated "as the organ generally competent to rule on administrative disputes. . . . [including] disputes related to the implementation of contracts for concessions, public works, supplies or any other administrative contracts" (Rady, 2002, 248–249), State Council courts were instrumental for labor rights groups, activists, and the political opposition to derail the privatization of public assets, be they desert land or privatized and divested SOEs (Adly, 2012b). This contentious setting had occasionally created shock waves that directly threatened the stability of private property rights under Mubārak. For instance, Talaat Moustafa's "Madinaty," Egypt's largest urban development project during the Mubārak era, was subject to a State Council court verdict in 2009 that essentially annulled the public contract allocating the land to the group (Adly, 2012b, 9).

This sense of uncertainty was exacerbated by the multiplicity of power centers within and between state bodies in charge of implementing economy-related regulations and laws. This made it difficult to reach and sustain stable and durable agreements and reduce abrupt policy changes. Such is the Egyptian state bureaucracy, characterized by a vast size and competing elite networks (Shehata, 2011; Roccu, 2013), encompassing the military, security, intelligence, the former NDP, the presidential family, and a relatively independent judiciary (Moustapha, 2007). In such a setting, it never sufficed to establish strong ties with only one group, network, or agency while ignoring others.

Even later instances of seemingly beneficial (from the business perspective) changes in State Council courts did not seem to emerge from effective private sector lobbying or any cronyistic dynamic. For instance, a presidential decree during the term of ʿAdly Mansour (2012–2013) curbed the oversight of the courts over public contracts by confining the right to challenge them to direct parties to the agreement. The amendment happened at a time when big private businesses lacked virtually all-political leverage and was rather driven by the political leadership, with the direct backing of the military, after the July 2013 coup, in a desperate attempt to provide some minimal guarantees for foreign and domestic investors (Adly, 2017, 19).

Thus, private businesses did not generally have the power to make formal rules and regulations in any direct manner, either individually or collectively. However, they had the resources to influence how such rules and regulations were implemented (or not) by devising informal rules and mechanisms that substituted, completely or partly, for these formal rules. This high level of adaptation is affordable only to those who have the resources and has enabled these firms to navigate their way through ambiguous and sometimes conflicting laws and regulations, as well as a costly tax administration (World Bank, 2015).

Indeed, navigating the Egyptian taxation system is a case in point. As indicated in Chapter 5, tax authorities have focused their collection efforts on the large and medium-sized enterprises in the private sector (al-ʿArabī, 2013). More specifically, it is the enterprises without the requisite political connection (i.e., dandy firms) that are expected to pay these taxes. The enterprises that embody the financial interests of the ruling elite (e.g., military-affiliated enterprises) are legally or effectively exempt.

Given the high dependence on rough estimates amid the absence of reliable data about business annual turnover or sales, most businesses appeal their tax bills before administrative committees. This serves as a means for renegotiating the final amounts of money due, though it is costly in terms of time consumed, informal payments to corrupt officers, and the fees paid to lawyers and auditors (ʿAbdel-Moḥsen, 2015). While this increases the discretion given to the tax authorities, it also allows for localized compromise based on connections within the bureaucracy and informal side payments.

In these instances, private information about how the system works can prove valuable. For instance, former employees in local government units generally have better access to building permits and licenses due to their previous professional experience and connections. This is of course the same logic that big businesses, including MNCs in areas like oil and gas extraction (Ḥamūda, 2015), follow in hiring former army and security generals and colonels once they are out of office.

State-Enabled Twisted Formality

Rule twisting refers to an institutionalized use of loopholes in formal rules and regulations that serves ends other than the ones they were originally set for. While twisted formality certainly is a defining feature of baladi capitalism, not only do state agencies tolerate or sanction twisted formality under dandy capitalism, but they also play an active central role. Such an active role by state agencies in this environment of semiformality is crucial for sustaining the depth and breadth of impersonal market transactions.

An example of state-enabled twisted formality is the use of checks to finance long-term investment in the real estate sector (among others). Crucial for financing large construction companies that cater to the upper and upper-middle classes, checks have been converted from unsecured short-term debt commercial papers into long-term security instruments. The state, through the Central Bank, has become a third-party enforcer of this twisted implementation of formal rules by institutionally integrating them into the formal regulations governing the banking sector.

In 1999, a new commercial code was issued that made the Central Bank an active regulator and de facto guarantor of these long-term secured checks between real estate developers and final consumers. Initially, it tightened the use of commercial paper, with a special emphasis on checks, by setting stringent, formalistic, and substantive standards and conditions for the issuance, circulation, and collection of checks with the aim of subjecting their issuance and use to the regulatory supervision of the Central Bank (Mūssa, 2018). As Article 503(1) reads: "The check shall be payable upon sighting. All statements otherwise added shall be null and non-existent. . . . If the check is presented for honoring before the date mentioned in it the issue date, it shall be honored on the day it is presented, with the exception of the lined checks [a check that can be paid only on a designated future date] prescribed in article (515) of this law." The original intent of the drafters of this new law was to stress the use of checks as payment rather than as long-term security instruments (Ḥamdi, 2014, 32); however, this collided with the already prevalent uses of checks among private market actors as security instruments since the 1970s and 1980s. Almost four years after the issuance of the new commercial code, parliament struck a compromise that provided for an exceptional use of lined or crossed checks (shīkāt moṣaṭara) as long-term rather than short-term debt instruments (Law No. 156 of 2004). This exception was added to a subsequent clause holding that lined checks, unlike normal open checks, "shall not be paid except on the date indicated therein as their date of issue."

Interestingly, this exceptional use of checks is in fact their most prevalent use in Egypt. However, the role of the state did not stop at legalizing the common practice of checks as security instruments; it went even further into the regulation and enforcement of these legally exceptional yet practically predominant uses, contributing to the expansion of anonymous market transactions in key sectors like real estate and construction.

For instance, before building housing units, real estate developers sign preliminary contracts with their buyers while simultaneously having them write lined checks for the total price of the contracted unit (Gabr, 2014; Palm Hills Group, 2014). These lined checks bear future due dates that act as installments to finance the construction of the contracted units in periods that extend on average for five to seven years (hence, medium term in nature). Buyers hand all of these long-term checks to the developer at the moment of signing the contract, and the developer deposits the lined checks in the bank and discounts each on the designated date.

Hence, lined checks have become the principal means of financing real estate investment in Egypt (Gabr, 2014). This mechanism is distinct from a mortgage because it involves the medium-term debt financing of nonexisting housing units. Indeed, while the mortgage market in Egypt remains negligible (less than half a percent of GDP; World Bank, 2015c, 23), check-based debt financing constituted by far the largest channel.

Nonetheless, this twisted use of formal rules and instruments (checks) can work only on a large scale thanks to the de facto role of the Central Bank as enforcer. In 2008, the board of the Central Bank issued Decree No. 906 that specifically regulated the use of lined checks for medium-term financing of the construction of housing units. The decree reconfirmed the exceptional uses of lined checks, acknowledging and enforcing the use of checks as long-term debt instruments (Sulaymān, 2010). Moreover, real estate developers reportedly used the long-term checks they collected from buyers as collateral to secure bank loans, technically known as invoice factoring (Paragon Financial Group, 2018). This suggests that the twisted use of checks as security instruments is no longer essential just for company financing and transactions with final consumers. It is also critical for the stability of credit relations between banks and real estate developers.

The financial reports of two of the largest publicly traded real estate developers, Talaat Moustafa (2014) and Palm Hill (2014), reveal the relative weight of long-term checks for company financing. Both became publicly traded in 2007, and hence their financial reports provide interesting data, especially in the few years preceding the outbreak of the January revolution that disrupted the economy significantly. For Talaat Moustafa (2014), checks collected from contracted buyers stood for 80.57 percent of the group's capital and around 36 percent of its total investment from 2007 through 2010. The same ratios can be found with Palm Hills during the same interval: checks stood for 148 percent of the group's capital and 33.44 percent of total investment. Long-term checks were significantly more important in financing investment in building housing units than long-term bank loans. In fact, long-term checks were nearly six times as great as long-term loans, while two-thirds of the commercial paper issued were long-term (230 percent of short-term checks), confirming their use as reliable security instruments.

THE DANDY ENCLAVE AND THE PERSISTENCE OF CLEFT CAPITALISM

Dandy capitalism was at best a high adaptation to state institutions that were often hostile to the development of a competitive and robust private sector in Egypt. Whereas it allowed the emergence of an entrepreneurial and viable private sector that could exploit its potential to grow with relative autonomy of political power, it did not lead to further market integration through the creation of backward and forward linkages with SSEs at the base of the private sector or raising the share of big business in employment. The complementarity this class of enterprises was able to develop with capital-regulating organizations, namely the banking sector and some bureaucratic bodies within the Egyptian state, was largely a function of their large initial capital endowments that allowed them to conduct impersonal transactions and ultimately disembed much of their economic dealing from the concrete social identities of their owners. This separation allowed them to operate at scales and levels of administrative sophistication that were for both foreign and domestic capital in the form of MNCs and Egyptian banks, respectively, and created a mutually reinforcing institutional structure that was beneficial to all involved. Of course, the problem is that the broad base of SSEs was not involved in this institutionalized system of credit circulation, rendering the Egyptian private sector persistently cleft and unintegrated.

Ultimately the main challenge facing any capitalist transformation has never been creating an enclave of well-functioning large enterprises. Rather, it is how to have a more competitive base of private sector enterprises that could achieve the task of market integration. The prevailing challenge of Egypt's transformation is thus how to break this exclusionary institutional arrangement and finally free the broad base of SSEs from their own dilemma that has precluded them from capital, growth, and the elusive Egyptian dream.

EPILOGUE

THE STORY OF EGYPT'S FAILED MARKET MAKING IS ROOTED IN deep socioeconomic misalignments rather than collusion between the state and big business. Despite economic liberalization and private sector development, designed to serve as the neoclassical solutions to Egypt's economic woes, entrenched levels of social marginalization and exclusion derived from earlier attempts at top-down modernization and colonial rule persisted after independence. Throughout most of Egypt's contemporary history, including social reform eras in the 1950s and 1960s, state institutions maintained ties with only limited segments of society. This implied the absence of complementarity between social evolution that involved the vast majority of the people, on the one hand, and state attempts to deliver development on the other. As Dorman (2013, 4) eloquently put it, the Egyptian state has been trying "to transform Egyptian society without actually engaging it." Such is the overarching concept for understanding the historical lack of complementarity and intermediate institutions between capital-regulating organizations and small-scale enterprises (SSEs), the missing-middle syndrome, rampant economic informality, and cleft capitalism as the general condition for underdevelopment throughout the past four decades of attempted market making.

Contrary to popular and simplistic diagnoses, Egypt's problem has never been an inability to produce political, economic, or cultural elites at the top, who could integrate and compete globally. Rather, the problem was how this "top" was related to the "bottom"—state-society relations that seemed to have evolved independently and, at times, at the expense of each other.

The root of this discomplementarity is historical. As Tignor (1984) and Vitalis (1995) have shown, a big business class that was made up of Egyptian and Egyptianized elements emerged in the early twentieth century, as the temporary interruption of international trade caused by World War I (1914–1918) attracted capitalists from the agricultural sector (the traditional bastion of wealthy Egyptians) into manufacturing. The shift was enabled further by the nationalist sentiment of the 1920s and Egypt's formal independence in 1922, which created some space for state protection and subsidization of burgeoning national industry. This state-business coordination was greatly characterized by rent seeking and state patronage and was rife with bitter competition among private cartels (see Vitalis, 1995). However, even in these early days, these businesses had sources of accumulation independent of state rents, largely derived from their control of the agricultural sector where they had enjoyed well-established private property rights since the second half of the nineteenth century (Cuno, 1980).

The private sector remained a basic feature of Egypt's economy even during the heyday of Nasserist nationalization and state-led development in the 1960s. Private sector micro and small (and to a lesser extent medium) establishments were left to not only operate but to dominate key sectors like wholesale and retail trading, as well as construction. In 1973, after almost fifteen years of state-led development, the private sector still supplied 56.18 percent of total output compared to 43.8 percent for the public sector. Small, private producers dominated agriculture (98 percent), trade (60 percent), and housing (88.2 percent) and had a significant presence in light manufacturing and services (O'Brien, 1966, cited in Waterbury, 1983, 160).

Private sector SSEs especially dominated labor-intensive manufacturing sectors like leather, furniture, wooden products, clothing and apparel, and printing ('Abdel-Faḍīl, 1980, 82). According to Mabro and Radwan (1976, 119), "In the middle of [the] 1970s, 93 percent of the total 116,000 private sector firms were artisanal, employing fewer than five workers. Half of them employed no workers at all." Waterbury (1983, 163–164) further noted that only ten private sector firms could be classified as "large-scale, with 500 or more employees."

In turn, public sector expansion was concentrated in capital- and technology-intensive industries and services.

By the 1970s and 1980s, Egypt and other (primarily non-oil-rich) Middle East and North Africa (MENA) countries underwent economic liberalization and private sector expansion schemes wherein state action, formal and informal, played a significant role in capitalizing early market actors through net transfers from public resources, in what, two centuries ago, Marx called primitive accumulation. Close relations between the state and some private sector actors opened avenues for primitive capital accumulation, though not necessarily in ways that were fully exclusive from entrepreneurship and market relations (Yāsīn, 2015). By the 1990s, Egypt ended up with a formidable class of large and concentrated private enterprises that were mainly family owned and sectorally diversified.

Despite inefficiencies from rampant corruption and rent seeking, not all transactions were predatory and unproductive. Linkages between the state and big business allowed coordination and even upgrading in certain sectors under Mubārak, such as manufactured and agricultural exports, as well as tourism and construction in new towns throughout the 1990s and 2000s. However, such coordination failed to catapult the economy in a fashion similar to the Korean or Taiwanese miracles, or even relatively humbler developmental cases like Turkey and Malaysia, as both business and state elites were cut off from the broad base of the private sector and labor force. This precluded the latter from being exploited in the neoclassical and Marxian senses, which would have led to a more developmental and politically sustainable capitalist transformation.

Thus, the divergence of Egypt's developmental path from more successful cases had less to do with rent seeking, corruption, and cronyism and more to do with the system of cleft capitalism that deprived the business elite of a robust and competitive base of small and medium enterprises (SMEs)—the missing middle. This access would have enabled the dominant classes to exploit the one abundant factor of production in Egypt: cheap labor directly, as well as indirectly, through employment in the SSE sector. Instead, cleft capitalism denied the Egyptian economy as a whole the chance for a more integrated capitalist order with an accessible and exploitable base of SSEs and labor. While some degree of exploitation has been rampant, especially with the progressive proletarianization of Egyptians throughout the second half of the twentieth century, this largely remained in the domain of subsistence-driven microunits with virtually no potential for scaling up or growing beyond their immediate localized markets.

The problem was not how Egyptian politics and economics were articulated in any exceptional ways compared to more successful cases in the Global South, nor were political factors such as rent seeking, cronyism, or state patronage primarily responsible for delivering Egypt's suboptimal development. Indeed, politics remains central to capital accumulation in the Global South as well as North (Bonefield, 2001; Glassman, 2006; Harvey, 2007). It would be hard to imagine how capitalism could function without governance and regulation on the national and global levels through state and interstate authoritative arrangements (Panitch and Gindin, 2012). In market democracies, the economy has become progressively differentiated from politics through the firm establishment of the rule of law and the even protection of property rights, a fairly recent process that signifies only one phase of capitalist development.

In contrast, capitalist development in much of the Global South did not necessitate the reproduction of the same kind of institutional differentiation between politics and the economy. Indeed, China, South Korea, Taiwan, and others in Southeast Asia demonstrate high levels of interpenetration and collusion between economic and political elites while formal market institutions have remained underdeveloped. In their place, alternative politically and socially embedded institutions have delivered high growth, competitiveness, and an overall favorable integration into world trade and capital markets.

WHEN SMALL IS BIG

The historical record of economic modernization in the late nineteenth and early twentieth centuries demonstrates that such development was less about "industrial gigantism," usually associated with modern economic elites in control of concentrated capital. Rather, Deborah Cohen (2018, 5) cites evidence that historically "small and medium-sized plants formed the bedrock of the economy" in Great Britain, France, Germany, the United States, and Japan back then. These firms were then able to form multiple linkages with large capital. The same story unfolded later with the newly industrializing nations of East and Southeast Asia. As Chapter 1 showed, SMEs have played a central role in the development journeys of Taiwan, South Korea, China, and Malaysia. Hence, the key lies not in engendering a few large "modern enterprises," but in the existence of a robust and competitive base of SMEs through a myriad of institutional arrangements.

The lack of these institutional arrangements points to an institutional explanation for the less successful cases of capitalist transformation in the MENA and other parts of the Global South. These intermediate institutions generate complementarities between public capital-regulating organizations governing access to credit and land and the broader base of private enterprises. Rather than the neoclassical institutions—formal private property protection and the rule of law—it was the absence of these intermediate institutions that led to largely unintegrated capitalist orders.

Similarly, the Weberian bureaucracies idealized as prerequisites for development in the literature on developmental states have either been very exceptional to a handful of cases or totally nonexistent in the Global South. The ability of states to influence their economies has been consistently overstated given the rampant informality and general lack of state autonomy from powerful societal groups. The Egyptian case shows that the broad base of the private sector emerged in the absence of intentional state action, as the marketization and proletarianization processes that engulfed millions of Egyptians by the 1970s have resulted from long-term demographic and social changes little regulated by the state.

The launch of infitāḥ and the following market-making reforms of the 1980s and 1990s could not (and were not meant to) undo the legacy of socioeconomic marginalization, primarily due to the persistent absence of intermediate institutions that could have cultivated complementarities with the broad base of small-scale private establishments. Hence, cleft capitalism was not a product of infitāḥ; rather it resulted from a long-standing process extending back to Egypt's modernization process in the nineteenth century, which left a majority of the people behind.

Throughout Egypt's contemporary history, SSE owners and local entrepreneurial populations were neither politically nor socially empowered in a way that could have elevated them to fill the middle rungs of the private sector economy. Politically, the authoritarian dynamics of the 1952 regime allowed only for the incorporation of state-dependent constituencies, dynamics that persist today because they are denied space to collectively articulate their interests. Socially, Egypt, unlike successful cases of transformation, never experienced that type of social revolution capable of delivering for the marginalized and excluded majority. In contrast, Amartya Sen (2001, 94–98) underlined the positive yet unintended impact of China's social revolution under Mao in incorporating sizable rural and urban constituencies into market operations following Xiao Ping's economic opening in the late 1970s. Earlier improvements in health, education, and women's emancipation broadened the base of a skilled (and cheap) labor force that came to define China's competitive advantage in the capitalist global economy. Conversely, India's market-making reforms of the 1990s have not overcome the deep socioeconomic marginalization that marked the country's postindependence period in which the caste system has endured. Hence, by the time economic liberalization unleashed market forces, a majority of Indians remained marginalized on caste, sectarian, ethnic, and gender basis.

India slightly resonates with the experience of Egypt, where no social or democratic revolutions ever (successfully) took place, not even under Nasserism, which was ultimately more of a conservative middle-class-dominated project of modernization (Abdel-Malek, 1968). Nor has it witnessed episodes of mass mobilization or a deep transformation of social or economic relations. Any social mobility that did occur due to expanding education and public sector employment was tied to demobilization and incorporation rather than the transformation.

By the time market-based capitalism was sought in Egypt in the mid-1970s, deeply entrenched social and economic marginalization precluded full market integration. However, the deadweight of the past was not inescapable; intermediate institutions could have emerged in response to the political empowerment of segments of SSEs, which never took place. Conversely, SSE populations were never brought into political processes because their interests never aligned with the immediate interests of those at the top, nor could they follow the path of larger dandy capitalist firms and break in from the outside given their dearth of capital. Ultimately, state action in the economic area remained captive to a bureaucratic coalition that in spite of being tension ridden and generally uncoordinated nevertheless unleashed mechanisms that raised economic and political barriers to accessing capital for the broad base of private enterprises. Most SSEs could not adapt to these state institutional arrangements, instead scraping out the ability to survive rather than grow. Conversely, larger enterprises with large initial or acquired capital showed higher adaptation, using their financial, social, and cultural capital in order to jump these barriers and scale up.

MARXIAN RECIPES FOR CAPITALIST TRANSFORMATION

Contrary to neoclassical accounts, the contemporary ordeal of market integration in much of the Global South has been ironically Marxian rather than Hayekian. The neoclassical stance that holds the distribution of private property rights and enforcement of contracts as the prerequisites of market creation simply misses the point. What good would it do to distribute property rights when the vast majority have no property in the first place? Market creation is all about creating market actors— actors who need capital in all its forms to be able to produce, exchange, and grow. In the light of the roles played by SMEs in earlier and later experiences of economic modernization, the problems of capitalist transformation in Egypt seem to have been much more about material access to capital. However, above this material base, institutionalism remains relevant with the need to cultivate intermediate institutions that create complementarities between the broad base of private SSEs and public capital-regulating organizations.

Egypt, as well as other countries in the Global South, has shown that market coordination can occur in the absence of the universal rule of law and contract enforcement. In Egypt, social institutions and organizations proved central for the functioning and creation of markets beginning with infitāḥ . Family and friendship networks have served as pools for early capital accumulation, the circulation of reliable information, as well as access to credit, skilled labor, and entrepreneurial and managerial skills. This book has demonstrated that such nonmarket structures and constructs, while being socially embedded, can create markets through mechanisms of familiarization wherein entrepreneurs go beyond their immediate social networks into more price-oriented exchanges. Indeed, there is little doubt that individuals and families often use their social embeddedness to conduct market-oriented operations. This is what I have called "market-oriented embeddedness" and argued that such Polanyian forms of exchange need not always be mutually exclusive with market exchange. Rather, they may in fact constitute markets, especially at early stages of capitalism when formal state institutions cannot efficiently perform the role of a third-party contract enforcer or provider of cheap, reliable public information.

However, such market-oriented embeddedness is not sufficient for accomplishing the task of market integration, mainly due to the limited pools of capital made available for socially embedded entrepreneurs and SSE owners. In modern settings, unless there are institutional channels that allow private SSEs to access publicly regulated financial and physical capital, their capacity to grow and compete will always be hampered. This refers back to the deep material restraints that SSEs face given the lack of complementarities between them and capital-regulating organizations.

Not only is market integration key to economic success under a globalized capitalist division of labor; it is also imperative for the political sustainability of market making. The creation of broad constituencies of scalable small and medium-sized market actors is vital for supporting economic liberalization and the redefinition of the role of the state in the economy. The missing-middle enterprises in Egypt were a political liability through the last years of Mubārak's long reign. Economically liberalizing elites lacked any sizable social forces that could have upheld their market-making efforts. Conversely, the more successful and integrated cases of market making in East and Southeast Asian countries, as well as Turkey in the MENA (since 1980), lent themselves to market making with more political depth, while simultaneously proving capable of drawing more social forces and classes into the orbit of market exchange and exploitation. Crucially, this reframed social conflict within the cadre of market capitalism and competition over the place of these forces within it. Despite these tensions, the great majority of societal forces were in the arena of the market, while in Egypt, the great majority remains on the outside looking in.

Notes

CHAPTER ONE

1. According to the Heritage Foundation, the index measures economic freedom based on ten quantitative and qualitative factors grouped into four broad categories, or pillars, of economic freedom: rule of law (property rights, freedom from corruption), limited government (fiscal freedom, government spending), regulatory efficiency (business freedom, labor freedom, monetary freedom), and open markets (trade freedom, investment freedom, financial freedom). Each of the ten economic freedoms within these categories is graded on a scale of 0 to 100. Averaging these freedoms, with equal weight being given to each, derives a country's overall score.

2. Distribution refers to the shares of different factors of production in the value created out of the production process—for example, wages for workers, profits, dividends and interest for capital holders, and rents for landowners. Redistribution is a political process through which the value created is reallocated among different groups, usually through taxation and public expenditure.

3. East Asian developmental breakthroughs did indeed enjoy favorable access to US markets in the 1960s and 1970s out of geostrategic considerations in the context of the Cold War. However, this does not explain why Japan, South Korea, and Taiwan could make use of this privileged access to a much greater extent than other prioritized Asian countries like Thailand, Indonesia, and Malaysia. This, once again, underlines the importance of domestic political and institutional arrangements. Egypt is in fact

a case in point. Egyptian textile and clothing manufacturers could never fill their quotas in the US market under the Multi-Fiber Agreement. Similarly, Egypt made little use of an unreciprocated access to the EU markets under the 1972 cooperation agreement, which granted manufactured products preferential treatment.

4. Following North (1990, 4), organizations are distinct from institutions: institutions are formal and informal rules and norms that constrain human behavior, whereas organizations are collective agents that garner preferences and objectives, like firms, households, and states. All organizations are institutions in the sense of being governed internally and externally with rules and norms, but not all institutions are organizations.

5. Egypt has never been a major attraction to foreign direct investment (FDI). The ratio of net FDI to GDP averaged 1 percent in the period between 1989 and 2004. The exception that proves the rule was that between 2005 and 2009, when the ratio increased to 5 percent (World Bank, 2017e). Moreover, more than two-thirds of net FDI has been concentrated in extractive industries, with minimal presence in important sectors like agriculture, tourism, and manufacturing. This means that big business in Egypt is mainly Egyptian, with a few exceptions of multinationals here and there.

6. This study does not equate capitalist transformation and market-based development with industrialization, as was held in the modernization theories of the 1960s and 1970s. Given the post-Fordist changes that underwent industry in the past decades, services can be as important and are usually closely related to industrial upgrading.

CHAPTER THREE

1. According to the World Bank (2017k), Egypt's urban population increased from 10.25 million in 1960 to 35.3 million in 2010. The percentage of urban dwellers of the total population jumped from 37.86 percent in 1960 to 43.85 percent in 1980 and stabilized around 43 percent through 2017. The urban population, however, is thought to be significantly larger in absolute and relative terms than official figures. The size of the urban population of Egypt is a matter of definition as well as counting. The government depends on outdated maps from the 1940s to distinguish urban from rural areas. Consequently, many people listed as living in "rural" areas are in fact not in those areas (Pagès-El Karoui, 2008).

2. Conversely, three-quarters of private establishments were made up of self-employed people. One-person enterprises constituted more than 50 percent of the total population of enterprises, followed by 26 percent for two-person enterprises. The

vast majority of these tiny enterprises were informally operating (Ministry of Foreign Trade, 2003) in predominantly low-capital and low-skill sectors like trade and social and personal services (OECD, 2013, 4).

3. The sample on which this book has depended included only enterprises that operated within fixed physical premises, which excluded menial activities such as peddling, street vending, and household-based activities. It was also confined to enterprises that employed at least six nonfamily paid employees, to the exclusion of the self-employed, who usually employ nobody or work through unpaid family employees. Moreover, 87 percent of respondents had some postsecondary or tertiary degree, which has generally been associated with higher income and less necessity-driven entrepreneurship.

4. I am indebted to my friend Moḥamed Gabr for coming up with the term *baladi capitalism.*

5. *Shiyāka* is a word in Egyptian slang that indicates a dandy or fancy conduct or style of life (dwelling, clothing, consumption pattern). It is derived from the French word *chic.*

6. *Sharika* literally means a company in Arabic or a share in an economic enterprise that involves more than one person. However, in the Egyptian common use of the term, it refers to a market organization that stands on its own financially, legally, and operationally.

CHAPTER FOUR

1. Egypt has a system of courts that specializes in administrative cases. Administrative courts are attached to the State Council (*Majlis al-Dawla*), established in 1946, which is an independent branch of the judicial system. (See Brown, 2001, 10, 17–18.)

CHAPTER FIVE

1. Basel I and II are sets of international banking prudential regulations set by the Basel Committee on Bank Supervision

CHAPTER SIX

1. Available data cover only SME financing as microenterprises are usually removed from the jurisdiction of banks and are expected instead to deal with special funds and programs like the SFD. The minuscule share of SMEs in bank financing, however, is a case in point as it shows that even the biggest enterprises within the ranks of SSEs have a hard time securing loans from banks.

2. Commercial or merchant banks are financial institutions that receive deposits from the public and extend loans, whereas central banks are usually the banks of issue, authorized by law to issue banknotes, regulate and monitor banking institutions, and manage monetary policy (e.g., interest rate, inflation, exchange rate).

3. Nominal transfers (*ḥiwāla ismiyya*)take place through exchange companies and Western Union offices, all supervised by the Central Bank.

4. "Nonbanking institutions" refers to financial organizations that offer various services including loans but are not authorized to receive deposits and hence, unlike banks, do not mediate between savers and investors.

CHAPTER SEVEN

1. The only notable exceptions are the internal cities within the delta that have no direct access to any desert space, leading to more urban densification. See Pagès-El Karoui (2012).

2. Under state capitalism, the state controls the production process and decides on the uses of capital. It also exploits the workers and extracts the surplus value for further accumulation. State capitalism is about accumulation and direct engagement with production (Bradley, 1983; Waterbury, 1983, 17).

3. El-Kadi (2009, 61–62) indicates that the vast majority of residents of informal settlements were workers. The motive behind migrating to the city and choosing the location was to access the labor market. Only a minor percentage were self-employed or engaged in household or enterprise work.

CHAPTER EIGHT

1. In 2010/2011, the Central Agency for Public Mobilization and Statistics reported that 37.6 percent of Egyptian families were made up of three to four members, followed by 21.3 percent of five members; 16.6 percent of the families had fewer than three members (al-Ḥūty, 2015).

2. For a rich account of Egypt urban economic life under the Ottomans, see the iconic work of André Raymond (2014).

3. "Knowing people is a treasure" (*maʿrifat al-nās kunūz*) is an Egyptian folk saying.

4. This chapter relies on a survey that I conducted with Lina Khatib (Adly and Khatib, 2014) for the Center for Democracy, Development and the Rule of Law at Stanford University in 2013 as part of the report "Reforming the Entrepreneurship." For details about the Egypt sample and the methodology and definitions used for the survey, see Adly and Khatib (2014, 50–59).

5. *Working capital* can be defined as the capital of a business used in its day-to-day trading operations, calculated as current assets minus current liabilities.

6. According to the median figures reported in the survey (conducted in mid-2013), registered microenterprises fall in between small, registered enterprises and micro-unregistered enterprises in terms of start-up capital. The median start-up capital of small, registered enterprises was 400,000 Egyptian pounds (approximately $73,000 in 2013 exchange rates) followed by 50,000 pounds(approximately, $9,000 in 2013 exchange rates) for micro-registered enterprises and 10,000 pounds (around $1,800 in 2013 exchange rate) for unregistered ones. The same observation applies to the reported values of the start-up capital of micro-registered and micro-unregistered enterprises. The reported figures are nominal, and because the firm age of each category differs (an average of nine years for small, registered enterprises and five years for micro-registered and micro-unregistered ones), it is difficult to compare them accurately without accounting for inflation. Nonetheless, even in nominal terms, they clearly show that small, registered enterprises retained much larger amounts of capital from the beginning, while accounting for inflation would show even larger disparities rather than smaller.

CHAPTER NINE

1. Dandy capitalism should not be confused as a simple reflection of business size. To the extent that this chapter serves as an in-depth exploration of the inner workings and interrelations of dandy firms and emphasizes big Egyptian enterprises, this is purely for practical considerations. These larger enterprises that have managed to grow through the previous decades are, by virtue of their current size, the most visible as they are often publicly traded and covered by the business media and advertisements.

2. Elsewedy electric is majority owned by the Ṣādiq Elsewedy branch of the bigger Elsewedy family. Ṣādiq Elsewedy's two sons Moḥamed and Aḥmed not to be confused with their cousin Moḥamed Zaki Elsewedy, who is currently the head of the Egyptian Federation of Industries and a member of parliament in the Pro-Sisi "Support Egypt" coalition. The two are economically unrelated.

Bibliography

ʿAbdalla, N. (2018). The Independent Union Movement in Egypt between Effort at Organization and Limited Impact [al-ḥaraka al-niqābiyya al-mustaqilla fī miṣr bayna juhūd al-tanẓīm wa taḥadiyyāt al-ta'thīr]. In A. Adly & F. Ramadan (eds.), *The Rise and Fall of Egypt's Labor Movement (2006–2016): Workers, Politics and the State* [ṣuʿūd wa ufūl al-ḥaraka al-ʿummāliyyah fī miṣr (2006–2016): al-ʿummāl, w-al-siyāsa wa-l-dawla], 39–79. Cairo: Dar al-Maraya.

ʿAbdel-Aẓīm, A., & Fawzy, A. (2015, September 15). President of the Egyptian Businessmen Associations: The Experience of "Madinaty" Frightened Investors from Partnership with the State [ra'īs jamʿiyyat rijāl al-aʿmāl al-miṣriyīn: tajrubat "Madinaty" akhāfat al-mustathmirīn min al-sharāka maʿa al-dawla], *Elbalad News*. [Online] http://www.elbalad.news/1705795

ʿAbdel-Bāri, M. (2015, September 1). Can Egypt Control the Balance of Payment Deficit? [hal tastaṭīʿ miṣr al-sayṭara ʿalā al-ʿajz al-muzmin fī mīzān al-madfūʿāt?]. *Tahrirnews*. [Online] https://www.tahrirnews.com/Story/292908/ المدفوعات/اقتصاد
هل-تستطيع-مصر-السيطرة-على-العجز-المزمن-لميزان-

ʿAbdel-Faḍīl, M. (1980). *The Egyptian Economy Between Central Planning and Open Door Policy* [al-iqtiṣād al-miṣrī bayna al-takhṭīṭ al-markazi wa-l-infitāḥ al-iqtiṣādī]. Cairo: Maʿhad al-Inmā' al-ʿarabī.

ʿAbdel-Ḥay, A., ʿOmar, K., al-Sawy, A., & Fouad, W. (2006). *Violated Opposition* [*al-muʿāraḍa al-mustabaḥa*]. Cairo: Sawasiya Center for Human Rights.

Abdelkhalek, G. (2007). *MDG-Based Debt Sustainability Analysis*. Country discussion paper prepared for a Joint UNDP/UNDESA Initiative on Defining a More MDG-Consistent Debt Sustainability Framework.

Abdel-Latif, A., & Schmitz, H. (2010). Growth Alliances: Insights from Egypt. *Business and Politics*, 12(4), 1–27.

Abdel-Malek, A. (1968). *Egypt, Military Society*. London: Vintage Books.

ʿAbdel-Moḥsen, M. (2015, April 2). Interview with A. Adly.

ʿAbdel-Nāṣer, G. (2015, October 1). Ḥussein Narrates His Journey with Business: I Moved from Building Apartments to Building Factories Because of ʿAbdel-Nāṣer, G. [Ḥussein Ṣabbour yarwī rihlatah maʿa al-business: intaqalt min bināʾ al-shuqaq ila tashyīd al-maṣaniʿ bi-sabab ʿAbdel-Nāṣer], *Vetogate*. [Online] https://www.vetogate.com/1836019

ʿAbdel-Wahāb, S. (2014, October 21). CAPMAS: 99.97% of Economic Enterprises in Egypt Are "Private" [al-iḥṣāʾ: 99.97% min al-munshaʾāt al-iqtiṣādiyya fī miṣr "khāṣṣa"]. *Almasryalyoum*. [Online], https://www.almasryalyoum.com/news/details/551769

Abdulhaq, N. (2016). *Jewish and Greek Communities in Egypt: Entrepreneurship and Business Before Nasser*. London: IB Tauris.

Abul-Magd, Z. (2017). *Militarizing the Nation: The Army, Business, and Revolution in Egypt*. New York: Columbia University Press.

Achcar, G. (2013). *The People Want: A Radical Exploration of the Arab Uprising*. Berkeley: University of California Press.

Acs, Z. J., Carlsson, B., & Karlsson, C. (eds.). (1999). *Entrepreneurship, Small and Medium-Sized Enterprises and the Macro-Economy*. Cambridge: Cambridge University Press.

Adler, P. S. (2001). Market, Hierarchy, and Trust: The Knowledge Economy and the Future of Capitalism. *Organization Science*, 12(2), 215–234.

Adly, A. (2009). Politically-Embedded Cronyism: The Case of Post-Liberalization Egypt. *Business and Politics*, 11(4), 1–26.

———. (2012a). *State Reform and Development in the Middle East: Turkey and Egypt in the Post-Liberalization Era*. New York: Routledge.

———. (2012b). Mubarak (1990–2011): The State of Corruption. *Amman, Arab Reform Initiative*. [Online] http://www. arab-reform. net/sites/default/files/Mubarak_1990–2011_The_State_of_Corruption

———. (2012c). *Energy Subsidies in the Egyptian Budget: A Model for Economic Injustice* [daʿm al-tāqa fī al-muwāzana al-miṣriyya: namūdhajan li-l-ẓulm al-ijtimāʿī]. Egyptian Initiative for Personal Rights policy paper.

———. (2015, January 31). The Triumph of the Bureaucracy: A Decade of Aborted Social and Political Change in Egypt. *Jadaliyya*. [Online] http://www.jadaliyya.com/Details/31735/Triumph-of-the-Bureaucracy-A-Decade- of Aborted-Social-and-Political-Change-in-Egypt

———. (2016). Between Social Populism and Pragmatic Conservatism. In B. Rougier & S. La Croix(eds.) *Egypt's Revolutions*. New York: Palgrave Macmillan, 61–78.

———. (2017). Too Big to Fail: Egypt's Large Enterprises After the 2011 Uprising. *Carnegie Endowment for International Peace*. [Online] https://carnegie-mec.org/2017/03/02/too-big-to-fail-egypt-s-large-enterprises-after-2011–uprising-pub-68154

Adly, A., & Khatib, L. (2014). *Reforming the Entrepreneurship Ecosystem in Post-Revolutionary Egypt and Tunisia*. Stanford, CA: Center for Democracy, Development and the Rule of Law

Adly, A., & Palluelo, M. (2013). *Corruption in Natural Gas Contracts Under Mubarak: A Legal and Economic Analysis* [fasād taʿāqudāt al-ghāz fī ʿaṣr Mubarak: taḥlīl qānūnī wa iqtiṣādī]. Egyptian Initiative for Personal Rights policy paper.

Aguiar, M., & Gopinath, G. (2007). Emerging Market Business Cycles: The Cycle Is the Trend. *Journal of Political Economy*, 115(1), 69–102.

Ahram Gate. (2013, May 16). CAPMAS: 18.9 Million Families in Egypt in 2012 and 53.8% of Egyptians Live in the Countryside [al-iḥṣāʾ: 18.9 miliyunān ʿadad al-usar fī miṣr khilāl 2012 wa 53.8% min al-miṣriyīn yaʿishūn bi-l-rīf]. *Ahram Gate*. [Online] http://gate.ahram.org.eg/News/347239.aspx

Alff, K. (2018). Levantine Joint Stock Companies: Trans-Mediterranean Partnerships and Nineteenth-Century Capitalist Development. *Comparative Studies in Society and History*, 60(1), 150–177.

Almal. (2017, July 3). Cement [al-Asmant]. *Almāl News*. [Online] http://www.almal-news.com/tag/257/1/الأسمنت#.WLKNXBhh2CQ

Almeida, H. V., & Wolfenzon, D. (2006). A Theory of Pyramidal Ownership and Family Business Groups. *Journal of Finance*, 61(6), 2637–2680.

ʿAmer, I. (1958). *The Land and the Peasant: The Agrarian Question in Egypt* [*al-arḍ wa-l-fallāḥ: al-masʾala al-zirāʿiyya fī miṣr*]. Cairo: al-Dar al-Miṣreiyya li-l-Nashr wa-l-Tawzīʿ.

Amer Group Official website. [Online] http://www.amer-group.com. [Accessed August 1, 2018]

Amin, G. (2009) *Egypt and the Egyptians Under Mubarak (1981–2008)* [*miṣr w-al-miṣriyūn fī ʿahd Mubarak (1981–2008)*]. Cairo: Dar Mirit.

Amin, G. (2000). *Whatever Happened to the Egyptians? Changes in Egyptian Society from 1850 to the Present.* Cairo: American University in Cairo.

Amsden, A. H. (1992). *Asia's next giant: South Korea and late industrialization. New York:* Oxford University Press.

———. (1997). Bringing Production Back in Understanding Government's Economic Role in Late Industrialization. *World Development*, 25(4),469–480.

———. (2001) *The Rise of "The Rest": Challenges to the West from Late-Industrializing Economies.* New York: Oxford University Press.

Anderson, A. R., Li, J. H., Harrison, R. T., & Robson, P. J. (2003). The Increasing Role of Small Business in the Chinese Economy. *Journal of Small Business Management*, 41(3), 310–316.

al-ʿAntarī, S. (2005). *The Financial Sector and Financing Development in Egypt: Evolution and Prospects till 2020* [al-qiṭāʿ al-māli wa tamwīl al-tanmiya fī miṣr: al-taṭawur wa-l-istishrāf ḥata ʿām 2020]. Cairo: al-Maktaba al-Akādimiyyah

al-ʿArabī, A. (2013, June 6). Interview with A. Adly.

Arrighi, G., Silver, B. J., & Brewer, B. D. (2003a). Industrial Convergence, Globalization, and the Persistence of the North-South Divide. *Studies in Comparative International Development*, 38(1), 3.

Arrighi, G., Silver, B. J., & Brewer, B. D. (2003b). Response. *Studies in Comparative International Development*, 38(1), 39–42.

ʿAskar, M. (2010, October 10). Expert: The Susceptibility of the Stock Market to Businessmen's Lawsuits Rendering It Captive to Political Decisions [Khabīr: ḥasāsiyyat al-borṣa li qaḍāyā rijāl al-aʿmāl jaʿalaha asīrat al-qarārāt al-siyāsiyya]. *Youm7*. [Online] https://www.youm7.com/Article/NewsPrint/288106

Assaad, R. (ed.). (2010). *The Egyptian Labor Market in the New Millennium* [*sūq al-ʿamāl al-miṣriyya fī al-alfiyya al-jadīda*]. Cairo: Economic Research Forum and al-Ahram Center.

Awlād al-Arḍ Center and the Egyptian Center for Economic and Social Rights. (2011). *Workers and the Revolution: A Rights-Based Vision.* [al-ʿummāl wa al-thawra: ru'ya huqūqiyya]. Cairo: Egyptian Center for Economic and Social Rights. [Online] http://ecesr.org/?p=2967. [Accessed July 17, 2017]

Ayubi, N. N. (1995). *Overstating the Arab State*. London: IB Tauris.

Bairoch, P. (1995). *Economics and World History: Myths and Paradoxes*. Chicago: University of Chicago Press.

Bairoch, P., & Kozul-Wright, R. (1998). Globalization Myths: Some Historical Reflections on Integration, Industrialization and Growth in the World Economy. In P. Bairoch & R. Kozul-Wright (eds.), *Transnational Corporations and the Global Economy*, 37–68. London: Palgrave Macmillan.

Banerjee, A., Duflo, E., Glennerster, R., & Kinnan, C. (2015). The Miracle of Microfinance? Evidence from a Randomized Evaluation. *American Economic Journal: Applied Economics*, 7(1), 22–53.

Banfield, E. C. (1958). *The Moral Basis of a Backward Society*. Glencoe, IL: Free Press.

Barayez, A. (2016, January 25). This Land Is Their Land: Egypt's Military and the Economy. *Jadaliyya*. [Online] http://www.jadaliyya.com/Details/32898 [Accessed May 17, 2017]

Barsoum, G., Ramadan, M., & Mostafa, M. (2014). *Labor Market Transitions of Young Women and Men in Egypt*. Geneva: International Labor Office.

Barth, J. R., Caprio Jr., G., & Levine, R. (2001). Banking Systems Around the Globe: Do Regulation and Ownership Affect Performance and Stability? In F. S. Mishkin (ed.), *Prudential Supervision: What Works and What Doesn't*, 31–96. Chicago: University of Chicago Press.

Baumol, W. J. (1969). Macroeconomics of Unbalanced Growth: Comment on the Comment. *American Economic Review*, 59(4), 632–633.

Bayat, A. (1993). Populism, Liberalization and Popular Participation: Industrial Democracy in Egypt. *Economic and Industrial Democracy*, 14(1), 65–87.

———. (2010). *Life as Politics: How Ordinary People Change the Middle East*. Palo Alto, CA: Stanford University Press.

Bayat, A., & Denis, E. (2000). Who Is Afraid of *ʿashwāʾiyyāt*? Urban Change and Politics in Egypt. *Environment and Urbanization*, 12(2), 185–199.

Beatty, S. E., Mayer, M., Coleman, J. E., Reynolds, K. E., & Lee, J. (1996). Customer-Sales Associate Retail Relationships. *Journal of Retailing*, 72(3), 223 – 247.

Beck, T., & Demirgüç-Kunt, A. (2006). Small and Medium-Size Enterprises: Access to Finance as a Growth Constraint. *Journal of Banking and Finance*, 30 (11), 2931– 2943.

Beck, T., Demirgüç-Kunt, A., Laeven, L., & Levine, R. (2008). Finance, Firm Size, and Growth. *Journal of Money, Credit and Banking*, 40(7), 1379– 1405.

Beck, T., Demirgüç-Kunt, A., & Martinez Peria, M. S. (2008). Banking Services for

Everyone? Barriers to Bank Access and Use Around the World. *World Bank Economic Review*, 22(3), 397– 430.

Beckhard, R., & Dyer, W. G. (1983). Managing Continuity in the Family-Owned Modern Diaspora. *Organizational Dynamics*, 12(1), 5–12.

Beinin, J. (1998). *The Dispersion of Egyptian Jewry: Culture, Politics, and the Formation of a Modern Diaspora*. Cairo: American University in Cairo Press.

Beinin, J. (2016). *Political Economy and Social Movement Theory Perspectives on the Tunisian and Egyptian Uprisings of 2011*. LSE Middle East Center paper series 14. [Online] http://eprints.lse.ac.uk/65291/ [Accessed April 13, 2019]

Beinin, J., & Duboc, M. (2015). The Egyptian Workers' Movement Before and After the 2011 Popular Uprising. *Socialist Register*, 51, 1-22.

Beinin, J., and Lockman, Z. (1987). *Workers on the Nile*. Princeton, NJ: Princeton University Press.

Beinin, J., & Vairel, F. (eds.). (2013). *Social Movements, Mobilization, and Contestation in the Middle East and North Africa*. Palo Alto, CA: Stanford University Press.

Beshāy, Y. (2015, June 9). Interview with A. Adly.

Bianchi, R. (1989). *Unruly Corporatism: Associational Life in Twentieth-Century Egypt*. New York: Oxford University Press.

Boisot, M., & Child, J. (1996). From Fiefs to Clans and Network Capitalism: Explaining China's Emerging Economic Order. *Administrative Science Quarterly*, 41(4), 600– 628.

Bonefeld, W. (2011). Primitive Accumulation and Capitalist Accumulation: Notes on Social Constitution and Expropriation. *Science and Society*, 75(3), 379– 399.

Bourdieu, P., & Nice, R. (1980). The Production of Belief: Contribution to an Economy of Symbolic Goods. *Media, Culture and Society*, 2(3), 261– 293.

Bradley, C. (1983). State Capitalism in Egypt: A Critique of Patrick Clawson. *Journal of Revolutionary Socialists of the Middle East* [*Khamasin*], 1, 73–99.

Brown, N. J. (2001). *Arab Judicial Structures*. New York: Program on Governance in the Arab Region, United Nations Development Programme.

Browne, M. N., & Blank, L. A. (1997). The Contrast Between Friendship and Business-Consumer Relationships: Trust Is an Earned Attribute. *Business and Professional Ethics Journal*, 16(1/3), 155– 170.

Buğra, A. (1994). *State and Business in Modern Turkey: A Comparative Study*. Albany: State University of New York Press.

Bush, R. (1999). *Economic Crisis and the Politics of Reform in Egypt*. Boulder, CO: Westview Press.

Caballero, R. J., Hoshi, T., & Kashyap, A. K. (2008). Zombie Lending and Depressed Restructuring in Japan. *American Economic Review*, 98(5), 1943–1977.

Cai, H., & Treisman, D. (2006). Did Government Decentralization Cause China's Economic Miracle? *World Politics*, 58(4), 505–535.

Caprio, G., & Cull, R. (2000). *Bank Privatization and Regulation for Egypt*. Egyptian Center for Economic Studies. [Online] http://www.eces.org.eg/MediaFiles/Uploaded_Files/%7B59E6E144-5EBD-427E-95CC-253F5B2787C2%7D_ECESDLS15e.pdf

Carbó-Valverde, S., Rodriguez-Fernandez, F., & Udell, G. F. (2009). Bank Market Power and SME Financing Constraints. *Review of Finance*, 13(2), 309–340.

Central Bank of Egypt (CBE). (2002–2012). *Annual Reports*. Cairo: Central Bank of Egypt. [Online] http://www.cbe.org.eg/en/EconomicResearch/Publications/Pages/AnnualReport.aspx?p=2. [Accessed July 2–23, 2017]

———. (2018a). *The Central Bank of Egypt Time Series Domestic Debt of Government and Economic Authorities (2005–2014)—Constant Prices (Millions of Egyptian Pounds)*. Cairo: Central Bank of Egypt. [Online] http://www.cbe.org.eg/_layouts/xlviewer.aspx?id=/Time%20Series%20Documents/Domestic%20Debt/Domestic%20Debt%20of%20Government%20and%20Economic%20Authorities%20Debt/Domestic%20Debt%20Annual.xlsx&DefaultItemOpen=1 [September 18, 2018]

———. (2018b). *The Central Bank of Egypt Time Series Domestic Debt: National Investment Bank (2005–2014)—Constant Prices (Millions of Egyptian Pounds)*. Cairo: Central Bank of Egypt. [Online] http://www.cbe.org.eg/_layouts/xlviewer.aspx?id=/Time%20Series%20Documents/Domestic%20Debt/National%20Investment%20Bank/NIB%20Annual.xlsx&DefaultItemOpen=1 [Accessed September 18, 2018]

———. (2018c). *The Central Bank of Egypt Time Series State Budget: Expenditure (2006–2014)—Constant Prices (Millions of Egyptian Pounds)*. Cairo: Central Bank of Egypt. [Online] http://www.cbe.org.eg/_layouts/xlviewer.aspx?id=/Time%20Series%20Documents/State%20Budget/Expenditures/Expenditures%20Annual.xlsx&DefaultItemOpen=1 [Accessed September 20 2018]

———. (2018d) *The Central Bank of Egypt Time Series State Budget: Revenues (2006–2014)—Constant Prices (Millions of Egyptian Pounds)*. Cairo: Central Bank of Egypt. [Online] http://www.cbe.org.eg/_layouts/xlviewer.aspx?id=/Time%20Series%20

Documents/State%20Budget/Revenues/Revenues%20Annual.xlsx&DefaultItemOpen=1 [Accessed September 20, 2018]

Chandler Jr., A. D. (1993). *The Visible Hand: The Managerial Revolution in American Business*. Cambridge, MA: Belknap Press of Harvard University Press.

Chekir, H., & Diwan, I. (2014). Crony Capitalism in Egypt. *Journal of Globalization and Development*, 5(2), 177–211.

Chen, H., & Rozelle, S. (1999). Leaders, Managers, and the Organization of Township and Village Enterprises in China. *Journal of Development Economics*, 60(2), 529–557.

Chen, M. A. (2005). *Rethinking the Informal Economy: Linkages with the Formal Economy and the Formal Regulatory Environment*. United Nations University, Department of Economic and Social Affairs (DESA) working paper 46. https://www.un.org/esa/desa/papers/2007/wp46_2007.pdf

Chen, X. P., & Chen, C. C. (2004). On the Intricacies of the Chinese Guanxi: A Process Model of Guanxi Development. *Asia Pacific Journal of Management*, 21(3), 305–324.

Chen, X. P., & Peng, S. (2008). Guanxi Dynamics: Shifts in the Closeness of Ties Between Chinese Coworkers. *Management and Organization Review*, 4(1), 63–80.

Claessens, S., & Fan, J. P. (2002). Corporate Governance in Asia: A Survey. *International Review of Finance*, 3(2), 71–103.

Coase, R. H. (1990). Accounting and the Theory of the Firm. *Journal of Accounting and Economics*, 12(1–3), 3–13.

Cohen, D. (2018, September 27). Missing the Satanic Mills. *New York Review of Books*. [Online] https://www.nybooks.com/articles/2018/09/27/factory-missing-dark-satanic-mills/ [Accessed November 18, 2018]

Conte, É., & Walentowitz, S. (2009). Kinship Matters: Tribals, Cousins, and Citizens in Southwest Asia and Beyond. *Études rurales*, 184, 217–250.

Court of Cassation. (1952, October 18). Challenge number 869.

———. (2003, May 28). Case number 2595.

Cox, R. W. (1992). Global Perestroika. *Socialist Register*, 28. [Online] https://socialistregister.com/index.php/srv/article/view/5606

Crossley-Holland, K. (1980). *The Norse Myths: Gods of the Vikings*. New York: Pantheon Books.

Crozier, M. (1964). *The Bureaucratic Phenomenon*. Chicago: University of Chicago Press.

Cull, R., Davis, L. E., Lamoreaux, N. R., & Rosenthal, J. L. (2006). Historical Financing of Small- and Medium-Size Enterprises. *Journal of Banking and Finance*, 30(11), 3017–3042.

Cuno, K. M. (1980). The Origins of Private Ownership of Land in Egypt: A Reappraisal. *International Journal of Middle East Studies*, 12(3), 245–275.

Das, T. K., & Teng, B. S. (1998). Between Trust and Control: Developing Confidence in Partner Cooperation in Alliances. *Academy of Management Review*, 23(3), 491–512.

Dasgupta, P. (2000). Trust as a Commodity. *Trust: Making and Breaking Cooperative Relations*, 4, 49–72.

David, P. A. (1994). Why Are Institutions the "Carriers of History"? Path Dependence and the Evolution of Conventions, Organizations and Institutions. *Structural Change and Economic Dynamics*, 5(2), 205–220.

Davis, P. S., & Harveston, P. D. (1998). The Influence of Family on the Family Business Succession Process: A Multi-Generational Perspective. *Entrepreneurship Theory and Practice*, 22, 31–54.

Dawar, N. D. N., & Chattopadhyay, A. (2002). Rethinking Marketing Programs for Emerging Markets. *Long Range Planning*, 35(5), 457–474.

Dawūd, M. (2014, August 29). The Story of a Garage Called al-Turguman [ḥikāyet garāj ismuh al-turgumān]. *al-Ahram.* [Online]http://www.ahram.org.eg/News/41289 /12/323009/ملفات-الاهرام/حكاية-جراج-اسمه-»الترجمان.aspx

De Groot, A. H. (2003). The Historical Development of the Capitulatory Regime in the Ottoman Middle East from the Fifteenth to the Nineteenth Centuries. *Oriente moderno*, 22(3), 575–604.

De Soto, H. (2000). *The Mystery of Capital: Why Capitalism Triumphs in the West and Fails Everywhere Else.* London: Bantam Books.

———. (2002). *The Other Path: The Economic Answer to Terrorism.* New York: Basic Books.

———. (2012). On Entrepreneurship and the Arab Spring. *Stiftung Entrepreneurship.* [Online] https://www.youtube.com/watch?v=7P-osmWWM_M [Accessed January 2, 2016].

De Vries, M. F. K. (1993). The Dynamics of Family Controlled Firms: The Good and the Bad News. *Organizational Dynamics*, 21(3), 59–71.

Dean, B. A. E., and Mohieldin, M. (2001). On the Formulation and Enforcement of Competition Law in Emerging Economies: The Case of Egypt. *Business Law International,* no. 3, 289–316

Deane, P. (1965). *The First Industrial Revolution. Cambridge:* Cambridge University Press.

Decker, M., Schiefer, G., & Bulander, R. (2006). Specific Challenges for Small and Medium-Sized Enterprises (SME) in M-Business. In *Proceedings of the International Conference on E-Business (ICE-B 2006)*, 169–174. Portugal: INSTICC Press.

De la Campa, A. (2011). *Increasing Access to Credit Through Reforming Secured Transactions in the MENA Region.* Policy Research working paper WPS 5613. World Bank. [Online] https://openknowledge.worldbank.org/handle/10986/3379.

Demir, F. (2004). A Failure Story: Politics and Financial Liberalization in Turkey: Revisiting the Revolving Door Hypothesis. *World Development*, 32(5), 851–869.

Demir, Ö., Acar, M., & Toprak, M. (2004). Anatolian Tigers or Islamic Capital: Prospects and Challenges. *Middle Eastern Studies*, 40(6), 166–188.

Demirag, I., & Serter, M. (2003). Ownership Patterns and Control in Turkish Listed Companies. *Corporate Governance: An International Review*, 11(1), 40–51.

Diwan, I. (2013). Understanding Revolution in the Middle East: The Central Role of the Middle Class. *Middle East Development Journal*, 5(1), 1–30.

Dong, X. Y. & Putterman, L. (1996). China's Rural Industry and Monopsony: An Exploration. *Pacific Economic Review*, 1(1), 59–78.

Doner, R. F., & Ramsay, A. (1997). Competitive Clientelism and Economic Governance: The Case of Thailand. In S, Maxfield & B. R. Schneider (eds.), *Business and the State in Developing Countries*, 237–276. Ithaca, NY: Cornell University Press.

Doney, P. M., & Cannon, J. P. (1997). Trust in Buyer-Seller Relationships. *Journal of Marketing*, 61, 35–51.

Dorman, W. J. (2013). Exclusion and Informality: The Praetorian Politics of Land Management in Cairo, Egypt. *International Journal of Urban and Regional Research*, 37(5), 1584–1610.

Dowla, A., & Barua, D. (2006). *The Poor Always Pay Back: The Grameen II Story.* Sterling, VA: Kumarian Press.

Dyck, A., & Zingales, L. (2004). Private Benefits of Control: An International Comparison. *Journal of Finance*, 59(2), 537–600.

Elaraby Group Official Website. [Online] https://www.elarabygroup.com/ar/elaraby-profile)

Elaraby, M. (2015). *My Life's Secret: Elaraby's Story* [sirr ḥayātī: ḥikāyāt El ʿarabī]. Cairo: Dār Nahḍit Miṣr.

Elaraby, M. (2016, February 27). Interview with A. Adly.

Elsewedy Electric. (2010). *Financial Statement of 2010/2011*. Cairo: Elsewedy Electric. [Online] http://resources.inktankir.com/swdy/Year-End-2010–Consolidated.pdf

———. (2014). *Financial Statement of 2014/2015*. Cairo: Elsewedy Electric. [Online] http://resources.inktankir.com/swdy/EE-consolidation-english-Q4–2014.pdf

Elyachar, J. (2005). *Markets of Dispossession: NGOs, Economic Development, and the State in Cairo*. Durham, NC: Duke University Press.

Endress, M. (2004). Foundations of Trust: Introductory Remarks on the Sociology of Trust. In H. Schrader (ed.), *Trust and Social Transformation: Theoretical Approaches and Empirical Findings from Russia*, 15–30. New Brunswick, NJ: Transaction.

Erdle, S. (2010). *Ben Ali's' "New Tunisia" (1987–2009): A Case Study of Authoritarian Modernization in the Arab World*. Berlin: Klaus Schwarz.

Evans, G. (2018, July 20). Who Is Nassef Sawiris? The Egyptian Billionaire behind Aston Villa Takeover. *Mirror*. [Online] https://www.mirror.co.uk/sport/football/news/who-nassef-sawiris-egyptian-billionaire-12955564

Evans, P. (2003). Beyond "Institutional Monocropping": Institutions, Capabilities, and Deliberative Development. *Sociologias*, 9, 20–63.

———. (2012). *Embedded Autonomy: States and Industrial Transformation*. Princeton, NJ: Princeton University Press.

Evans, D. S., & Leighton, L. S. (1989). The Determinants of Changes in US Self-Employment, 1968–1987. *Small Business Economics*, 1(2), 111–119.

———. (1990). Small Business Formation by Unemployed and Employed Workers. *Small Business Economics*, 2(4), 319–330.

ʿEzz al-dīn, N. (2003). *Labor and Businessmen: The Changing Political Opportunities in Egypt* [al-ʿummāl wa rijāl al-aʿmāl: taḥawwulāt al-furaṣ al-siyāsiyya fī miṣr]. Cairo: Markaz al-Ahrām li-l-dirāsāt al-siyāsiyya wa-l-istirātijiyya.

Fahmi, K. (2010). *All the Pasha's Men: Mehmet Ali, His Army and the Making of Modern Egypt*. Trans. S. Younis. Cairo: Dar al-Shorouk.

Fahmi, W. S. (2005). The Impact of Privatization of Solid Waste Management on the Zabaleen Garbage Collectors of Cairo. *Environment and Urbanization*, 17(2), 155–170.

Fan, S., Zhang, L., & Zhang, X. (2002). *Growth, Inequality, and Poverty in Rural China: The Role of Public Investments*. Washington, DC: International Food Policy Research Institute.

Fargues, P. (2001). *The Generation of Change, Maghred-Machrek* [La génération du changement, Maghreb-Machrek]. La Documentation Française, numéro spécial sous la direction de Fargues, P., Jeunesse du Monde Arabe: Défis et Opportunité, 3 (11), 171–192

Farsoun, S. K. (1988). Oil, State, and Social Structure in the Middle East. *Arab Studies Quarterly*, 102 155–175.

Fay, C. K., & Jomo, K. S. (2000). Financial Sector Rents in Malaysia. In M. H. Khan & J. K. Sundaram (eds.), *Rents, Rent-Seeking and Economic Development—Theory and Evidence in Asia*, 304–326. Cambridge, Cambridge University Press.

Ferguson, N. (2008). *The Ascent of Money: Financial History of the World.* New York: Penguin.

Fischer, S. (2001). *Ten Years of Transition: Looking Back and Looking Forward.* IMF staff papers 48(1), 1–8.

Forbes Middle East. (2015). The World's Richest Arabs 2015. [Online] https://archives.forbesmiddleeast.com/en/list/the-world-richest-arabs-2015/ [Accessed May 15, 2018]

Foucault, M., Davidson, A. I., & Burchell, G. (2008). *The Birth of Biopolitics: Lectures at the Collège de France, 1978–1979*. London: Palgrave Macmillan.

France 24. (2012, February 7). Businessman Ṭalʿat Muṣṭafa Is Sentenced to 15 Years in Prison [ḥukm nihāʾī bi-l-sajn 15 ʿāman ʿalā rajul al-aʿmāl al-miṣrī Ṭalʿat Muṣṭafa]. *France 24*. [Online] https://www.france24.com/ar/20100928–egypt-talat-mustafa-case-jail-15–years

François, P. (2004). *Social Capital and Economic Development.* London: Routledge.

Frenzen, J. K., & Davis, H. L. (1990). Purchasing Behavior in Embedded Markets. *Journal of Consumer Research*, 17(1), 1–12.

Fukuyama, F. (1989). The End of History? *Interest*, 16 (Summer), 3–18.

Gabr, H. (2018). Egyptian Trade Union Federation: Deep Unions Confronting the Revolution [al-ittiḥād al-ʿām li-niqābāt ʿummāl miṣr: al-niqābāt al-ʿamīqa tuwājih al-thawra]. In A. Adly & F. Ramadan (eds.), *The Rise and Fall of Egypt's Labor Movement (2006–2016): Workers, Politics and the State* [ṣuʿūd wa ufūl al-ḥaraka al-ʿumāliyya fī miṣr (2006–2016): al-ʿummāl, wa-l-siyāsa wa-l-dawla], 287–333. Cairo: Dar al-Maraya.

———. (2014, May 5). Interview with A. Adly.

———. (2017, September 19). Interview with A. Adly.

Gabriel, S., Resnick, S. A. and Wolff, R. D. (2011). What Happened to Chinese Communism: The Transition From State Feudalism To State Capitalism. In V. Pollard (ed.),

State Capitalism, Contentious Politics and Large-Scale Social Change, 119–133. Leiden: Brill

Gād, A. (2015, May 2, October 13, 25). Interview with A. Adly.

Gād, M. (2016). *Changes in Public Employer's Wage Policies: From Nasserism to Civil Service* [taḥawwulāt siyāsāt al-ujūr al-ḥukūmiyya min al-nāṣiriyya ila-l-khidma al-madaniyya]. Cairo: Egyptian Center for Economic and Social Rights. [Online] http://ecesr.org/?p=775153

al-Gebāly, A. (1999). *Domestic Public Debt in Egypt: Causes and Solutions* [al-dayn al-ʿām al-maḥalī fī miṣr: al-asbāb wa-l-ḥulūl]. Cairo: Ahram Center for Political and Strategic Studies.

Gerschenkron, A. (1962). *Economic Backwardness in Historical Perspective: A Book of Essays*. Cambridge, MA: Belknap Press of Harvard University Press.

Ghazaleh, P. (2010). *Urban Fortunes and Social Strategies: Patrimonial Geneologies in Cairo 1780–1830* [Fortunes Urbaines et Stratégies Sociales: Généalogies Patrimoniales au Caire, 1780–1830]. Cairo: Institut Français D'archéologie Orientale.

Ghoneim, A. F. (2005). *Promoting Competitive Markets in Developing Economies (The Case of Egypt)*. Cairo: International Development Research Center (IDRC). [Online] https://idl-bnc-idrc.dspacedirect.org/bitstream/handle/10625/35100/127158.pdf?sequence=1

Glassman, J. (2006). Primitive Accumulation, Accumulation by Dispossession, Accumulation by "Extra-Economic" Means. *Progress in Human Geography*, 30(5), 608–625.

Global Entrepreneurship Monitor (GEM). (2008). Egypt Entrepreneurship Report. *Global Entrepreneurship Monitor*. [Online] https://www.gemconsortium.org/report/47257

———. (2010). Egypt Entrepreneurship Report. *Global Entrepreneurship Monitor*. [Online] https://www.gemconsortium.org/report/48361.

———. (2012). Egypt Entrepreneurship Report. *Global Entrepreneurship Monitor*. [Online] https://www.gemconsortium.org/report/gem-egypt-2012-report

Goldberg, E. (2004). *Trade, Reputation, and Child Labor in Twentieth-Century Egypt*. New York: Palgrave Macmillan.

Görmüş, E. (2017). Economic Liberalisation Policies and (Non-Islamic) Market Coalition in Egypt. *Journal of North African Studies*, 22(1), 60–77.

Granovetter, M. S. (1973). The Strength of Weak Ties. *American Journal of Sociology*, 78(6), 1360–1380.

———. (1985). Economic Action and Social Structure: The Problem of Embeddedness. *American Journal of Sociology*, 91(3), 481–510.

———. (1990). The Myth of Social Network Analysis as a Special Method in the Social Sciences. *Connections*, 13(1–2), 13–16.

Grayson, K. (2007). Friendship Versus Business in Marketing Relationships. *Journal of Marketing*, 71(4), 121–139.

Greif, A. (2006). History Lessons: The Birth of Impersonal Exchange: The Community Responsibility System and Impartial Justice. *Journal of Economic Perspectives*, 20(2), 221–236.

———. (2006). *Institutions and the Path to the Modern Economy: Lessons from Medieval Trade*. Cambridge: Cambridge University Press.

Guinnane, T. W. (2011). The Early German Credit Cooperatives and Microfinance Organizations Today: Similarities and Differences. In B. Armendariz and M. Labie (eds.), *The Handbook of Microfinance*, 77–100. Singapore: World Scientific.

Haber, S. H., North, D. C., & Weingast, B. R. (eds.). (2008). *Political Institutions and Financial Development*. Palo Alto, CA: Stanford University Press.

Haddad, B. S. (2011). *Business Networks in Syria: The Political Economy of Authoritarian Resilience*. Palo Alto, CA: Stanford University Press.

Halpern, J. J. (1994). The Effect of Friendship on Personal Business Transactions. *Journal of Conflict Resolution*, 38(4), 647–664.

Ḥamdi, K. (2014). *On the Rules Governing Checks and Trust Receipts* [sharḥ aḥkām al-shīk wa'īṣāl al-amāna]. Cairo: Haydar Group.

el-Hamidi, F., & Baslevent, C. (2013). *Micro and Small Enterprises (MSEs) in Urban Economies: A Comparative Study of Egypt and Turkey at the Province Level*. Economic Research Forum working paper 761.

Hammad, H. (2016). *Industrial Sexuality: Gender, Urbanization, and Social Transformation in Egypt*. Austin: University of Texas Press.

Ḥammād, I. (2015, September 18). Union of Egypt's Banks: 90 Percent of Egyptians Do Not Deal with Banks [bunūk miṣr: 90% min al-miṣriyīn la yata'amalūn ma'a al-maṣāref]. *Elwatan News*. [Online] https://www.elwatannews.com/news/details/805673

Ḥamūda, A. (2015, August 23, October 15). Interview with A. Adly.

Hanafy, S. (2015). *Sectoral FDI and Economic Growth: Evidence from Egyptian Governorates*. Joint Discussion Paper Series in Economics 37-2015.

Handler, W. C. (1994). Succession in Family Business: A Review of the Research. *Family Business Review*, 7(2), 133–157.

Haney, L., & Pollard, L. (2003). In a Family Way: Theorizing State and Familial Relations. In L. Haney & L. Pollard (eds.)*Families of a New World: Gender, Politics, and State Development in a Global Context*. New York: Routledge.

Hanieh, A. (2013). *Lineages of Revolt: Issues of Contemporary Capitalism in the Middle East*. Chicago: Haymarket Books.

Hansen, B. (1991). *The Political Economy of Poverty, Equity, and Growth: Egypt and Turkey*. New York: Oxford University Press.

Harders, C. (2003). The Informal Social Pact: The State and the Urban Poor in Cairo. In E. Kienle (ed.), *Politics from Above, Politics from Below: The Middle East in the Age of Economic Reform*, 191–213. London: Saqi Books.

Harveston, P. D., Davis, P. S., & Lyden, J. A. (1997). Succession Planning in Family Business: The Impact of Owner Gender. *Family Business Review*, 10(4), 373–396.

Harvey, D. (2007). *A Brief History of Neoliberalism*. New York: Oxford University Press.

Hashim, M. K. (2005). *Small and Medium-Sized Enterprises in Malaysia: Problems and Prospects*. Sintok: Universiti Utara Malaysia Press.

Ḥassan, S. (2017, November 8). Sawiris: The Central Bank Denied Me the License of Establishing a Bank to Finance Project . . . So I Pursued the Idea in Europe [Sawiris: al-markazī rafaḍa manḥī rukhṣat inshā' bank li tamwīl al-mashrū'āt, fanaffadht al-fikra fī ūrūbba]. *Elwatan News*. [Online] https://www.elwatannews.com/news/details/2689929

Heide, J. B., & Wathne, K. H. (2006). Friends, Businesspeople, and Relationship Roles: A Conceptual Framework and a Research Agenda. *Journal of Marketing*, 70(3), 90–103.

Helāl, H. (2016, February 22). Interview with A. Adly.

Hellman, J. S., Jones, G., & Kaufmann, D. (2000). *Seize the State, Seize the Day: An Empirical Analysis of State Capture and Corruption in Transition*. Policy Research working paper 2444.

Hendy, R., & Zaki, C. (2013). On Informality and Productivity of Micro and Small Enterprises: Evidence from MENA Countries. *International Journal of Entrepreneurship and Small Business*, 19(4), 438–470.

Henry, C. M., & Lamm, J. E. (2009). *Islamic Finance*. Oxford: Oxford University Press.

Henry, C. M., & Springborg, R. (2010). *Globalization and the Politics of Development in the Middle East*. Cambridge: Cambridge University Press.

Heydemann, S. (ed.). (2004). *Networks of Privilege in the Middle East: The Politics of Economic Reform Revisited.* New York: Palgrave Macmillan.

Hirschman, A. O. (1957). Investment Policies and "Dualism" in Underdeveloped Countries. *American Economic Review,* 47(5), 550–570.

Hoodfar, H. (1997). *Between Marriage and the Market: Intimate Politics and Survival in Cairo.* Berkeley: University of California Press.

Hoogvelt, A. M. (1978). *The Sociology of Developing Societies.* London: Palgrave.

Hopkins, N. S. (ed.). (1992). *Informal Sector in Egypt.* Cairo: American University in Cairo Press.

Hoshi, T. (2001). What Happened to Japanese Banks? *Monetary and Economic Studies,* 19(1), 1–29.

Hourani, A. (1981). *The Emergence of the Modern Middle East.* Berkeley: University of California Press.

Huang, L. Y., & Carraher, S. (2004). How Effective Are Expatriate Management and Guanxi Networks? Evidence from Chinese Industries. *International Journal of Family Business,* 1(1), 1–23.

Ḥussein, A. (1982). *The Egyptian Economy from Independence to Dependency* [al-iqtiṣād al-miṣrī min al-istiqlāl ilā-l-tabaʿiyya]. Cairo: Dar al-Mustaqbal al-ʿArabī.

———. (2017). *Austerity or Reform for the Government Administration?* [taqashshuf am iṣlāḥ li-l-jihāz al-ḥukūmī?]. In W. Gamal (ed.), *The Egyptian Economy in the Twenty First Century* [al-iqtiṣād al-miṣrī fī al-qarn al-ḥādī wa-l-ʿishrīn]. Cairo: Dar al-Maraya.

al-Ḥūty, H. (2015, March 8). CAPMAS: 51% of the Population Is Male and 24 Years the Average Marriage Age for Females [al-iḥṣāʾ: 51% min ʿadad al-sukkān dhukūr wa naḥwa 24 ʿāman sin al-zawāj li-l-fatayāt]. *Youm7.* [Online] http://www.youm7.com/story/2015/3/8/%09%09%09%09%09%09الإحصاء-51-من-عدد-السكان-ذكور-و24-عاما-متوسط-سن/2096867

Ikram, K. (2007). *The Egyptian Economy, 1952–2000: Performance Policies and Issues.* New York: Routledge.

Imām, S. S. (1986). *Who Owns Egypt: An Analytical Study of the Social Roots of the Open Door Elite in the Egyptian Society* [man yamluk miṣr dirāsa taḥlīliyya li nukhbat al-infitāḥ]. Cairo: Dar al-Mustaqbal al-Arabi.

International Monetary Fund (IMF). (2007, December). IMF Country Report Article IV Consultation, 07/380. Washington. DC: International Monetary Fund

Ismail, A. (2009). *Private Equity and Venture Capital in Emerging Markets: A Case Study of Egypt and the MENA Region*. PhD diss., MIT.

Isma'īl, S. M. (2016). *Arab Stock Markets* [*al-burṣāt al-'arabiyya*]. Cairo: Arab Center for Political and Strategic Studies.

Issawi, C. P. (1947). *Egypt: An Economic and Social Analysis*. Oxford: Oxford University Press.

Jessop, B. (1990). *State Theory: Putting the Capitalist State in Its Place*. State College: Pennsylvania State University Press.

Jin, H., Qian, Y., and Weingast, B. R. (2005). Regional Decentralization and Fiscal Incentives: Federalism, Chinese Style. *Journal of Public Economics*, 89(9-10),1719–1742.

Johnson, C. (1982). *MITI and the Japanese Miracle: The Growth of Industrial Policy: 1925–1975*. Palo Alto, CA: Stanford University Press.

Joseph, S. (ed.). (2000). *Gender and Citizenship in the Middle East*. Syracuse, NY: Syracuse University Press.

el-Kabbani, R. N., & Kalhoefer, C. (2011). *Financing Resources for Egyptian Small and Medium Enterprises*. IDEAS working paper 28.

el-Kadi, G. (2009). *Random Urbanization* [al-taḥaddur al-'ashwa'ī]. Trans. M. al-Baṭrāwi. Cairo: al-Markaz al-Qawmī li-l-Tarjama.

el-Kalioubi, S. (2002). Company Laws. In N. Bernard-Maugiron and B. Dupret (eds.), *Egypt and Its Laws*. London: Kluwer Law International.

Kandil, H. (2012). Why Did the Egyptian Middle Class March to Tahrir Square? *Mediterranean Politics*, 17(2), 197–215.

Kang, D. C. (2002). *Crony Capitalism: Corruption and Development in South Korea and the Philippines*. Cambridge: Cambridge University Press.

Karl, T. L. (1997). *The Paradox of Plenty: Oil Booms and Petro-States*. Berkeley: University of California Press.

Kassem, M. (2004). *Egyptian Politics: The Dynamics of Authoritarian Rule*. Boulder, CO: Lynne Rienner.

Kaufman, H. (2015). *Red Tape: Its Origins, Uses, and Abuses*. Washington, DC: Brookings Institution Press.

Khafaji, I. (2013) *Tormented Births: Passages to Modernity in Europe and the Middle East* [wilādāt muta'athira: al-'ubūr ilā-l-ḥadātha fī ūrūbbā wal-mashreq]. Trans. I. Khafaji. Cairo: al-Markaz al-Qawmī li-l-Tarjamah.

Khalil, E. L. (1995). Organizations Versus Institutions. *Journal of Institutional and*

Theoretical Economics (JITE)/Zeitschrift für die gesamte Staatswissenschaft, 151(3), 445–466.

Khan, M. H., & Jomo, K. S. (eds.). (2000). *Rents, Rent-Seeking and Economic Development: Theory and Evidence in Asia*. Cambridge: Cambridge University Press.

Khanna, T., & Palepu, K. (2000). Is Group Affiliation Profitable in Emerging Markets? An Analysis of Diversified Indian Business Groups. *Journal of Finance*, 55(2), 867–891.

Khanna, T., & Yafeh, Y. (2007). Business Groups in Emerging Markets: Paragons or Parasites? *Journal of Economic literature*, 45(2), 331–372.

Kharoufi, M. (1991). The Informal Dimension of Urban Activity in Egypt: Some Recent Work. *Cairo Papers in Social Science*, 14, 8–20.

El-Khawaga, D., & Ferrié, J. N. (2010). Egypt in the Hour of Succession [L'Egypte à l'heure de la succession]. Études, 413(9), 163–173.

Khayri, M., & al-Amīn, S. (2011). *Commercial Sales and Endorsement of Promissory Notes: Promissory Notes and Checks* [al-buyūʿ al-tijāriyya wa-l-taẓhīr fī al-kimbiyāla: al-sanad al-idhnī wa-l-shīk]. Cairo: al-Markaz al-Qawm*ī* li-l-iṣdārāt al-qānūniyya.

King, S. J. (2009). *The New Authoritarianism in the Middle East and North Africa*. Bloomington: Indiana University Press.

Klein, B., Crawford, R. G., & Alchian, A. A. (1978). Vertical Integration, Appropriable Rents, and the Competitive Contracting Process. *Journal of Law and Economics*, 21(2), 297–326.

Kramer, R. M., Brewer, M. B., & Hanna, B. A. (1996). Collective Trust and Collective Action. In R. M. Kramer & T. R. Tyler (eds.), *Trust in Organizations: Frontiers of Theory and Research*, 357–389. Thousand Oaks, CA: Sage.

Krueger, A. O. (1987). *The Importance of Economic Policy in Development: Contrasts Between Korea and Turkey*. National Bureau of Economic Research working paper 2195.

Krugman, P. (1991). Increasing Returns and Economic Geography. *Journal of Political Economy*, 99(3), 483–499.

La Porta, R. (2001). *Comment on "Ownership Structure, Legal Protections and Corporate Governance by I: J. Alexander Dyck."* In Proceedings of the Annual World Bank Conference on Development Economics, 361–370. Washington, DC: International Bank for Reconstruction and Development.

Leff, N. H. (1978). Industrial Organization and Entrepreneurship in the Developing

Countries: The Economic Groups. *Economic Development and Cultural Change*, 26(4), 661–675.

Lewis, W. A. (1979). The Dual Economy Revisited. *Manchester School*, 47(3), 211–229.

Lin, N. (1995). Local Market Socialism: Local Corporatism in Action in Rural China. *Theory and Society*, 24(3), 301–354.

———. (1999). Building a Network Theory of Social Capital. *Connections*, 22(1), 28–51.

Luo, Y. (2003). Industrial Dynamics and Managerial Networking in an Emerging Market: The Case of China. *Strategic Management Journal*, 24(13), 1315–1327.

Mabro, R., & Radwan, S. (1976). *The Industrialization of Egypt 1939–1973: Policy and Performance*. New York: Oxford University Press.

al-Mahdi, A., & Rashed, A. (2010). The Changing Environment and the Development of Small and Micro Projects in Egypt 2006 [al-munākh al-mutaghayyer wa tanmiyat al-mashrūʿāt al-ṣaghīra wa-l-mutanāhiyat al-ṣighar fī miṣr 2006]. In R. Assaad (ed.), *The Egyptian Labor Market in the New Millennium* [sūq al-ʿamal al-miṣriyya fī al-alfiyya al-jadīda]. Cairo: Economic Research Forum and al-Ahram Center.

Mahdi, F. (2016, September 19). Missing Facts Are the Secret of Special Funds [al-ḥaqāʾiq al-ghāʾiba sir al-ṣanādīq al-khāṣṣa]. *al-Ahram*. [Online] http://www.ahram.org.eg/NewsPrint/551689.aspx

Makram Ebeid, D. (2012). *Manufacturing Stability: Everyday Politics of Work in an Industrial Steel Town in Helwan, Egypt*. PhD diss., London School of Economics and Political Science.

Maxfield, S., & Schneider, B. R. (eds.). (1997). *Business and the State in Developing Countries*. Ithaca, NY: Cornell University Press.

Mayer, R. C., Davis, J. H., & Schoorman, F. D. (1995). An Integrative Model of Organizational Trust. *Academy of Management Review*, 20(3), 709–734.

McMillan, J., & Woodruff, C. (1999). Dispute Prevention Without Courts in Vietnam. *Journal of Law, Economics, and Organization*, 15(3), 637–658.

McNally, C. A., & Chu, Y. W. (2006). Exploring Capitalist Development in Greater China: A Synthesis. *Asian Perspective*, 30(2), 31–64.

el-Meehy, A. (2010). *Rewriting the Social Contract: The Social Fund and Egypt's Politics of Retrenchment*. PhD diss., University of Toronto.

Menza, M. F. (2012). *Patronage Politics in Egypt: The National Democratic Party and Muslim Brotherhood in Cairo*. London: Routledge.

al-Merghani, I. (2010). Labor Relations [Awḍāʿ ʿilāqāt al-ʿamal]. In Al-Hilāli Foundation (ed.), *Egyptian Workers in a Changing World: History and Struggle* [al-ʿommāl al-miṣriyyūn fī ʿālam mutaghayyir: tārīkh, niḍāl], 131–165. Cairo: al-Hilāli Foundation.

Merton, R. K. (1968). *Social Theory and Social Structure.* New York: Simon and Schuster.

Migdal, J. S. (1988). *Strong Societies and Weak States: State-Society Relations and State Capabilities in the Third World.* Princeton, NJ: Princeton University Press.

Miller, D., Steier, L., & Le Breton-Miller, I. (2003). Lost in Time: Intergenerational Succession, Change and Failure in Family Business. *Journal of Business Venturing,* 18(4), 513–531.

Ministry of Finance (Egypt). (2004). *Enhancing Competitiveness for SMEs in Egypt: General Framework and Action Plan.* Cairo: Ministry of Finance.

———. (2009). *Financial Monthly,* 4(12).

Ministry of Foreign Trade (Egypt). (2003). *Profile of M/SMEs in Egypt.* Cairo: Ministry of Foreign Trade.

Minor, M. S. (1994). The Demise of Expropriation as an Instrument of LDC Policy, 1980–1992. *Journal of International Business Studies,* 25(1), 177–188.

Mitchell, T. (1999). Dreamland: The Neoliberalism of Your Desires. *Middle East Report,* 29(1), 28–33.

———. (2002). *Rule of Experts: Egypt, Techno-Politics, Modernity.* Berkeley: University of California Press.

Mohieldin, M., & Nasr, S. (2003). *On Bank Privatization in Egypt.* Economic Research Forum working paper 032.

Mohieldin, M. S., & Wright, P. W. (2000). Formal and Informal Credit Markets in Egypt. *Economic Development and Cultural Change,* 48(3), 657–670.

Mokhtār, A. (2010). *The New Check According to Commerce Law* [al-shīk al-jadīd wafqan li qānūn al-tijāra]. Cairo: Ḥaydar Group.

Montgomery, C. A. (1994). Corporate Diversification. *Journal of Economic Perspectives,* 8(3), 163–178.

Montgomery, J. D. (1998). Toward a Role-Theoretic Conception of Embeddedness. *American Journal of Sociology,* 104(1), 92–125.

Moorman, C., Zaltman, G., & Deshpande, R. (1992). Relationships Between Providers and Users of Market Research: The Dynamics of Trust Within and Between Organizations. *Journal of Marketing Research,* 29(3), 314–328

Morck, R., & Nakamura, M. (1999). Banks and Corporate Control in Japan. *Journal of Finance,* 54(1), 319–339.

Morck, R., Nakamura, M., & Shivdasani, A. (2000). Banks, Ownership Structure, and Firm Value in Japan. *Journal of Business*, 73(4), 539–567.

Morsi, F. (1980). *This Economic Opening* [hādhā al-infitāḥ al-iqtiṣādī]. Cairo: Dar al-Waḥda.

Moussa, M. (2018, April 2). Interview with A. Adly.

Moustafa, T. (2007). *The Struggle for Constitutional Power: Law, Politics, and Economic Development in Egypt*. Cambridge: Cambridge University Press.

Myant, M. (2007). The Czech Republic: From "Czech" Capitalism to "European" Capitalism. In D. Lane & M. Myant (eds.), *Varieties of Capitalism in Post-Communist Countries*, 105–123. Hampshire: Palgrave Macmillan.

Nahapiet, J., & Ghoshal, S. (1998). Social Capital, Intellectual Capital, and the Organizational Advantage. *Academy of Management Review*, 23(2), 242–266.

Naṣr, M. (2017, February 6). *Cain and Abel Are Still Among Us* [Qābīl wa Hābīl la yazālūna baynanā]. *Youm7*. [Online]] http://www.youm7.com/story/2017/2/6ليباق
3089637/ثاريملا-دصرت-لدعلا-ةرازول-ةسارد-اننيب-نولازي-ال-ليباهو-

Nasr, S. (2008). *Access to Finance and Economic Growth in Egypt: World Bank, Middle East and North African Region*. Washington, DC: World Bank.

Neidik, B., & Gereffi, G. (2006). Explaining Turkey's Emergence and Sustained Competitiveness as a Full-Package Supplier of Apparel. *Environment and Planning A*, 38(12), 2285–2303.

Nenova, T. (1999). *The Value of a Corporate Vote and Private Benefits: A Cross-Country Analysis*. Unpublished working paper, Harvard University.

North, D. (1990). Institutions and Their Consequences for Economic Performance. In K. S. Cook & M. Levi (eds.), *The Limits of Rationality*, 383–401. Chicago: University of Chicago Press.

Oh, I., & Varcin, R. (2002). The Mafioso State: State-Led Market Bypassing in South Korea and Turkey. *Third World Quarterly*, 23(4), 711–723.

al-ʿOkda, F. (2013, May 23). Interview with A. Adly.

ʿOlama, A. (2015, January 6). Interview with A. Adly.

Olson, M. (1993). Dictatorship, Democracy, and Development. *American Political Science Review*, 87(3), 567–576.

Önis, Z. (1999). *State and Market: The Political Economy of Turkey in Comparative Perspective*. Working paper, Boğazçi University, Faculty of Economics and Administrative Sciences, Department of Economics.

Organization for Economic Co-operation and Development (OECD). (2004). *Promoting Entrepreneurship and Innovative SMEs in a Global Economy.* Paris: OECD Publishing.

———. (2013). *Competitiveness and Private Sector Development: New Entrepreneurship and High Performance Enterprises in the Middle East and North Africa.* Paris: OECD Publishing.

Ouchi, W. G. (1980). Markets, Bureaucracies, and Clans. *Administrative Science Quarterly,* 25(1), 129-141.

'Ouda, G. (2004). *Gamāl Mubārak and the Renewal of National Liberalism* [Gamāl Mubārak wa tajdīd al-librāliyya al-waṭaniyya]. Cairo: Kitāb al-Ḥoriyya.

Owen, R. (2014). *The Rise and Fall of Arab Presidents for Life: With a New Afterword.* Cambridge, MA: Harvard University Press.

Pagès-El Karoui, D. (2008). *Cities of the Nile Delta: Tanta, Mahalla, Mansûra, Cities of Density* [Villes du delta du Nil: Tantâ, Mahalla, Mansûra, cités de la densité]. Paris: Karthala Editions.

———. (2012). Geography of Social Change in Egypt [Géographie du Changement Social en Égypte] *EchoGéo,* 12 (September 2012). [Online] https://journals.openedition.org/echogeo/13204

Palm Hills Group. (2014). *Annual Financial Report 2014.* [Online] http://www.palmhillsdevelopments.com/Cms_Data/Contents/PalmHillsDevelopmentsCD/Media/Investors/PDF/Financial_Statements/2014/4Q/FY14%20–%20Consolidated%20–%20IFRS.pdf [Accessed June 8, 2017]

Panitch, L., & Gindin, S. (2012). *The Making of Global Capitalism: The Political Economy of American Empire.* London: Verso Books.

Paoli, L. (2002). The Paradoxes of Organized Crime. *Crime, Law and Social Change,* 37(1), 51–97.

Paragon Financial Group. (2018). What Is Invoice Factoring? [Online] https://www.paragonfinancial.net/how-factoring-works/articles-resources/factoring-articles/what-is-invoice-factoring/) [Accessed September 17, 2018]

Park, S. H., & Luo, Y. (2001). Guanxi and Organizational Dynamics: Organizational Networking in Chinese Firms. *Strategic Management Journal,* 22(5), 455–477.

Peck, J., & Theodore, N. (2007). Variegated Capitalism. *Progress in Human Geography,* 31(6), 731–772.

Peck, J., & Zhang, J. (2013). A Variety of Capitalism . . . with Chinese Characteristics? *Journal of Economic Geography,* 13(3), 357–396.

Peng, M. W., Lee, S. H., & Wang, D. Y. (2005). What Determines the Scope of the Firm over Time? A Focus on Institutional Relatedness. *Academy of Management Review*, 30(3), 622–633.

Peng, Y. (2004). Kinship Networks and Entrepreneurs in China's Transitional Economy. *American Journal of Sociology*, 109(5), 1045–1074.

Perotti, E. C., & Gelfer, S. (2001). Red Barons or Robber Barons? Governance and Investment in Russian Financial–Industrial Groups. *European Economic Review*, 45(9), 1601–1617.

Perotti, E. C., & Suarez, J. (2002). Last Bank Standing: What Do I Gain If You Fail? *European Economic Review*, 46(9), 1599–1622.

Piketty, T. (2016). *Capital in the 21st Century*. Trans. W. Gamal & S. Ḥussein. Cairo: Dar al-Fikr.

Platteau, J. P. (1994). Behind the Market Stage Where Real Societies Exist—Part II: The Role of Moral Norms. *Journal of Development Studies*, 30(4), 753–817.

Polanyi, K. (1957). *The Great Transformation: The Political and Economic Origin of our Time*, 2nd ed. Boston: Beacon Press.

Pollard, L. (2005.) *Nurturing the Nation: The Family Politics of Modernizing, Colonizing, and Liberating Egypt, 1805–1923*. Berkeley: University of California Press.

Porta, R. L., Lopez-de-Silanes, F., Shleifer, A., & Vishny, R. W. (1998). Law and Finance. *Journal of Political Economy*, 106(6), 1113–1155. Posusney, M. P. (1997). *Labor and the State in Egypt, 1952–1994: Workers, Unions, and Economic Restructuring*. New York: Columbia University Press.

Prinz, M. (2002). German Rural Co-Operatives, Friedrich Wilhelm Raiffeisen and the Organization of Trust. In *Eighth Proceedings of the International Economic History Association Congress*. Buenos Aires: International Economic History Association.

Qotb, M., & Ghāleb, G. (2016, March 8). I Wish I Could Buy a Bank in Egypt [kuntu atamannā shirā' bank fī miṣr]. *Almasryalyoum*. [Online] https://www.almasryalyoum.com/news/details/906339

Rady, M. (2002). Administrative Justice. In N. Bernard-Maugiron & B. Dupret (eds.), *Egypt and Its Laws*. London: Kluwer Law International.

Rauch, J. E. (1993). Productivity Gains from Geographic Concentration of Human Capital: Evidence from the Cities. *Journal of Urban Economics*, 34(3), 380–400.

Ravallion, M., & Chen, S. (2007). China's (Uneven) Progress Against Poverty. *Journal of Development Economics*, 82(1), 1–42.

Raymond, A. (2014). *Artisans and Merchants in Cairo in the 18th Century* (Artisans et

Commerçants au Caire au XVIIIe Siècle). Damas: Presses de l'institut Français du Proche Orient.

Redding, G. (2005). The Thick Description and Comparison of Societal Systems of Capitalism. *Journal of International Business Studies*, 36(2), 123–155.

Rettberg, A. (2005). Business Versus Business? Grupos and Organized Business in Colombia. *Latin American Politics and Society*, 47(1), 31–54.

Reynolds, K. E., & Beatty, S. E. (2000). A Relationship Customer Typology. *Journal of Retailing*, 75(4), 509–523.

Reynolds, P., Storey, D. J., & Westhead, P. (1994). Cross-National Comparisons of the Variation in New Firm Formation Rates. *Regional Studies*, 28(4), 443–456.

Richards, A. (1991). The Political Economy of Dilatory Reform: Egypt in the 1980s. *World Development*, 19(12), 1721–1730.

Riddle, L. A., & Gillespie, K. (2003). Information Sources for New Ventures in the Turkish Clothing Export Industry. *Small Business Economics*, 20(1), 105–120.

Rijkers, B., Freund, C., & Nucifora, A. (2014). *All in the Family: State Capture in Tunisia*. World Bank Policy Research working paper 6810.

Ritchie, B., & Brindley, C. (2000). Disintermediation, Disintegration and Risk in the SME Global Supply Chain. *Management Decision*, 38(8), 575–583.

Robinson, J. A., & Acemoglu, D. (2012). *Why Nations Fail: The Origins of Power, Prosperity, and Poverty*. New York: Crown.

Roccu, R. (2013). *The Political Economy of the Egyptian Revolution: Mubarak, Economic Reforms and Failed Hegemony*. London: Palgrave Macmillan.

Rocha, R. D. R., Farazi, S., Khouri, R., & Pearce, D. (2011). *The Status of Bank Lending to SMES in the Middle East and North Africa Region: The Results of a Joint Survey of the Union of Arab Bank and the World Bank*. World Bank Policy Research working paper WPS5607.

Rodrik, D. (1998). Has Globalization Gone Too Far? *Challenge*, 41(2), 81–94.

———. (2004). *Industrial Policy for the Twenty-First Century*. Prepared for UNIDO, Harvard University

Roll, S. (2013). *Egypt's Business Elite After Mubarak: A Powerful Player Between Generals and Brotherhood*. SWP research paper, 8/2013). Berlin: Stiftung Wissenschaft und Politik -SWP- Deutsches Institut für Internationale Politik und Sicherheit. https://nbn-resolving.org/urn:nbn:de:0168–ssoar-385620.

[al-]Sadat, A. (1974). *The October Working Paper*. Ministry of Information, State Information Service (Egypt)

Sadowski, Y. M. (1991). *Political Vegetables? Businessmen and Bureaucrats in the Development of Egyptian Agriculture*. Washington, DC: Brookings.

Sa'īd, S. (2017, January 22). A Capitalist in the House of the Left . . . Ḥussein Ṣabbour Fires from the Headquarter of al-Tajamo'Party [ra'smālī fī bayt al-yasār . . . Ḥussein Ṣabbour yutliq qadhā'ifahu miṇ maqar al-Tajammu']. *Youm7*. [Online] https://www.youm7.com/story/2017/1/22/رأسمالى-فى-بيت-اليسار-حسين-صبور-يطلق-قذائفه-من-مقر/3066510

al-Sa'īd, D. (2013, June 2). Interview with A. Adly.

el-Said, H., al-Said, M., & Zaki, C. (2013). Access to Finance and Financial Problems of SMEs: Evidence from Egypt. *International Journal of Entrepreneurship and Small Business*, 20(3), 286–309.

Sahnoun, H., Keefer, P., Schiffbauer, M., Sy, A., & Hussain, S. (2014). *Jobs or Privileges: Unleashing the Employment Potential of the Middle East and North Africa*. Washington DC: International Bank for Reconstruction and Development/World Bank.

Saleḥ, A. (2016, October 18). Ahsraf al-'Arabī: Maḥmoud Moḥeildin Was the First to Consider the One-Stop-Shop [Ashraf al-'Arabī: Maḥmoud Moḥeildin awwal man bada'a fikrat al-shubbāk al-wāḥid]. *Youm7*. [Online] http://www.youm7.com/story/2016/10/18/أشرف-العربى-محمود-محيى-الدين-أول-من-بدأ-فكرة-الشباك/2925538

Saleh, A. S., & Ndubisi, N. O. (2006). An Evaluation of SME Development in Malaysia. *International Review of Business Research Papers*, 2(1), 1–14.

Sanabel (Microfinance Network of Arab Countries) (January 2010) Microfinance Industry Profile: Egypt. Tunisia. *Sanabel (The Microfinance Network of Arab Countries)*.[Online] https://www.sanabelnetwork.org/SanabelFiles/Publications/TransparencyPublications/Sanabel_Profile_Egypt_Eng.pdf

Sánchez, O. (2003). The Rise and Fall of the Dependency Movement: Does it Inform Underdevelopment Today? *EIAL: Estudios Interdisciplinarios de America Latina y el Caribe*, 14(2), 31–50.

al-Sayyed, M. K. (1983). *Society and Politics in Egypt: The Role of Interest Groups in the Egyptian Political System (1952–1981)* [al-mujtama' wa-l-siyāsa fī miṣr: dawr jamā'āt al-maṣāliḥ fī al-niẓām al-siyāsī al-miṣrī (1952–1981)]. Cairo: Dar al-Mostaqbal al-'Arabī.

al-Sharqāwi, M. S. (1990, November 30). Guarantee Checks: Are These Checks? [Shīk al-ḍamān hal huwa shīk?].

al-Shawārby, L. (2015, January 8). Interview with A. Adly.

Schmitter, P. C. (1989) Corporatism Is Dead! Long Live Corporatism! *Government and Opposition*, 24(1), 54–73.

Schneider, B. R. (2004). *Business Politics and the State in Twentieth-Century Latin America*. Cambridge: Cambridge University Press.

———. (2009). Hierarchical Market Economies and Varieties of Capitalism in Latin America. *Journal of Latin American Studies*, 41(3), 553–575.

Schneider, F. (2012). *The Shadow Economy and Work in the Shadow: What Do We (Not) Know?* IZA discussion paper 6423. [Online] https://papers.ssrn.com/sol3/papers.cfm?abstract_id=2031951 [Accessed July 11, 2017]

Schneider, F., Buehn, A., & Montenegro, C. E. (2010). *Shadow Economies All Over the World*. World Bank policy research working paper 5356.

Schumacher, E. F. (2011). *Small Is Beautiful: A Study of Economics as If People Mattered*. London: Blond & Briggs.

Selim, T. H. (2006). Monopoly: The Case of Egyptian Steel. *Journal of Business Case Studies*, 2(3), 85–92.

Selznick, P. (1943). An Approach to a Theory of Bureaucracy. *American Sociological Review*, 8(1), 47–54.

Sen, A. K. (2001). *Development as Freedom*. New York: Oxford University Press.

Sfakianakis, J. (2004). The Whales of the Nile: Networks, Businessmen, and Bureaucrats During the Era of Privatization in Egypt. In S. Heydemann (ed.), *Networks of Privilege in the Middle East: The Politics of Economic Reform Revisited*, 77–100. New York: Palgrave Macmillan.

Shamsān, H. (1994). Dissolution of Partnerships: A Comparative Study [taṣfiyat sharikāt al-ashkhāṣ al-tijariyya: dirasa muqarana]. PhD diss., Cairo University.

Shapiro, S. P. (1987). The Social Control of Impersonal Trust. *American Journal of Sociology*, 93(3), 623–658.

Sharabi, H. (1988). *Neopatriarchy: A Theory of Distorted Change in the Arab Society*. New York: Oxford University Press

Sharma, P., Chrisman, J. J., and Chua, J. H. (2003). Succession Planning as Planned Behavior: Some Empirical Results. *Family Business Review*, 16(1), 1–15.

Sharp, J. M. (2009). *Egypt: Background and US Relations*. Washington DC: Congressional Research Service. [Online] https://apps.dtic.mil/docs/citations/ADA501061 [Accessed May 25, 2017]

Shawkat, Y. (2012). *Social Justice and Urbanity: Egypt's Map* [al-ʿadāla al-ijtimāʿiyya wa-l- ʿumrān: kharīṭat miṣr]. Cairo: Wizārat Iskān al-Ẓil.

———. (2014, October 26). Interview with A. Adly.

Shehata, D. (2011). The Fall of the Pharaoh: How Hosni Mubarak's Reign Came to an End. *Foreign Affairs*, 90(3), 26–32.

Shehata, I. (1996). The *Legal Framework of Economic Reform in Egypt* [al-iṭār al-qānūnī lil Hiṣlāḥ al-iqtiṣādī fī miṣr]. Distinguished Lecture 5. Cairo: Egyptian Centre for Economic Studies.

Shuhayb, A. (1989). *The Breach: The Story of Capital Investment Companies* [al-Ikhtirāq: qiṣat sharikāt tawẓīf al-amwāl]. Cairo: Sīna li-l-Nashr.

Shukri, G. (1987). *The Counterrevolution in Egypt* [al-thawra al-muḍādda fī miṣr]. Cairo: al-Ahāli.

Silver, A. (1990). Friendship in Commercial Society: Eighteenth-Century Social Theory and Modern Sociology. *American Journal of Sociology*, 95(6), 1474–1504.

Sims, D. (2015). *Egypt's Desert Dreams: Development or Disaster?* Cairo: American University in Cairo Press.

Singerman, D. (1995). *Avenues of Participation: Family, Politics, and Networks in Urban Quarters of Cairo*. Princeton, NJ: Princeton University Press.

Singerman, D., and Hoodfar, H. (eds.). (1996). *Development, Change, and Gender in Cairo: A View from the Household*. Bloomington: Indiana University Press.

Siu, W. S. (2005). An Institutional Analysis of Marketing Practices of Small and Medium Sized Enterprises (SMEs) in China, Hong Kong and Taiwan. *Entrepreneurship and Regional Development*, 17(1), 65–88.

Skaperdas, S. (2001). The Political Economy of Organized Crime: Providing Protection When the State Does Not. *Economics of Governance*, 2(3), 173–202.

Smith, R. (2009). Understanding Entrepreneurial Behavior in Organized Criminals. *Journal of Enterprising Communities: People and Places in the Global Economy*, 3(3), 256–268.

Søderberg, A. M., & Worm, V. D. (2011). Communication and Collaboration in Subsidiaries in China: Chinese and Expatriate Accounts. *European Journal of Cross-Cultural Competence and Management*, 2(1), 54–76.

Soliman, S. (2006). The Strong Regime and the Weak State: Managing the Fiscal Crisis and Political Change Under Mubarak [al-niẓām al-qawī wa-l-dawla al-ḍaʿīfa: idārat al-azma al-māliyya wa al-taghayyur al-siyāsī fī miṣr]. Cairo: al-Dar Press.

———. (2011). *The Autumn of Dictatorship: Fiscal Crisis and Political Change in Egypt Under Mubarak*. Palo Alto, CA: Stanford University Press.

Soskice, D. W., and Hall, P. A. (2001). *Varieties of Capitalism: The Institutional Foundations of Comparative Advantage*. Oxford: Oxford University Press.

Soule, E. (1998). Trust and Managerial Responsibility. *Business Ethics Quarterly*, 8(2), 249–272.

Springborg, R. (1989). *Mubarak's Egypt: Fragmentation of the Political Order*. Boulder, CO: Westview Press.

———. (2012). Gas and Oil in Egypt's Development. In R.

Looney (ed.), *Handbook of Oil Politics*, 295–311. London: Routledge.

Stallings, B., Haggard, S., & Kaufman, R. (1992). *The Politics of Economic Adjustment*. Princeton, NJ: Princeton University Press.

Stark, D. (1996). Recombinant Property in East European Capitalism. *American Journal of Sociology*, 101(4), 993–1027.

Stark, D., & Bruszt, L. (1998). *Post-Socialist Pathways: Transforming Politics and Property in East Central Europe*. Cambridge: Cambridge University Press.

Stauth, G. (1991). Gamaliyya: Informal Economy and Social Life in a Popular Quarter of Cairo. In Nicholas S. Hopkins (ed.), *Informal Sector in Egypt*. Cairo Papers in the Social Sciences, Cairo, American University in Cairo, 78–103.

Steerb, L., & Senc, K. (2008). *Informal Institutions in Transition: How Vietnam's Private Sector Boomed Without Legal Protection*. London: Department of International Development.

Steinmo, S., Thelen, K., & Longstreth, F. (eds.). (1992) *Structuring Politics: Historical Institutionalism in Comparative Analysis*. Cambridge: Cambridge University Press.

Stepan, A. C. (2000). Religion, Democracy, and the "Twin Tolerations." *Journal of Democracy*, 11(4), 37–57.

Stevenson, L. (2011). *Private Sector and Enterprise Development: Fostering Growth in the Middle East and North Africa*. Northampton, MA: Elgar.

Stevenson, L., & 'Abdel Aziz, M. (2008). *Influencing Policy Key Factors in the Case of a SME Policy Project in Egypt*. Cairo: International Council for Small Business World

Stiglitz, J. E. (1996). *Whither Socialism?* Cambridge, MA: MIT Press.

Streeck, W., & Schmitter, P. C. (eds.). (1985). *Private Interest Government: Beyond Market and State*. London: Sage.

Sulaymān, S. (1999). *State and Industrial Capitalism in Egypt*. Cairo: American University in Cairo Press.

Sulaymān, 'Abdel-Fattah (2010, June 2). Cross Checks in Egypt Are Security Instruments and Not Checks [al-ṣak al-muṣaṭṭar fī miṣr adāt i'timān wa laysa shīkan].

al-Iqtiṣādiyya. [Online] http://www.aleqt.com/2010/06/02/article_401208.html

Sulṭān, M. (2015, May 12). Interview with A. Adly.

Talaat Moustafa Group Official. History and Evolution. [Online] http://www.talaatmoustafa.com/?AspxAutoDetectCookieSupport=1 (Accessed August 2, 2018]

Talaat Moustafa Group. (2014). *Annual Financial Report.* [Online] http://www.talaatmoustafa.com/Upload/Financial/%D8%AA%D9%82%D8%B1%D9%8A%D8%B1%20%D9%85%D8%AC%D9%84%D8%B3%20%D8%A7%D9%84%D8%A5%D8%AF%D8%A7%D8%B1%D8%A9%20%D8%A7%D9%84%D8%B3%D9%86%D9%88%D9%89%20%D8%B9%D9%86%20%D8%A7%D9%84%D8%B3%D9-%86%D8%A9%20%D8%A7%D9%84%D9%85%D8%A7%D9%84%D9%8A%D8%A9%20%D8%A7%D9%84%D9%85%D9%86%D8%AA%D9%87%D9%8A%D8%A9%20%D9%81%D9%89%2031-12-2014%20pdf.pdf [Accessed August 2, 2018]

Tarbush, N. (2012). Cairo 2050: Urban Dream or Modernist Delusion? *Journal of International Affairs*, 65 (2),171–186.

el-Tarouty, S. (2016). *Businessmen, Clientelism, and Authoritarianism in Egypt.* New York: Palgrave Macmillan.

al- Tawịla , A. (1988). *Capital Investment Companies and Their Ambiguous Future* [sharikāt tawẓīf al-amwāl wa-l-mustaqbal al-ghāmiḍ]. Cairo: al-Ṣawi Publishing House.

Teoh, W. M. Y., & Chong, S. C. (2008). Improving Women Entrepreneurs in Small and Medium Enterprises in Malaysia: Policy Recommendations. *Communications of the IBIMA*, 2(5), 31–38.

Thābet, A. (1996). Money and Politics in Egypt: A Study of the Mechanisms of Political Participation of Interest Groups [al-māl wa-l-siyāsa fī miṣr: dirāsa fī āliyyāt al-mushāraka al-siyāsiyya liba'ḍ al-jamā'āt]. In M. K. Elsayed (ed.), *The Truth About Political Pluralism in Egypt: Studies in Capitalist Transformation and Political Participation* [ḥaqīqat al-ta'addudiyyh al-siyāsiyya fī miṣr: dirāsa fī al-taḥawwul al-ra'asmālī wa-l mushāraka al-siyāsiyya]. Cairo: Madbouli Publishers.

Tignor, R. L. (1984). *Capitalism and Nationalism at the End of Empire: State and Business in Decolonizing Egypt, Nigeria, and Kenya, 1945–1963.* Princeton, NJ: Princeton University Press.

Trading Economics. (2018). *Egypt: Government Debt to GDP.* [Online] https://tradingeconomics.com/egypt/government-debt-to-gdp. [Accessed January 8, 2018]

Tsai, K. S. (2004). *Back-Alley Banking: Private Entrepreneurs in China*. Ithaca, NY: Cornell University Press.

United Nations Development Program. (2011). *Arab Development Challenges Report 2011: Towards the Developmental State in the Arab Region*. Cairo: United Nations Development Program.

US Agency for International Development. (2009). *The Legal and Regulatory Environment for Microfinance in Egypt: Diagnostic Study with Focus on NGO-MFI Transformation Issues*. Cairo: Microenterprise Finance.

Uzzi, B. (1996). The Sources and Consequences of Embeddedness for the Economic Performance of Organizations: The Network Effect. *American Sociological Review*, 61(4), 674–698.

———. (1997). Social Structure and Competition in Interfirm Networks: The Paradox of Embeddedness. *Administrative Science Quarterly*, 42(1), 35–67.

Vandevelde, K. J. (2009). *US International Investment Agreements*. Oxford: Oxford University Press.

Van Stel, A., & Storey, D. (2004). The Link Between Firm Births and Job Creation: Is There a Upas Tree Effect? *Regional Studies*, 38(8), 893–909.

Vitalis, R. (1995). *When Capitalists Collide: Business Conflict and the End of Empire in Egypt*. Berkeley: University of California Press.

Volkov, V. (2016). *Violent Entrepreneurs: The Use of Force in the Making of Russian Capitalism*. Ithaca, NY: Cornell University Press.

Wade, R. (1990). *Governing the Market: Economic Theory and the Role of Government in East Asian Industrialization*. Princeton, NJ: Princeton University Press.

al-Wafd. (2016, April 18). Onsi Sawiris: My Father Was a Lawyer and My Mother "Badīʿa" Could Run a Country by Herself [Onsi Sawiris: abī kāna muḥāmiyyan wa ummī "Badīʿa" kanat tasṭatīʿ an taḥkum baladan bimufradihā]. *al-Wafd*. [Online] https://alwafd.news/تحقيقات-وحوارات/1134872أنسي-ساويرس-أبي-كان-محاميًا-وأمي«بديعة»-كانت-تستطيع-أن-تحكم-بلدًا-بمفردها

Wahba, A. (2013, June 3). Interview with A. Adly.

Wahba, J. (2010). A General Look at Internal and External Migration in Egypt [naẓra ʿāmma ʿalā al-hijra al-dākhiliyya wa-l-khārijiyya fī miṣr]. In R. Assaad (ed.), *The Egyptian Labor Market in the New Millennium* [*sūq al-ʿamal al-miṣriyya fī al-alfiyya al-jadīda*]. Cairo: Economic Research Forum and al-Ahram Center.

Wahba, R. (2013). *Land and All That Is on It* [al-arḍ wa man ʿalayhā]. Cairo: Shabakat Hukuk al-Arḍ wa-l-Sakan.

Waḥīd, T. (2016, February 18). Interview with A. Adly.

Walder, A. G. (1995). Local Governments as Industrial Firms: An Organizational Analysis of China's Transitional Economy. *American Journal of Sociology*, 101(2), 263–301

Walker, G., Kogut, B., & Shan, W. (1997). Social Capital, Structural Holes and the Formation of an Industry Network. *Organization Science*, 8(2), 109–125.

Wang, J. (2005). Going Beyond Township and Village Enterprises in Rural China. *Journal of Contemporary China*, 14(42), 177–187.

Wang, Y. (2004). Financing Difficulties and Structural Characteristics of SMEs in China. *China and World Economy* 12(2), 34–49

Waṣfi, N., Waṣfi, H., & Shawqi, N. (2013, June 4). Interview with A. Adly.

Waterbury, J. (1983). *The Egypt of Nasser and Sadat: The Political Economy of Two Regimes*. Princeton, NJ: Princeton University Press.

———. (1992). The Heart of the Matter? Public Enterprise and the Adjustment Process. In S. Haggard and R. R. Kaufman (eds.), *The Politics of Economic Adjustment*, 182–220. Princeton, NJ: Princeton University Press.

Weiss, L. (ed.). (2003) *States in the Global Economy: Bringing Domestic Institutions Back*. Cambridge: Cambridge University Press.

Wicks, A. C., Berman, S. L., and Jones, T. M. (1999). The Structure of Optimal Trust: Moral and Strategic Implications. *Academy of Management Review*, 24(1), 99–116.

Williamson, O. E. (1971). The Vertical Integration of Production: Market Failure Considerations. *American Economic Review*, 61(2), 112–123.

Windolf, P. (1998). Privatization and Elite Reproduction in Eastern Europe. *European Journal of Sociology/Archives Européennes de Sociologie*, 39(2), 335–376.

Whitley, R. (1999). *Divergent Capitalisms: The Social Structuring and Change of Business Systems*. New York: Oxford University Press.

World Bank (1997). *The State in a Changing World*. Washington. DC: World Bank.

———. (2006). *Egypt Public Land Management Strategy*. 2 vols. Washington, DC: World Bank.

———. (2009). *From Privilege to Competition: Unlocking Private-Led Growth in the Middle East and North Africa*. Washington DC: International Bank for Reconstruction and Development/World Bank.

———. (2015a). *Privatization Database (1990–2008): World Bank*. [Online] https://data.worldbank.org/data-catalog/privatization-database [Accessed May 8, 2017]

———. (2015b). *Doing Business Report, 2015*. Washington, DC: World Bank.

———. (2015c). *Project Performance Assessment Report: Arab Republic of Egypt: Mortgage Finance Project.* IBRD 73960. Washington, DC: World Bank.

———. (2017a). *Gross Capital Formation (% of GDP): China, Egypt, India and Vietnam.* [Online] https://data.worldbank.org/indicator/NE.GDI.TOTL.ZS?locations=EG-IN-VN-CN [Accessed June 12, 2017]

———. (2017b) *GDP per Capita Growth* (annual) (1961–2016): Egypt. [Online] https://data.worldbank.org/indicator/NY.GDP.PCAP.KD.ZG?locations=EG [Accessed June 12, 2017]

———. (2017c). *Vulnerable Employment, Total (% of total employment): Egypt.* [Online] https://data.worldbank.org/indicator/SL.EMP.VULN.ZS?locations=EG [Accessed June 13, 2017]

———. (2017d). *Personal Remittances Received: Brazil, Egypt and Turkey (Current US Dollars).* [Online] https://data.worldbank.org/indicator/BX.TRF.PWKR.CD.DT?locations=EG [Accessed June 12, 2017]

———. (2017e). *Foreign Direct Investment Net Inflows (BoP, Current US Dollars): Brazil, China, Chile, Czech, Egypt, India, Mexico and Turkey.* [Online] https://data.worldbank.org/indicator/BX.KLT.DINV.CD.WD?locations=EG-BR- CN- CL-CZ-IN-MX-TR [Accessed June 16, 2017]

———. (2017f). *Net ODA Received Per Capita: Egypt (Current US Dollars). World Bank Data.* [Online] https://data.worldbank.org/indicator/DT.ODA.ODAT.PC.ZS?locations=EG. [Accessed June 12, 2017]

———. (2017g). Commercial Bank Branches (per 100,000 adults): Brazil, Egypt, India, Indonesia, Thailand, Tunisia and Turkey (2004–2014). *World Bank Data.* [Online] https://data.worldbank.org/indicator/FB.CBK.BRCH.P5?locations=BR-EG-IN- ID-TH-TN-TR [Accessed June 16, 2017]

———. (2017h). Domestic Credit to Private Sector by Banks: Brazil, Egypt, Poland and Turkey (% of GDP). *World Bank Data.* [Online] https://data.worldbank.org/indicator/FD.AST.PRVT.GD.ZS?locations=EG-PL-BR- TR [Accessed June 16, 2017]

———. (2017i). Market Capitalization of Listed Domestic Companies: Egypt, East Asia and Pacific, Lower-Middle Income Countries and OECD (% of GDP). *World Bank Data.* [Online] https://data.worldbank.org/indicator/CM.MKT.LCAP.GD.ZS?locations=EG-Z4– XN- OE [Accessed June 13, 2017]

———. (2017j). International Tourism: Number of Arrivals: Egypt. *World Bank Data.* [Online] https://data.worldbank.org/indicator/ST.INT.ARVL [Accessed June 18, 2017]

———. (2017k). Urban Population (% of Total): Egypt. *World Bank Data.* [Online] https://data.worldbank.org/indicator/SP.URB.TOTL.IN.ZS?locations=EG [Accessed September 8, 2017]

World Economic Forum. (2012). Global Competitiveness Report 2011–2012. *World Economic Forum.* [Online] http://reports.weforum.org/global-competitiveness-report-2012–2013/ [Accessed May 9, 2015]

Worldwide Governance Indicators (WGI). (2017). *World Bank Interactive Database.* [Online] http://info.worldbank.org/governance/wgi/#reports. [Accessed July 21, 2017]

World Trade Organization. (2017). Times Series—Trade Flow Selection, Egypt's Merchandize Trade (1990–2010). [Online] http://stat.wto.org/StatisticalProgram/WSDBViewData.aspx?Language=E [Accessed May 8, 2017]

Wright, M., Liu, X., Buck, T., & Filatotchev, I. (2008). Returnee Entrepreneurs, Science Park Location Choice and Performance: An Analysis of High Technology SMEs in China. *Entrepreneurship Theory and Practice*, 32(1), 131–155.

Wu, R. I., & Huang, C. C. (2003). Entrepreneurship in Taiwan: Turning Point to Restart. *Open Journal of Business and Management*, 3(4), 389–402.

Wu, W. P., & Leung, A. (2005) Does a Micro-Macro Link Exist Between Managerial Value of Reciprocity, Social Capital and Firm Performance? The Case of SMEs in China. *Asia Pacific Journal of Management*, 22(4), 445–463.

Xin, K. K., & Pearce, J. L. (1996). Guanxi: Connections as Substitutes for Formal Institutional Support. *Academy of Management Journal*, 39(6), 1641–1658.

Ya'qoub, A. (2016, January 10). The Central Bank Announces a Comprehensive Program for the Financing of Small and Medium Project [al-bank al-markazī yuʿlin tafāṣīl barnamig shamil li tamwīl al-mashrūʿāt al-saghīra wa al-mutawassiṭa] *Youm7.* [Online] https://www.youm7.com/story/2016/1/10/البنك-المركزى-يعلن-تفاصيل-برنامج-شامل-لتمويل-المشروعات-الصغيرة-والمتوسطة/2532252 [Accessed September 18, 2018]

Yāsīn, M. (2015, October 27). Interview with A. Adly.

Yeh-Yun Lin, C., & Yi-Ching Chen, M. (2007) Does Innovation Lead to Performance? An Empirical Study of SMEs in Taiwan. *Management Research News*, 30(2), 115–132.

Yunus, M. (2007) Remarks by Muhammad Yunus, Managing Director, Grameen Bank. *Microcredit Summit E-News*, 5(1), 167–192

Zaalouk, M. (1989). *Power, Class, and Foreign Capital in Egypt: The Rise of the New Bourgeoisie.* London: Zed Books.

Zaki, R. (1980). *The Problem of Inflation in Egypt: Causes and Effects with a Program to Fight It* [mushkilāt al-taḍakhkhum fī miṣr: asbābuhā wa natā'ijuhā maʿa barnāmij muqtaraḥ li mukāfaḥat al-ghalā']. Cairo: al-Ha'ia al-ʿAma li-l-Kitāb.

Zaki, M. (1999). *Egyptian Business Elites: Their Visions & Investment Behavior.* Cairo: Arab Center for Development and Future Research.

Zhu, Y. M., & Sanderson, J. W.(2009). The Key Obstacles and Countermeasure Against Development of Innovative SMEs in CHINA. *China Soft Science*, 9, 23–31.

Zimmer, C., & Aldrich, H. (1987). Resource Mobilization Through Ethnic Networks: Kinship and Friendship Ties of Shopkeepers in England. *Sociological Perspectives*, 30(4), 422–445.

Zubaida, S. (1990). The Politics of the Islamic Investment Companies in Egypt. *British Society for Middle Eastern Studies. Bulletin*, 17(2), 152–161.

Zulkifli-Muhammad, M., Char, A. K., bin Yasoa, M. R., & Hassan, Z. (2009). Small and Medium Enterprises (SMEs) Competing in the Global Business Environment: A Case of Malaysia. *International Business Research*, 3(1), 66–75.

Index

Note: page numbers followed by *f* and *t* refer to figures and tables respectively. Those followed by n refer to notes, with note number.

Stanford Studies *in* Middle Eastern
***and* Islamic Societies *and* Cultures**

Joel Beinin and Laleh Khalili, editors

The Universal Enemy: Jihad, Empire, and the Challenge of Solidarity 2019
DARRYL LI

Waste Siege: The Life of Infrastructure in Palestine 2019
SOPHIA STAMATOPOULOU-ROBBINS

Heritage and the Cultural Struggle for Palestine 2019
CHIARA DE CESARI

Banking on the State: The Financial Foundations of Lebanon 2019
HICHAM SAFIEDDINE

Familiar Futures: Time, Selfhood, and Sovereignty in Iraq 2019
SARA PURSLEY

Hamas Contained: The Rise and Pacification of Palestinian Resistance 2018
TAREQ BACONI

Hotels and Highways: The Construction of Modernization Theory in Cold War Turkey 2018
BEGÜM ADALET

Bureaucratic Intimacies: Human Rights in Turkey 2017
ELIF M. BABÜL

Impossible Exodus: Iraqi Jews in Israel 2017
ORIT BASHKIN

Brothers Apart: Palestinian Citizens of Israel and the Arab World 2017
MAHA NASSAR

Revolution without Revolutionaries: Making Sense of the Arab Spring 2017
ASEF BAYAT

Soundtrack of the Revolution: The Politics of Music in Iran 2017
NAHID SIAMDOUST

Copts and the Security State: Violence, Coercion, and Sectarianism in Contemporary Egypt 2016
LAURE GUIRGUIS

Circuits of Faith: Migration, Education, and the Wahhabi Mission 2016
MICHAEL FARQUHAR

Morbid Symptoms: Relapse in the Arab Uprising 2016
GILBERT ACHCAR

Imaginative Geographies of Algerian Violence: Conflict Science, Conflict Management, Antipolitics 2015
JACOB MUNDY

Police Encounters: Security and Surveillance in Gaza under Egyptian Rule 2015
ILANA FELDMAN

Palestinian Commemoration in Israel: Calendars, Monuments, and Martyrs 2015
TAMIR SOREK

Digital Militarism: Israel's Occupation in the Social Media Age 2015
ADI KUNTSMAN and REBECCA L. STEIN

Official Stories: Politics and National Narratives in Egypt and Algeria 2014
LAURIE A. BRAND

The Reckonings of Pluralism: Citizenship and the Demands of History in Turkey 2014
KABIR TAMBAR